Gardening with Color

BY THE EDITORS OF SUNSET BOOKS

*Striking combination of hues in 'Raging Tiger'
daylily (Hemerocallis) adds drama to borders.*

Sunset Publishing Corporation ■ Menlo Park, California

Two clematis vines intertwine on a fence: rosy lilac 'Gypsy Queen' and pink 'Duchess of Albany'.

SUNSET BOOKS

President and Publisher
Susan J. Maruyama

Director, Finance & Business Affairs
Gary Loebner

Director, Sales & Marketing
Richard A. Smeby

Marketing & Creative Services Manager
Guy C. Joy

Production Director
Lory Day

Director, New Business
Kenneth Winchester

Editorial Director
Bob Doyle

EDITORIAL STAFF FOR GARDENING WITH COLOR

Coordinating Editor
Suzanne Normand Eyre

Research and Text
Susan Lang

Copy Editor
Rebecca LaBrum

Design
Joe di Chiarro

Illustrations
Lois Lovejoy, Lucy Sargeant

Production Coordinator
Sally Lauten

SUNSET PUBLISHING CORPORATION

Chairman
Jim Nelson

President/Chief Executive Officer
Robin Wolaner

Chief Financial Officer
James E. Mitchell

Publisher
Stephen J. Seabolt

Circulation Director
Robert I. Gursha

Vice President, Manufacturing
Lorinda B. Reichert

Editor, Sunset Magazine
William R. Marken

Fourth printing May 1998

ISBN Hardcover edition 0-376-03158-1
Softcover edition 0-376-03157-3
Library of Congress Catalog Card Number: 95-69103
Printed in the United States

Front cover: Colorful landscape includes 'Dreamland' zinnias and various types of sages. Cover design by Susan Bryant Caron. Photography by Saxon Holt.
Back cover, clockwise from top: Photography by Susan Roth, Jerry Pavia, Susan Roth, Michael S. Thompson, Susan Roth.

The Possible Dream

Like most home gardeners, you probably dream of a picture-perfect garden bursting with vibrant, long-lasting color. Whether the image in your mind's eye is exquisitely detailed or a bit hazy, you can turn it into reality with the help of this book. We take a "can-do" approach, providing you the inspiration and practical advice necessary for success.

For reviewing the manuscript, we extend sincere thanks to Charles O. Cresson, John R. Dunmire, and Jim Wilson. All are known not only for considerable plant expertise but also for gardening with an impeccable color sense.

We also acknowledge Pamela Evans for carefully proofreading the manuscript. Finally, thanks to Redwood City Nursery for allowing us to stage photographs on their premises.

 Printed on recycled paper

Contents

Color in the Garden 4

Sources of Color 7
Flowers, Fruit, Foliage & More

Where Color Goes 19
A Pictorial Tour of Gardens

Understanding Color 29
Principles & Practices

A Rainbow of Garden Colors 41
From Delicate to Dynamic

Planning a Colorful Garden 87
Design Basics & Garden Plans

Choosing Plants 105
Shopping for Seeds & Transplants

An Encyclopedia of Plants 113
Exceptional Color from A to Z

Index 206

SPECIAL FEATURES

Experimenting with Color 38

Making the Most of Fall Color 91

Designing Drifts 93

Instant Color 95

Quick Color from Seeds 111

Color in the Garden

A well-arranged garden brimming with radiant hues, creamy pastels, and soft tones can be as thrilling as a great work of art. Fortunately, you don't have to visit a grand public garden to experience such excitement and inspiration. A skillful use of color in your own outdoor space—whether a half-acre or a small sliver of land ringing the house—will gratify you and lift your mood every time you come and go, walk through the yard, sit on the patio, or look out the windows.

Creating this kind of garden means selecting carefully from a host of plants and landscaping materials, then combining your choices in an appealing way. Unlike a painting or photograph, which freezes an image in time, the picture you compose will change with the seasons—and over the long term, as the plants grow. The effect will also vary each year, since you can never completely control living things subject to natural forces. The spectacle may be lackluster one year after a cold snap kills new growth or storms batter blossoms, but glorious the next, when nature cooperates. Gardeners tolerate this uncertainty only because they feel doubly exhilarated when the picture is perfect!

Developing your garden so that it fills out nicely and unfolds its panorama of color on cue (or nearly so) takes time. Realize that you're embarking on a journey that may take many years to accomplish. However, you'll have fun deciding where to go, fun while you're getting to your destination, and fun once you're there.

This book provides the basic information you'll need for successful gardening with color. We begin by displaying the various sources of color: not only flowers, but also foliage, fruit, bark and stems, and landscaping materials. Next comes a photographic tour of garden areas enlivened by color. A chapter on color theory gives you the fundamentals for developing a pleasing scheme; this is followed by overviews of the diverse hues and the various moods they express.

Next is a design chapter that provides guidelines for translating your vision into fact; to help you along, we've included eight professionally designed garden plans featuring assorted color schemes. We then give some hints on shopping for seeds and transplants. The final section of the book is an illustrated encyclopedia describing hundreds of colorful plants.

As you'll discover, there is no single correct way to create the garden of your dreams. The routes to your goal are as varied as the color combinations you can choose. Regardless of the path you take, however, you must become conscious of color—so much so that you'll automatically consider it before putting a plant (or anything else) in your garden.

Most important, don't be afraid to play with color, even if you don't get it right the first time. Just learn from your mistakes and make adjustments. Let this book be your companion throughout the process; it provides practical information, inspiring ideas, and the confidence to dig in and create the garden you've always wanted!

Left to right: Annual border flaunts bright hues; orange-red fall foliage of 'Diane' witch hazel (Hamamelis × intermedia) is paired with pink-marbled leaves of 'Rose Glow' Japanese barberry (Berberis thunbergii); and perennial garden features cream and orange shades.

Sources of Color

The finest ornamental gardens draw oohs and aahs in every season. Brightly hued blossoms account for much of the spectacle, but they don't carry the show alone. Brilliant or variegated foliage, vivid fruit, and showy bark all grab attention too, especially during lulls in blooming. These great gardens also take advantage of landscaping materials, such as brick, flagstones, and painted wood, for lasting color.

Many deciduous trees and shrubs explode into spectacular color before dropping their leaves in autumn.

Flowers

These marvels of nature are amazingly diverse. The myriad configurations and colors we see today have evolved over millions of years to attract pollinators—though one might be forgiven for thinking their purpose is simply to delight the gardener. The countless shapes include trumpets, bells, cups, globes, and pinwheels; blossoms may be borne singly or in clusters, in sizes ranging from less than an inch to more than a foot across. Every color of the rainbow is represented—in fact, shades such as violet, lavender, and goldenrod owe their names to flowers. And many blossoms display such exquisite color combinations that they seem designed by artists.

Top row, left to right: Globe thistle (Echinops), 'Blue Wave' hydrangea, and 'Seashells' cosmos.

Middle row, left to right: Kousa dogwood (Cornus kousa), lupine (Lupinus), 'Headlight' lily (Lilium), Oriental poppy (Papaver orientale), and columbine (Aquilegia).

Bottom row, left to right: Gazania, pocketbook plant (Calceolaria crenatiflora), gooseneck loosestrife (Lysimachia clethroides), and 'Diane' witch hazel (Hamamelis × intermedia).

Foliage

Leaves are a rich, sometimes surprising source of garden color. You'll find plants with yellow, red, purple, blue, or gray foliage, as well as choices offering various gradations of green. Some plants have leaves speckled, marbled, streaked, splashed, or edged with a contrasting color.

A particular plant's foliage display may be temporary, occurring at the beginning or end of the growing season. New spring growth is often brightly colored, creating a two-tone effect. In autumn, the leaves of many deciduous trees and shrubs take on brilliant hues before dropping.

Top row, left to right: 'Crimson Queen' Japanese maple (Acer palmatum), Virginia creeper (Parthenocissus quinquefolia), and Korean stewartia.

Middle row, left to right: 'Candidum' fancy-leafed caladium, witch hazel (Hamamelis), group of hostas, 'Maculata' evergreen silverberry (Elaeagnus pungens), and ginkgo.

Bottom row, left to right: Flowering cabbage (Brassica oleracea), smoke tree (Cotinus coggygria) with Bethlehem sage (Pulmonaria saccharata), and 'Tricolor' culinary sage (Salvia officinalis).

Fruit

On some plants, flowers don't provide the main spectacle; they're merely the prelude to a more glittering show. They bloom and fade— and then develop into bright-colored fruits that may appear singly or in large clusters. Some hang on for a long time, while others are soon harvested by humans or cleared out by birds, squirrels, or other animals. There's a wide range of shapes, sizes, and colors, though fruits used decoratively in gardens—such as those of holly *(Ilex)*, firethorn *(Pyracantha)*, and cotoneaster—tend to be round, shiny, fairly small, and red or orange in color.

Top row, left to right: Strawberry tree (Arbutus unedo), mountain ash (Sorbus), and 'Mohave' firethorn (Pyracantha).

Middle row, left to right: Oregon grape (Mahonia aquifolium), Chinese lantern plant (Physalis alkekengi), 'Dolgo' crabapple (Malus), 'Fuyu' Japanese persimmon (Diospyros kaki), and 'Fructo-Albo' skimmia.

Bottom row, left to right: Cranberry bush viburnum, Washington thorn (Crataegus phaenopyrum), and cotoneaster.

Bark & Stems

Drab brown and gray are the colors usually associated with bark and stems, but some trees and shrubs display much more colorful, often beautifully textured or patterned exteriors. The woody outer layer of certain trees flakes off in irregular patches or peels off in papery sheets to expose one or more colors beneath. On deciduous species, multicolored or mottled bark is especially conspicuous in fall and winter, when the branches are bare. In fact, some deciduous shrubs with brilliant stems and twigs are prized for the way they illuminate the otherwise somber winter garden.

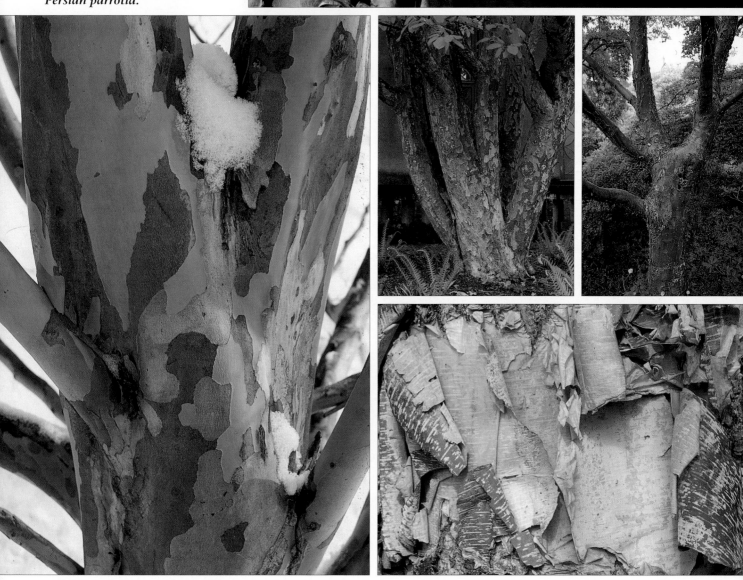

Facing page, clockwise from top: 'Sango Kaku' Japanese maple (Acer palmatum), paper birch (Betula papyrifera), madrone (Arbutus menziesii), and 'Flaviramea' dogwood (Cornus stolonifera).

This page, clockwise from top: birch bark cherry (Prunus serrula), paperbark maple (Acer griseum), river birch (Betula nigra), and Japanese stewartia. Middle: Persian parrotia.

Landscaping Materials

Flagstone patios, brick paths, porcelain pots, wrought-iron benches, painted wood arbors—these garden features are a steady source of color the year around. Paving materials offer sophisticated choices; for example, stone is sold in a medley of soft colors, and brick is available in tones including rosy red, purplish, and earthy orange. Wood structures such as decks and fences can be coated with a preservative, allowed to weather to gray, or painted a bright color. Garden furniture made of wood, metal, and plastic comes in various colorful finishes to complement any landscape.

Facing page, clockwise from top: Bamboo fence supporting a clematis vine; blue-painted wood arbor in a harmonious scheme; pink-toned rocks lining a streambed; and terra-cotta pots flanking a sky blue bench on a brick terrace backed by a wall made of concrete, rocks, and brick. Middle: Whimsical wood figure.

This page, clockwise from top: Rustic "pole" fence; painted concrete walkway; Elizabeth Rose's sculpture "The Swimmer"; crushed gravel path through a perennial garden; and a rock stairway.

Where Color Goes

Color belongs everywhere! Don't restrict it to a lone flower bed or a particular area of the yard. Locate your colorful plantings in any area that can be viewed or traversed: streetside parking strip, front yard, side yard, entryway, walkway, foundation, patio or deck, poolside, and so on. And remember to use colorful nonplant elements too, such as garden furniture and stone paths.

An attractive Wedgwood blue arbor is the focal point in a planting of colorful dahlias, delphiniums, roses, and petunias.

19

The photographs on the facing page show how colorful plantings at the windows and entrances of a home hearten all who come and go. Clockwise from left: Daffodils (Narcissus) in pots and in the ground radiate springtime cheer; a window box overflowing with brightly hued plants signals "welcome"; flamboyant daylilies (Hemerocallis) brighten the path to a back entry; and sprightly, sun-loving perennials massed near a walled entrance salute visitors.

Break with the traditional lawn and let colorful mixed plantings enliven the front yard, as shown on this page. Top: A big, bold rock garden abounds with rosy pinks, blues, and silvery grays chosen to match the house colors. Bottom: a delightful hodgepodge of perennials and shrubs forms a privacy screen between the front door and street.

Dress up the house with colorful foundation plants arranged in beds and sent scampering up the facade. Clockwise from left: Various blue shades of delphinium echo the house trim; the vivid red fall foliage of Virginia creeper (Partheno-cissus quinquefolia) stands out boldly against a green-accented white window; and vining forms of nasturtium (Tropaeolum majus) and sweet pea (Lathyrus odora-tus) trained onto a net loosely attached to the build-ing enhance the reddish-stained clapboards.

Here are additional ways to frame your home with vibrant plantings. Above: Dazzling magenta, scarlet, and pink dahlias perk up a terra-cotta stucco wall and light pinkish flagstone walk. Right: Pastel delphiniums set the stage for radiant red and creamy white climbing roses secured to a wire lattice set in front of the house wall.

Surround yourself with color while relaxing outdoors. Left: This quiet seating area beneath an arbor is permeated with creams and pinks during spring. Bottom: Brilliant annuals and perennials spilling onto the slatted wood bench offer close-up enjoyment of hues and fragrances.

Colorful yards like those on the facing page will lure even the housebound outdoors. Clockwise from top left: Vibrant color begins right outside the door of this cabin; an unclipped low hedge of yellow-leafed Japanese barberry (Berberis thunbergii 'Aurea') demarcates the lawn; and flowering plants in delicate hues line a path from house to garden gate.

Create colorful beds and borders like those shown on the facing page. Clockwise from top left: A rectangular island bed dug into the lawn is filled with mixed plantings in soothing pastels; a meandering flower border skirts a small backyard lawn; and a large shrub border features azaleas and rhododendrons interplanted with spring-flowering bulbs.

There are no rigid rules for rock gardens. Right: The plants decorating these steps were chosen for subtle color as well as interesting shapes and textures. Bottom: Dry-laid rocks form a raised bed containing a lively mixture of yellow- and orange-flowering perennials.

Understanding Color

Some people have an intuitive grasp of color—give them a bare plot and, without much ado, they'll transform it into a garden filled with a pleasing combination of colors. But for most of us, such artistry doesn't come naturally; we need some background in color theory. Study the principles outlined in this chapter, but remember that they're meant to inspire you, not stifle you. Keep your own tastes in mind; survey gardens you admire to see how color principles work in practice.

Pale bluish purple delphinium and pink fleabane (Erigeron) contribute to a harmonious color scheme.

Light affects garden colors. The needles on this prostrate form of blue spruce (Picea pungens) appear dull blue in the shade; in direct sunlight, they're brighter, with a yellow overtone.

What Is Color?

Visible light from the sun consists of many wavelengths. When light hits an object, some of these waves are absorbed; others are reflected back from the surface. The human eye detects *only* the reflected waves. Depending on its frequency, each wavelength produces the sensation of a distinct color: when a certain reflected wavelength strikes the retina, the eye signals to the brain that it sees blue, orange, red, or some other color.

An object reflecting only one wavelength is said to have a pure color. Such colors are rare in nature, since most objects reflect not only the wave equivalent to their most evident hue, but

also varying amounts of adjacent waves. Objects reflecting almost all wavelengths look white— just as the combined rays of sunlight appear white to us. Those absorbing almost every wavelength, on the other hand, look black in color.

Surface texture alters reflection and, correspondingly, the colors we see. Green looks darker and purer if reflected from something smooth or shiny, but seems lighter and less intense if the surface is dull or rough. No leaf or flower is so flat and uniform that it reflects light evenly: its textural differences—tiny projections and hollows—create a blend of colors giving richness and depth.

But simple reflectance from the physical structures of leaves, stems, and blossoms isn't all that determines plant color. The biochemical compounds found in each plant also play an important role. We see the foliage of most plants as green because it contains *chlorophyll,* a pigment that reflects green. White or yellow variegation in green leaves results when chloroplasts (the bodies that contain chlorophyll) are absent: the areas where they're missing are perceived as white or yellow. Similarly, though there are white pigments, white flowers may also look white due to air spaces in the tissue that cause most light waves to be reflected.

Among other common pigments are *anthocyanins,* responsible for the reds, blues, and purples in some plants. *Xanthophylls* reflect yellow or orange, *carotenes* yellow-orange. *Anthoxanthins* produce colors from ivory to deep yellow. (For more on the role of pigments in fall color, see page 91.)

Garden colors aren't static. They vary with the time of day, the season, the weather, and the distance from which we view them. Another variable is the individual observer, for not all people with normal vision see colors exactly the same way. Plants themselves aren't constant—for example, hydrangea blooms often fade to dull pink or green; Santa Barbara daisy *(Erigeron karvinskianus)* opens white and ages to pink; and gaura's flowers are pink in bud, white when they open, then pink again as they fade.

Since color and light are inseparable, the quality of light—intense, bright, muted, dim, hazy—radically alters the way plants look. Most colors take on a yellowish tinge in strong light (although clear yellows look bleached) and a violet cast in shade. Whites, yellows, and pastels seem more vivid in low light. In overcast, misty, or foggy climates, soft colors—from pinks and creamy yellows to pale blues and lavenders—come alive. Strong colors, on the other hand, lose intensity and look bluer or blacker when light is dim.

As night approaches, bathing the earth in blues and violets, those plant colors are the first to fade from view. At other times of day, leaves and blossoms may take on a yellowish or reddish cast depending on the sun's position in the sky.

All colors are seen in relation to other colors and are modified by them. If you set a blue-

Close associations of very intense hues like scarlet sage (Salvia splendens) and purple lobelia appeal to some people but not to others.

flowered plant next to a red one, the colors tend to merge, making the red seem bluer and the blue redder. The contrast between yellow and violet is so stark that each color appears brighter than if it were positioned alone.

Of course, there are all kinds of reds, blues, yellows, and violets—and other colors. Before you categorize a color and decide how it relates to the others in your garden, you should know that all colors have three dimensions: hue, value, and intensity.

Hue is the quality by which we distinguish one color from another—a red from a blue, a green from an orange, and so on. However, simply knowing that a hue is yellow or orange or violet doesn't tell you whether it's light or dark, bright or dull. You need to know the value and intensity as well.

Value is the relative lightness or darkness of a color. Lighter values—those containing white—are called *tints*. Darker ones—those containing black—are known as *shades*. Grayed values are called *tones*. A single color has a range of values extending from the lightest tint to the darkest shade. A clear bright green (such as emerald green) is an example of a pristine hue; apple green is a tint, bottle green a shade, and olive green a tone. Varying the values of the colors you choose is one of the easiest ways to make a garden interesting.

Intensity refers to the strength or purity of a color—to its degree of saturation. A single wavelength of light produces a pure color; intermingling other waves reduces the purity. Electric blue is more intense (purer) than dull blue, fire-engine red more intense than pink. Strong colors seem most at home in clear, hot, sunny areas, where the bright light accentuates them. Such colors can be overwhelming in cloudy or overcast climates.

Ways of Looking at Color

Sir Isaac Newton made a major breakthrough in the understanding of color during the 1600s, devising the first color wheel and providing a practical view of color relationships. By directing a beam of sunlight through a prism, he had already split light into its component hues, from red at one end of the band to violet at the other (see the spectrum illustrated above). Newton then twisted the spectrum into a circle. He chose seven prominent spectral hues—red, orange, yellow, green, blue, indigo, and violet— and related them to the seven planets (all the planets known at that time) and to the seven notes of the diatonic musical scale.

Since Newton's time, color theorists have configured a variety of other models, including triangles, six-pointed stars, spheres, cubes, and hemispheres, but a wheel not unlike that of Newton remains the model most commonly used today.

The modern color wheel is shown below. Spaced equally around its perimeter are the three primary hues (blue, yellow, and red); these are "primary" because they cannot be produced by any mixture of other colors. Also on the wheel are three secondary hues—green, orange,

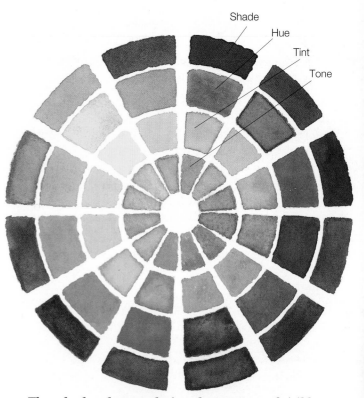

The color band at top depicts the sequence of visible light on the electromagnetic spectrum; the color wheel shows how the colors relate to each other.

and violet, produced by various mixtures of the primaries—and six intermediate hues made by mixing primaries and secondaries. The wheel also displays tints, shades, and tones.

Warm & Cool Colors

Botanically, colors are classified as *xanthic* (yellow-based) or *cyanic* (blue-based). Those with a yellow component are considered warm, while those based on blue are cool.

Warm colors tend to be more stimulating, dynamic, and noticeable from afar than cool hues, which are more calming and understated. Warm colors advance visually; cool ones recede. Notice, for example, how scarlets, oranges, yellows, and chartreuses seem to surge forward, while crimsons, violets, blues, and aquamarines retreat into the distance. Because warm hues dominate in this way, it takes a lot of cool color to balance them visually—you'll typically need to use four to five times as much cool color as warm color.

On the color wheel, the dividing line between warm and cool colors can be drawn between yellow-green and green on one side and red and red-violet on the other. Pure red appears on the warm side of the circle, but because it doesn't contain yellow or blue, it can fit into either a warm or a cool scheme. Other reds have clearer identities. Magenta is cool because of its strong blue component; scarlet is warm because of its yellow base.

Some plants have a mixed identity: they may have warm leaves and cool flowers, or vice versa. The combination may or may not please your eye, depending on the colors involved. You may find something vaguely unsatisfying about a geranium *(Pelargonium)* with purplish flowers and lime green leaves, yet consider a pansy with violet petals and a contrasting yellow center highly attractive.

Other plants change their color identity with the season. Leaves that are a cool, calm green in summer may heat up into blazing scarlet, yellow, or orange when autumn arrives. This sort of botanical split personality is almost always pleasing—in fact, it's one of the key reasons for putting such plants in your garden in the first place.

Warm colors dominate cool ones. Notice how a few bright orange tulips shout for attention among more numerous—but quieter—Virginia bluebells (Mertensia virginica).

Color Schemes

Gardens, like clothing and interior decor, are subject to color trends. Combinations of dazzlingly bright colors were all the rage in Victorian days, and even 20 or 30 years ago, popular schemes were a little brighter than they are now. Pastels are in vogue today, thanks in part to plant breeders who have developed a wider palette for gardeners to play with.

There are no rigid rules for color schemes. You can find ideas anywhere: in a friend's garden, displays at local nurseries, the exterior colors of your house, an Impressionist painting,

The harmonious arrangement at left, based on cool reds and blues, features delphiniums, monkshood (Aconitum), and roses. The complementary scheme at right combines peachy alstroemeria with lavender (Lavandula) and other pale blue–flowering perennials for a serene contrast.

an appealing fabric, a set of dishes. Or take your inspiration from nature: duplicate the colors of a sunset or a meadow filled with wildflowers, or use the component hues of your favorite multi-colored flower. Since the colors in nursery seed mixes usually go well together, you may want to pull your scheme directly from a mix you especially like—for example, the blue, lavender, purple, mauve, rose, and white of 'Persian Jewels' love-in-a-mist (*Nigella damascena*).

Four standard color schemes are reviewed below. Follow a scheme precisely, if you like; or use the information as a starting point and take it in any direction.

Harmonious

Also known as analogous, a harmonious scheme features colors adjacent on the color wheel, such as scarlets, oranges, and yellows. These hues are harmonious because they share a pigment—yellow, for the sunset colors.

Harmonious schemes can look flat and lifeless if all the colors you use have approximately the same value—the same degree of

lightness or darkness. To enliven the picture, vary your selections to include tints as well as deep or bright colors. If your scheme calls for blue through red-violet, for example, you might choose soft lavenders and pinks as well as touches of magenta.

Adding white is another way to energize the scene. White promotes harmony as long as tints are included in the scheme: tints harmonize both with both their basic hue and with white, since they contain both. In the absence of tints, white serves as punctuation.

A third option is to inject a touch of a contrasting color—for a blue-and-violet scheme, a dab of clear yellow. Even with that bit of contrast, you'll still have an essentially harmonious combination.

Complementary

A complementary (also called contrasting) scheme uses colors directly opposite each other on the color wheel, such as yellow and violet or orange and blue. One color is on the warm side, the other on the cool side.

The complementary scheme shown above contains two sophisticated, mixed-value pairings of yellow and violet: bright sunny yellow and light purple as well as creamy yellow and vivid purple. The monochromatic planting at right runs the gamut from rosy red to pale pink fading to white.

Unlike harmonious colors, complementary hues have no pigment in common. "Complementary" means that the two colors neutralize to a shade of gray when combined—as would happen if you mixed blue and orange paint, for example. With respect to plants, complementary hues contrast when placed side by side; in fact, the juxtaposition intensifies each color. Complementary colors are also known as such because of the afterimage effect: if you stare at one color in bright light for about 30 seconds and then look away, you'll see the contrasting color.

There are three types of contrasts. Nearly full values have the most startling effect (fire-engine red and emerald green); tints offer a calmer contrast (creamy yellow and lavender); and mixed values give a sophisticated look (pale peach and vivid blue). The total quantity of each color also governs the effect.

Beware of very intense contrasts in a small space. To tie complementary colors together and soften the contrast, use gray (recall that it results from the mixture of any two contrasting colors).

Monochromatic

Monochromatic plans are centered around one hue and encompass all the various tints, shades, and tones. For example, a red scheme might include pure reds, maroons, magentas, and various gradations of pink. Since there are few true blues in the plant kingdom, a blue scheme can embrace reddish blues, lavenders, mauves, plums, and purples. To keep the composition from sounding a single note, it's important to include a wide range of values and intensities.

Don't be slavish about sticking to a single color if you think that a splash of white or another color will set off your plan. Remember, no garden is truly monochromatic, since bark, foliage, landscaping materials, and even your house contribute color to the composition.

Kaleidoscopic

Following a kaleidoscopic approach, you mix all the colors of the rainbow; the effect, though always colorful, may range from downright riotous to slightly more sedate. Many bedding

These kaleidoscopic schemes, clockwise from top left, include a cottage garden with roses, foxglove (Digitalis purpurea), and California poppies (Eschscholzia californica); a perennial bed featuring penstemon and Italian bugloss (Anchusa azurea); and a raised bed with snapdragons (Antirrhinum majus) and pansies (Viola × wittrockiana).

plants are available in such a wide selection of tints and shades that it's possible to create an explosion of color using just one type of plant. For instance, a single seed packet of impatiens can yield apricot, salmon, blush, white, hot pink, burgundy, and lavender blossoms. Part of the fun is waiting to see what you'll get: more than any other color plan, a kaleidoscopic scheme allows for serendipity, the unexpectedly happy marriage of colors you would never have paired intentionally.

White is indispensable in kaleidoscopic plans, since it has the ability to separate strong or clashing colors—each color looks a little truer next to white than it does bordering other colors. If the garden appears too chaotic for your taste, use gray as a unifying element.

You don't have to worry about color clashes or chaos in a traditional cottage garden: the effect is supposed to be haphazard, as if you've simply stuck plants into the ground with no thought of a grand design.

Ways to Use Color

Although your gardening goal may be simply to surround yourself with colorful flowers and foliage, you should be aware that color can play special roles.

Color can evoke a mood. For example, sunny yellow creates a cheery atmosphere, blue a serene one, and red a stimulating one. See "A Rainbow of Garden Colors,"starting on page 41, for more about the moods associated with different colors.

You can also use color to manipulate perspective, since warm colors seem to advance while cool ones recede (see page 33). To enlarge a small garden visually, place cool colors in the rear and warm ones close up; the distance between the two will seem greater than it really is. Do the opposite—position warm colors at the back, cool colors in front—to make a large space feel more intimate.

If your time in the garden is limited to evenings, opt for colors that show up well in dim light. White is the most luminous choice, but other pale colors also shine through. Avoid dark colors, since these tend to vanish from view as light fades.

Color can be used for special effects. Utilize blues and blue-based greens on a hot patio or deck to make the area seem cooler and more inviting. Brighten a dark house exterior with light-colored foundation plants; temper a bright exterior with deep-colored plants. The contrast in values also serves to make each color stand out more than it would if used alone.

Perhaps there's no better use of color than as an accent. A splash of strong or luminous color draws the eye: it can highlight a positive feature, such as a birdbath or statuary, or divert attention from an offending view (in the latter case, place the accent opposite the undesirable element).

Because they're noticeable to start out with, warm colors make ideal accents. Bright reds and yellows are particularly effective, since we see these more quickly than we do other colors. White, silver, and gray are good accents as well. In general, tints are better choices than shades, but be sure the tint you use doesn't compete with similar ones for attention.

Use color to fulfill special functions in the landscape. Above: Golden-hubbed pink fleabane (Erigeron) brightens a dark house facade. Below: Red-flowered bougainvillea serves as an accent.

Experimenting with Color

Have fun with color! Don't be afraid to try new combinations, even those that seemingly defy the guidelines discussed in this chapter. If your notion succeeds, you'll feel great satisfaction; if it flops, chalk it up to experience and try a new idea. Don't be discouraged if others dispute the outcome: remember, color perception and taste are highly personal.

This page suggests some unlikely ways to use orange; the facing page features various other color alliances.

You might expect even soft orange to ring a discordant bell among rosy purples and pinks, but it doesn't in this primrose (Primula) planting. Such an alliance works best when the plants are of a single type and the colors intermingled rather than separated into blocks of color.

Orange is harmonious with scarlet and other yellowed reds, but it's also surprisingly compatible with dark red. Here, maroon roses and daylilies (Hemerocallis) temper the orange of the red-hot poker (Kniphofia uvaria) flower spikes. The yellow in the spikes is picked up in the daylily buds and blossom throats.

You might never think of linking orange with pink, but it's a pleasing combination in a planting built around the purple-and-orange 'Jolly Joker' pansy (Viola × wittrockiana). The pink of the primrose and flowering cabbage (Brassica oleracea) is analogous with the purple. Lavender-blue pansies are added to harmonize with the pinks and contrast with the orange.

In this complementary pairing of deep violet penstemon and yellow yarrow (Achillea), the visual dominance of either color produces a warm or cool effect. In the lefthand illustration, the impact is cool; in the righthand, it is warm. For a balanced look, use four to five times as much of the cool color as the warm.

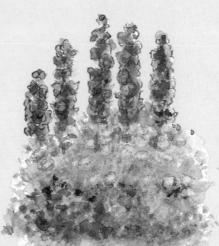

Dwarf delphinium, pincushion flower (Scabiosa caucasica), and a low-growing geranium combine beautifully, but the effect is lackluster when all of the blossoms are various shades of blue. Notice how the planting perks up when a rosy-flowered geranium is switched for the blue-blossomed one.

Let nature be your guide in constructing a colorful planting. This scheme uses as its starting point a multicolored primrose featuring rosy pink petals with red blotching around a yellow eye. The purple of the pansies and soft pink of the stock (Matthiola) harmonize with the rosy tints. Yellow pansies repeat the warm color of the primrose's eye and contrast with the purple pansies.

A Rainbow of Garden Colors

Shall it be a lavender or a scarlet rose here?

Bright yellow tulips or apricot ones there?

Choosing colors is one of the real pleasures

of gardening. And now that breeders have

expanded the color range of so many plants

to include subtle tints and bold shades, the

possibilities seem endless. In this chapter, we

consider six color categories: whites and creams; blues

and purples; pinks and reds; yellows and oranges;

greens; and silvers and grays. A chart in each section

lists some of the most colorful selections and indicates

their showiest season.

*A carpet of flower color includes
rosy 'Dreamland' zinnias and white
and blue types of sage (Salvia).*

41

Whites & Creams

White is the color associated variously with purity, sophistication, or coldness—depending on whether images of wedding gowns, white ties and tails, or glaciers leap to mind.

In gardens, the special appeal of white is luminosity. White reflects more light than any other color and is the last to fade as night descends. Indispensable for brightening dark corners, it's also splendid near a patio or along a pathway popular for evening strolls. In many ways, a white garden is even lovelier at dusk or in moonlight than during the day. For the ultimate effect, look for plants offering both luminous blossoms and a heavenly evening fragrance; one of the best such choices is old-fashioned flowering tobacco *(Nicotiana)*.

White has the advantage of being fairly easy to place. It combines nicely with both warm and cool colors, although it's more akin to cool ones. It's harmonious with tints, which are whitened hues, and provides a sharp contrast to dark or very bright colors. White is also an effective "peacemaker": colors that would clash or lose their own identities if placed side by side get along beautifully if separated by white.

Clockwise from top left: 'Alba', a white-flowering form of bleeding heart (Dicentra spectabilis), displays a delicate chain of puffy, pure white hearts; large-flowered 'Henryi' clematis twines along a picket fence for a charming white-on-white composition; and handsome leaves edged in creamy white are this variegated hosta's main glory, far outshining its summertime flower spikes.

Although white is most often used with other colors, it's powerful on its own. White-on-white gardens—inspired by Vita Sackville-West's famous garden at Sissinghurst, England—are fashionable today. The best such gardens, including Sissinghurst's, use greens and grays to great advantage. Grays are particularly companionable with white: in fact, some of the lightest grays, such as the dusty millers—among them *Centaurea cineraria, Senecio cineraria,* and *Artemisia stellerana* (also called beach wormwood)—can pass for powdery white.

Just about every plant species offers white forms. Look for botanical names that include *alba (albus, album, albo,* etc.)—Latin for "white." *Candida (candidissima, candidum,* etc.), too, is a Latin reference to white. The common or variety name of a plant may include the word "white" or allude to white, as in *Lamium maculatum* 'White Nancy', snow-in-summer *(Cerastium tomentosum),* and *Lavatera trimestris* 'Mont Blanc' *(blanc* is French for "white").

Although many plants are described as white, in truth the white is not always pure. It's often tinged with other colors, thus taking on a yellow, blue, pink, green, or gray cast. Since the English language doesn't provide us with precise terms for each of these subtle gradations, the descriptions we use refer to objects that approximate the colors we have in mind. The purest whites we call snow, fleece, swan, milk, or lily white. We refer to a whole range of off-whites by names such as cream, eggshell, alabaster, bone, ivory, and pearl.

Some white-flowered plants have variable color. Gaura's blossoms are rosy in bud, opening to pink-tinged white and fading to pink. The red buds of Sargent crabapple *(Malus sargentii)* unfold to small clear white flowers. The nodding white blossoms of Christmas rose *(Helleborus niger)* are often suffused with purplish pink, and grow pinker still with age.

Texture affects a color's quality. Thick, waxy petals, such as those of magnolia blossoms, seem to shine. Delicate, crinkly, tissue-papery petals—notably those of Matilija poppy *(Romneya coulteri),* Oriental poppy *(Papaver orientale),* and rockrose *(Cistus)*—look translucent.

Brightly hued stamens (the male reproductive parts in the flower's center) or colorful

Clockwise from top left: 'Sneezy' dwarf dahlia, baby's breath (Gypsophila paniculata), flowering tobacco (Nicotiana), and petunia make a pleasing jumble; a clipped hedge neatly frames Shasta daisies (Chrysanthemum × superbum); arching white-flowered spiraeas form a frothy mass behind creamy daffodils (Narcissus); and Shasta daisies, lilies (Lilium), and phlox comprise a radiant trio.

markings adorn many white flowers, often giving the blossoms a special glow. The pure white upturned petals of Madonna lily *(Lilium candidum)* flare back to reveal long orange stamens. Matilija poppy, with its luxuriant white petals and large golden center, looks like a gorgeous interpretation of a fried egg. 'Polka Dot' Madagascar periwinkle *(Catharanthus roseus)*, featuring five crisp white petals and a red center, resembles a pinwheel. A large black-tufted center makes the cupped petals of 'Perry White' Oriental poppy seem even whiter. Some rockroses have both a sunny yellow center and a crimson blotch at the base of each petal. Elegant white-flowered rhododendrons are often speckled with darker colors; the pink buds of 'Loder's White', for example, unfold into pink-edged white blossoms with mauve flecks.

Other pleasing plants bearing pure white flowers include honey-scented 'Carpet of Snow' alyssum *(Lobularia maritima)*. Snow-in-summer produces a blanket of pristine blooms above a mat of gray foliage; 'Mont Blanc' annual mallow *(Lavatera trimestris)* is a brilliant, shining white.

Goatsbeard *(Aruncus dioicus)*, with graceful, feathery plumes made up of hundreds of tiny cream flowers, is reminiscent of a large astilbe, though the latter's plumes are somewhat more solid and a little whiter. Baby's breath *(Gypsophila paniculata)* bears billowy clouds of delicate grayish white or pinkish blooms. Other plants with airy floral sprays—suggestive of a more substantial baby's breath—include the 'The Pearl' yarrow *(Achillea ptarmica)*, with pure white pearl-size blossoms, and ivory-flowered pearly everlasting *(Anaphalis margaritacea)*.

Many spring bulbs make a lovely show in white. The nodding, clear white blossoms of snowdrop *(Galanthus)* have delicate green tips. Daffodils *(Narcissus)* are available in solid white or with white petals centered by yellow, orange, or pink cups. Outstanding choices include 'Stainless', a clean white all over; 'Ice Follies', with ivory petals and a lemon cup that turns creamy with age; and 'Ice Wings', which opens pale cream and fades to snow white. White tulips are quite numerous as well, among them milky white 'White Emperor', delicately green-tinged 'Hibernia', and stark white, lily-flowered 'White Triumphator'.

Clockwise from top left: Creamy plumes of goatsbeard (Aruncus dioicus) softly illuminate a shade planting; the renowned white garden at Sissinghurst, England; and snowy white Shasta daisies keep peace between orange California poppies (Eschscholzia californica) and red Oriental poppies (Papaver orientale).

WHITES & CREAMS

	Height	Season of Color*				Sun or Shade
		Sp	Su	F	W	
Achillea ptarmica 'The Pearl' (yarrow)	2½'		▓			☼
Agapanthus (lily-of-the-Nile)	1'–5'		▓			☼ ◑
Amelanchier (serviceberry)	6'–30'	▓				☼
Anaphalis margaritacea (pearly everlasting)	1'–2½'		▓			☼ ◑
Anemone x hybrida (Japanese anemone)	3'–5'			▓		☼ ◑
Antirrhinum majus (snapdragon)	8"–3'	▓				☼
Arabis caucasica (wall rockcress)	6"	▓				☼ ◑
Arrhenatherum elatius 'Variegatum' (false oatgrass)	3'–4'	▓				☼ ◑
Aruncus dioicus (goatsbeard)	3'–6'	▓				☼ ◑
Astilbe	1½'–5'		▓			☼ ◑
Bougainvillea 'White Madonna'	climbing		▓			☼
Camellia	6'–20'			▓		◑ ●
Catharanthus roseus (Madagascar periwinkle)	4"–2'		▓			☼ ◑
Cerastium tomentosum (snow-in-summer)	8"		▓			☼
Chrysanthemum x morifolium	1'–4'			▓		☼
Cimicifuga racemosa (bugbane)	6'–7'		▓			◑
Cistus (rockrose)	1'–6'		▓			☼
Clematis	climbing		▓			☼ ◑
Cleome hasslerana (spider flower)	4'–5'		▓			☼ ◑
Clethra alnifolia (summersweet)	8'		▓			◑
Convallaria majalis (lily-of-the-valley)	6"–10"	▓				◑ ●
Convolvulus cneorum (bush morning glory)	2'–4'		▓			☼
Cornus mas 'Variegata' (Cornelian cherry)	12'–20'	▓				☼ ◑
Cosmos bipinnatus	2'–6'		▓			☼ ◑
Crataegus (hawthorn)	25'–30'	▓				☼

*Peak season of color shown is an average: it may start earlier or last longer in mild-winter climates, and start later or be briefer in cold-winter regions.

Some peonies are clear white, others flushed with pink or yellow. 'Festiva Maxima' is pure white with flecks of crimson; 'Bowl of Cream' resembles its name; and 'Top Brass' is a subtle blend of pale pink, creamy yellow, and ivory. Adding more interest—and beauty—is the variety in flower form, from simple, cup-shaped bowls with one or two rows of petals to frilly, ruffled spheres made up of crinoline-like layers of silky petals.

White roses offer just as much variation in color as peonies do. The floribunda 'Iceberg' is pure white, while 'French Lace', another floribunda, is ivory with overtones of peach and pink. The hybrid tea 'Garden Party' is ivory blended with cream, flushed with pink at the edges. The shrub rose 'Fair Bianca' is a yellowed white. The old garden rose 'Great Maiden's Blush' is tinged with pink, the miniature 'Green Ice' with green.

When planning whites in a garden, don't forget foliage: many plants have leaves that are marbled, spotted, or edged with white. In addition to crisp white flowers, 'Sissinghurst White' Bethlehem sage (Pulmonaria saccharata) features foliage speckled with silvery white. Among the many fine choices with cream- or white-margined foliage are 'Variegata' Cornelian cherry (Cornus mas), 'Silver Queen' euonymus, and 'Albomarginata' hosta.

	Height	Season of Color				Sun or Shade
		Sp	Su	F	W	
Dahlia	1'–7'		■			☼
Dianthus caryophyllus (border carnation)	1'–3'		■			☼
Dicentra spectabilis 'Alba' (bleeding heart)	2'–3'	■				◑
Dictamnus albus 'Albiflorus' (gas plant)	2½'–3'	■	■			☼ ◑
Digitalis purpurea 'Alba' (foxglove)	3'–5'		■			◑
Euonymus fortunei 'Silver Queen'	4'–6'	■	■	■	■	☼ ◑
Fothergilla gardenii (dwarf witch alder)	3'	■				☼ ◑
Galanthus (snowdrop)	6"–1'				■	☼ ◑
Gaura lindheimeri	2½'–4'		■	■		☼
Gypsophila paniculata (baby's breath)	1½'–4'		■			☼
Helleborus niger (Christmas rose)	1'–1½'				■	◑ ●
Heuchera (coral bells)	1'–2½'	■	■			☼ ◑
Hibiscus moscheutos (rose-mallow)	2'–8'		■			☼ ◑
Hosta undulata 'Albomarginata'	1½'		■			◑ ●
Hyacinthus (Dutch hyacinth)	6"–1'	■				☼ ◑
Hydrangea anomala petiolaris	climbing		■			☼ ◑
Iberis sempervirens (evergreen candytuft)	8"–1'	■				☼ ◑
Impatiens wallerana	8"–2'		■	■		◑ ●

	Height	Season of Color				Sun or Shade
		Sp	Su	F	W	
Iris (Dutch hybrids)	1½'–2'		■			☼ ◑
Lamium maculatum 'White Nancy' (dead nettle)	6"	■	■			◑ ●
Lavatera trimestris 'Mont Blanc' (annual mallow)	2'		■	■		☼
Lilium candidum (Madonna lily)	3'–4'		■			☼
Lobularia maritima (sweet alyssum)	2"–1'		■			☼ ◑
Lysimachia clethroides (gooseneck loosestrife)	3'		■			◑
Magnolia denudata (yulan magnolia)	35'	■				☼ ◑
Malus sargentii (Sargent crabapple)	10'	■				☼
Matthiola (stock)	1'–2½'	■				☼
Narcissus (daffodil)	6"–1½'	■			■	☼ ◑
Nerium oleander (oleander)	6'–12'		■			☼
Nicotiana (flowering tobacco)	10"–5'		■			☼ ◑
Paeonia (peony)	2'–6'	■	■			☼
Papaver orientale (Oriental poppy)	2'–4'		■			☼ ◑
Petunia x hybrida	8"–2½'		■			☼
Philadelphus coronarius (mock orange)	10'		■			☼ ◑

	Height	Season of Color				Sun or Shade
		Sp	Su	F	W	
Phlox	6"–4'		▓	▓		☼ ◐
Pieris japonica (lily-of-the-valley shrub)	6'–10'	▓			▓	◐
Primula (primrose)	9"–3'	▓				◐
Prunus 'Tai Haku' (flowering cherry)	25'	▓				☼
Pulmonaria saccharata 'Sissinghurst White' (Bethlehem sage)	1'	▓				◐ ●
Rhododendron	2'–20'	▓			▓	☼ ◐
Romneya coulteri (Matilija poppy)	6'–8'		▓			☼
Rosa (rose)	1'–15'		▓	▓		☼ ◐
Salvia farinacea 'Alba' (mealy-cup sage)	3'		▓			☼
Skimmia japonica 'Fructo-Albo'	2½'		▓	▓		◐ ●
Spiraea x vanhouttei	6'	▓				☼
Styrax japonicus (Japanese snowbell)	20'–30'	▓				☼ ◐

	Height	Season of Color				Sun or Shade
		Sp	Su	F	W	
Syringa (lilac)	4'–15'	▓				☼
Trachelospermum jasminoides (star jasmine)	climbing	▓				☼ ◐
Tulipa (tulip)	6"–3'	▓				☼ ◐
Verbascum chaixii 'Album' (mullein)	3'		▓			☼
Viburnum plicatum tomentosum (doublefile viburnum)	6'–15'	▓				☼ ◐
Viola x wittrockiana (pansy)	8"		▓			☼ ◐
Wisteria floribunda 'Alba'	climbing	▓				☼
Zantedeschia aethiopica (calla lily)	1'–3'	▓				☼ ◐
Zephyranthes candida (fairy lily)	1'			▓		☼ ◐

Right: The various white-barked species of birch (Betula) lend subtle grace and elegance to plantings. Here, the creamy bark brightens a woodland garden.

Below: The white garden at Sissinghurst has inspired gardeners the world over; see page 47 for another view.

Blues & Purples

This coolest of color ranges embraces primary blue, greenish blue, and the various gradations of blue-red that we call purple. Different values of these hues convey vastly different moods—from the pertness of clear radiant blue to the melancholy of misty lavender to the solemnity of deep bluish purple.

As a group, blues and purples are considered calming and tranquil. Blue is associated with truth, wisdom, and loyalty, though it also conveys sadness; purple is traditionally linked with pomp and royalty.

Regardless of how light or dark they are, blue-based colors seem to recede: when placed around the edges or at the back of a garden, they make the space appear wider or deeper. These are the colors of so many natural elements often viewed from afar: the sky, the ocean, lakes, rivers, distant mountains.

Although there are more than enough choices for an all-blue garden, such a scheme can be dreary. Blue and purple are more satisfying when brightened by white in what remains a cool color arrangement, or by orange or yellow in a complementary scheme. The great English gardener Gertrude Jekyll liked to use

Clockwise from top left: 'Freedom Blue' delphiniums put up majestic, intense blue flower spikes in front of a young purple-leafed smoke tree (Cotinus coggygria); a mass planting of blue-violet catmint (Nepeta × faassenii) encircles a hub of lavender (Lavandula) in this spoke garden; and a low hedge of bright green boxwood (Buxus) enlivens a cool-color border featuring blue-flowering speedwell (Veronica).

plants with golden leaves or clear yellow flowers to spice up blue gardens. Keep in mind that blues and purples, even those energized by brighter accents, are poor choices for plantings that you want to view at night, since they're the first colors to fade as darkness falls.

True blue—the color of blue poppy (*Meconopsis betonicifolia*) and 'Crater Lake Blue' speedwell (*Veronica*)—is rare. More common are reddened blues, including mauve, plum, and rosy purple. These colors are difficult to classify; some people see them as blues and purples, others as reds and pinks. The confusion just proves that blues and cool reds are compatible.

Among the terms we use for blues and purples are several that take their names from flowers: gentian (bright blue), lavender (pale bluish purple), lilac (medium pinkish purple), violet (various reddish blues), and orchid (light bluish to reddish purple). Delft and Wedgwood blue approximate the colors of the ceramic ware for which they were named. Cerulean and azure refer to the clear blue sky. Cobalt takes its name from a greenish blue pigment. Other blues owe their names to gemstones: sapphire is a deep purplish blue, turquoise a light greenish blue, and amethyst a medium purple. Electric blue is startlingly bright. Steel blue is a light grayish

Left to right: A trio of blue bloomers includes grape hyacinth (Muscari), Virginia bluebells (Mertensia virginica), and primrose (Primula); 'Blue Star' juniper (Juniperus squamata) stands out among green-leafed plants; brilliant blue lithodora forms a carpet for Spanish bluebell (Endymion hispanicus); and blue poppy (Meconopsis betonicifolia) lines a walkway.

blue; indigo—which Sir Isaac Newton classified as a separate spectral hue—is a dark grayish blue. Mauve usually refers to a pale or medium reddish purple, while grape and plum are names used for deep reddish as well as deep bluish purples. Mulberry describes a dark, even blackish, purple.

Not every member of a blue-flowered plant group has the selfsame shade. The color of ornamental allium, for example, is species-dependent—*Allium aflatunense* is pink-toned lavender, *A. caeruleum* sky blue, and *A. giganteum* bluish lavender. The large spherical blossoms of lily-of-the-Nile *(Agapanthus)* and the

blooms of many types of bellflower *(Campanula)* vary from pale blue to deep bluish violet. Two fine back-of-the-border plants are extremely variable: the stately spikes of delphinium range from true blue to purple, and the pea-shaped blossoms of false indigo *(Baptisia australis)* from lavender to deep purple.

Among ground covers, you'll find superb selections. In spring, periwinkle *(Vinca)* makes a lovely blanket of soft lavender-blue; *V. minor* 'Bowles' bears larger, deeper blue flowers. Another springtime delight, Siberian bugloss *(Brunnera macrophylla)*, produces airy sprays of forget-me-not flowers with clear blue petals and

yellow centers against a backdrop of large, heart-shaped leaves. In summer, dwarf plumbago *(Ceratostigma plumbaginoides)* unrolls a dazzling, intensely blue carpet.

Two of the best vines are wisteria, with long, drooping racemes of pea-shaped lavender or lilac-blue flowers, and Jackman clematis *(Clematis × jackmanii)*, with rich purple flowers so abundant they almost envelop the foliage.

Many denizens of the herb garden display blue or purple blooms. Among them are lavender *(Lavandula)*, rosemary *(Rosmarinus)*, mealy-cup sage *(Salvia farinacea)*, Russian sage *(Perovskia)*, catmint *(Nepeta × faassenii)*, columbine *(Aquilegia)*, delphinium, ornamental allium, rose, speedwell, and sweet violet *(Viola odorata)*.

There's no shortage of blues and purples among spring bulbs. Squill *(Scilla)* and bluebell *(Endymion)* both produce nodding bells in various blues. Grape hyacinth *(Muscari)* has tight little spikes of light to dark blue urn-shaped flowers resembling clusters of grapes. Dutch hyacinth comes in several blues, including the nearly navy 'Blue Surprise'. And breeders have produced many spectacular tulips in this color range, among them lily-flowered 'Ballade', a rich purple bordered in white, and double-flowered 'Lilac Perfection', which resembles a purplish peony.

Striking choices in rhododendrons include 'Blue Peter', a lavender-blue with purple splotches; 'Blue Diamond', an intense blue; 'Van Nes Sensation', a pale lilac fading to a white center; and 'Purple Splendour', a deep purple with black spots.

Although blue and purple don't constitute the largest color category in roses, you'll still find many fine selections. Among the floribundas are rosy lavender 'Angel Face' and deep plum 'Intrigue'. The grandiflora 'Lagerfeld' is a silvery lavender, as is the hybrid tea 'Paradise', which has a ruby edging that spreads deeper into the petals as the blossom unfolds.

Two superb flowers for drying are statice *(Limonium latifolium)* and globe thistle *(Echinops)*. The former bears a haze of tiny lavender flowers, each held in a papery base; the latter's spherical flower heads look like golfball-size pincushions stuck full of intense, metallic blue pins.

Clockwise from top left: The vivid spikes of blue cardinal flower (Lobelia siphilitica) contrast beautifully with yellow-blooming coreopsis; prolific 'Johnson's Blue' geranium manufactures bright blossoms from spring into early fall; and Serbian bellflower (Campanula poscharskyana) scrambles over and around a brick planter.

BLUES & PURPLES

	Height	Season of Color* Sp	Su	F	W	Sun or Shade
Aconitum (monkshood)	3'–6'		■	■		☼ ◐
Agapanthus (lily-of-the-Nile)	1'–5'		■			☼ ◐
Ageratum houstonianum (floss flower)	6"–2½'		■	■		☼
Ajuga reptans (carpet bugle)	6"–1½'	■	■			☼ ◐ ●
Allium	6"–6'	■	■			☼
Amsonia tabernaemontana (blue star)	2'–3'	■				☼ ◐
Anchusa azurea (Italian bugloss)	1½'–5'	■	■			☼
Aquilegia caerulea (Rocky Mountain columbine)	2'	■	■			☼ ◐
Aster	1'–6'		■	■		☼ ◐
Baptisia australis (false indigo)	3'–4'	■	■			☼
Brachycome (Swan River daisy)	1'		■			☼
Browallia speciosa (amethyst flower)	1'–2'		■	■		◐
Brunnera macrophylla (Siberian bugloss)	1½'	■				☼ ◐
Buddleia (butterfly bush)	10'–15'		■	■		☼
Campanula (bellflower)	4"–5'		■			☼ ◐
Catananche caerulea (cupid's dart)	2'		■			☼
Ceanothus (wild lilac)	1'–20'	■	■			☼
Centaurea cyanus (bachelor's button)	1'–3'		■			☼
Ceratostigma plumbaginoides (dwarf plumbago)	1'		■	■		☼ ◐
Clematis x jackmanii (Jackman clematis)	climbing		■	■		☼ ◐
Cobaea scandens (cup-and-saucer vine)	climbing		■	■		☼
Cotinus coggygria (smoke tree)	15'		■			☼
Crocus speciosus	4"			■		☼ ◐
Cynoglossum amabile (Chinese forget-me-not)	1½'–2'		■			☼ ◐
Delphinium	2½'–7'	■	■			☼ ◐

*Peak season of color shown is an average: it may start earlier or last longer in mild-winter climates, and start later or be briefer in cold-winter regions.

If you're looking for a large purple accent, there's no better choice than 'Royal Purple' or 'Velvet Cloak' smoke tree (*Cotinus coggygria*), clothed in purplish leaves that retain their color throughout the growing season. The tiny blossoms are greenish when they open—but as they fade in summer, they send out elongated stalks covered with pinkish gray hairs, giving the flower clusters the look of puffs of smoke.

Other exceptional blue-leafed plants include blue fescue (*Festuca ovina glauca*), blue carpet juniper (*Juniperus horizontalis* 'Wiltonii'), and many forms of blue spruce (*Picea pungens*). The bluish foliage of some hostas—including 'Blue Skies', 'True Blue', and 'Hadspen Blue'—is so striking that it overshadows the attractive lavender or white flower spikes.

	Height	Season of Color				Sun or Shade
		Sp	Su	F	W	
Echinops (globe thistle)	4'		▓			☀
Endymion (bluebell)	1'–1½'	▓				☽
Erigeron (fleabane)	1'–2'		▓	▓		☀
Eryngium (sea holly)	1½'–4'		▓			☀
Felicia amelloides (blue marguerite)	1½'–2'	▓	▓	▓		☀
Festuca ovina glauca (blue fescue)	10"	▓	▓	▓	▓	☀ ☽
Gentiana asclepiadea (willow gentian)	2'		▓	▓		☽
Heliotropium arborescens (heliotrope)	8"–2'		▓			☀
Hibiscus syriacus (rose of Sharon)	6'–10'		▓			☀ ☽
Hosta 'Hadspen Blue'	1'	▓	▓			☽ ●
Hyacinthus (Dutch hyacinth)	6"–1'	▓				☀ ☽
Hydrangea macrophylla (bigleaf hydrangea)	3'–8'		▓			☀ ☽
Ipomoea tricolor 'Heavenly Blue' (morning glory)	climbing		▓			☀
Iris sibirica (Siberian iris)	1'–4'	▓				☀ ☽
Jacaranda mimosifolia	25'–40'	▓				☀ ☽

	Height	Season of Color				Sun or Shade
		Sp	Su	F	W	
Juniperus horizontalis 'Wiltonii' (blue carpet juniper)	4"	▓	▓	▓	▓	☀
Lagerstroemia 'Muskogee' (crape myrtle)	20'		▓			☀
Lantana montevidensis	1½'		▓	▓		☀
Lavandula (lavender)	1½'–4'		▓			☀
Limonium latifolium (sea lavender)	2'		▓			☀
Linum (flax)	1½'–2'		▓			☀
Liriope muscari (big blue lily turf)	1'–1½'			▓		☽ ●
Lithodora diffusa	6"–1'		▓			☀
Lobelia erinus	4"–8"		▓	▓		☀ ☽
Lupinus (lupine)	1½'–5'	▓				☀
Mahonia aquifolium (Oregon grape)	2'–6'	▓				☀ ☽
Meconopsis betonicifolia (blue poppy)	3'–6'		▓			☽ ●
Mertensia virginica (Virginia bluebells)	1½'–2'	▓				☽ ●
Muscari (grape hyacinth)	6"–1'	▓			▓	☀ ☽
Nemophila menziesii (baby blue eyes)	6"–10"		▓			☀ ☽
Nepeta x faassenii (catmint)	1½'		▓			☀
Nierembergia hippomanica (cup flower)	6"–15"		▓			☀ ☽
Nigella damascena (love-in-a-mist)	2'		▓			☀ ☽
Penstemon	1'–3'		▓			☀ ☽
Perovskia (Russian sage)	3'–4'		▓	▓		☀
Phlox	6"–4'		▓			☀ ☽
Picea pungens 'Hoopsii' (blue spruce)	30'–50'	▓	▓	▓	▓	☀
Platycodon grandiflorus (balloon flower)	1'–3'		▓			☀ ☽
Plumbago auriculata (Cape plumbago)	6'		▓	▓		☀ ☽
Pulmonaria (lungwort)	8"–1½'	▓				☽ ●
Rhododendron	2'–20'	▓			▓	☀ ☽
Rosa (rose)	1'–15'		▓	▓		☀ ☽

	Height	Season of Color				Sun or Shade
		Sp	Su	F	W	
Rosmarinus officinalis (rosemary)	1½'–6'	■			■	☼
Salvia farinacea (mealy-cup sage)	1½'–3'		■			☼
Scabiosa (pincushion flower)	2½'		■			☼
Scaevola 'Mauve Clusters'	6"	■	■			☼
Scilla (squill)	6"–1'				■	☼ ◑
Stokesia laevis (Stokes' aster)	1½'–2'		■			☼
Syringa (lilac)	4'–15'	■				☼

	Height	Season of Color				Sun or Shade
		Sp	Su	F	W	
Thalictrum (meadow rue)	2'–6'		■			☼ ◑
Tulipa (tulip)	6"–3'	■			■	☼ ◑
Verbena rigida	1½'–2'		■	■		☼
Veronica (speedwell)	4"–4'	■	■			☼ ◑
Vinca (periwinkle)	6"–2'	■				◑ ●
Viola odorata (sweet violet)	2"–10"	■				◑ ●
Wisteria	climbing	■				☼ ◑

Clockwise from top left: Heat-resistant Crystal Bowl pansies (Viola × wittrockiana) are available in many clear colors, including this dazzling blue; the dainty lace cap blooms of 'Blue Wave' hydrangea are blue in acid soils but turn lilac or pink in neutral to alkaline soils; and purplish blue speedwell contrasts subtly with creamy yellow foxglove (Digitalis grandiflora).

Pinks & Reds

Vivid red is a stimulating, forceful, sometimes violent hue that grabs attention. The color of blood and fire, bright red is associated with extreme emotions—ardent love, recklessness, rage, cruelty. When red is darkened, it grows mysterious. Subdued and whitened into pink, it becomes simple, sweet, and fresh.

Many distinct reds and pinks, running the gamut from blush to deep burgundy, are found in the plant kingdom. A few are true colors—pure fire-engine red and its clear pastel pink tints—but most have either a yellow or a blue base.

Yellowed reds parade under names such as scarlet, cardinal, vermilion, flame, and copper, while yellowed pinks go by labels like coral, peach, salmon, and shrimp.

Blued reds include crimson, magenta, garnet, ruby, and wine red. Some blued pinks retain their obvious pink identity, while others straddle the line between red and blue. Whether you classify pale violet and mauve as pinks or pinkish blues doesn't really matter, since they're at home in either category.

Clockwise from top left: Ruffled, bright red herbaceous peonies (Paeonia) consort with large-flowered, rich rosy violet 'Barbara Dibley' clematis; the bright orange-red fruits of 'Winter King' green hawthorn (Crataegus viridis), striking against the peeling silver-gray bark, light up the winter landscape; and vibrant magenta blooms of crown-pink (Lychnis coronaria) combine with rosy pink foxglove (Digitalis purpurea), radiant deep pink geranium, and pink-tinged white penstemon.

Mixing the true, yellowed, and blued reds and pinks requires care, whether you're aiming for a monochromatic scheme or working with other hues as well. Combinations may or may not work, depending on the precise colors, the amounts of each, and their relative positions. If certain pinks or reds clash with their neighbors, the best solution may be to separate the combatants with white or to create a smooth transition with gray. When you're dealing with many hues of a single type of plant (for example, impatiens or zinnias in salmon, scarlet, mauve, clear pink, and crimson), you'll find that intermingling the colors is more pleasing than juxtaposing separate blocks.

Companionable reds and pinks are attractive against a green background in a complementary color scheme. Very bright reds are easier on the eyes against a true, deep, or blued green backdrop; yellowed greens only add to the glare.

Blazing scarlet sage (*Salvia splendens*) tends to eclipse other colors, as does magenta crownpink (*Lychnis coronaria*), although the latter's blooms are softened somewhat by the plant's felted silvery leaves. Pairing these glowing reds with green- or gray-leafed foliage plants is often the best way to bring them into line. On the other hand, the soft, romantic pinks and rosy reds of plants such as hollyhock (*Alcea rosea*) and stock (*Matthiola*) mix easily with other hues.

Above: Scarlet cockscomb (Celosia) and 'Disco Flame' French marigolds (Tagetes patula) make a hot twosome. Right: Graceful spider flower (Cleome hasslerana) planting contains both pink and white bloomers.

Facing page clockwise from top left: 'Apple Blossom' verbena harmonizes with magenta petunia; 'Sunnyside' camellia bears single pale pink blooms; and 'Fire King' yarrow (Achillea millefolium) produces clusters of rich red blossoms.

Some red and pink plants are so winning that they deserve a place in the garden whether or not they're team players. For sheer spectacle, try love-lies-bleeding *(Amaranthus caudatus)*: its long, tassel-like crimson flower spikes cascade like so many bellpulls. A striking red-on-pink pattern—mauvish pink petals, each marked by a carmine center stripe—accounts for the popularity of the large-flowered clematis 'Nelly Moser'. Another surprising color combination occurs in purple coneflower *(Echinacea purpurea)*: the rosy petals radiate from a bulbous, orange-brown center.

Some plants merit use for their changing color. A splendid case is 'Autumn Joy' stonecrop *(Sedum)*. Fresh green foliage is the main attraction until late summer; then the broad flower clusters appear, opening a pale pink before turning coppery pink and finally rosy rust. The spent flower heads can be left to dry in the garden for a wintertime show or brought indoors for decoration.

Two of the showiest back-of-the-border plants are queen-of-the-prairie *(Filipendula rubra)*, its towering stems topped by feathery bright pink plumes, and foxglove *(Digitalis purpurea)*, its lofty spikes decorated with drooping purplish pink blossoms. As the common name implies, foxglove's flowers resemble the fingertips of gloves.

Geraniums—both frost-tender *Pelargonium* (commonly known as geranium) and hardy *Geranium* (cranesbill)—offer numerous striking selections. Martha Washington geraniums *(P. × domesticum)* produce flashy flower clusters in many gradations of pink and red, the petals marked with brilliant blotches in darker shades. Some of the best cranesbills include *G. cinereum* 'Ballerina', which bears lilac-pink blooms with crimson veins and a reddish purple center, and magenta-flowering *G. sanguineum.*

Among the plants most closely identified with the pink and red category are the spicy-scented pinks *(Dianthus)*. Though the blossoms do come in a wide range of solid pinks and reds as well as bicolors, the common name actually derives from the delicately fringed petals, which look serrated—or "pinked."

"Rose," of course, is virtually synonymous with pink and red. The countless hybrid teas in this range include blood-red 'Precious Platinum', rich velvety maroon 'Mister Lincoln', and silvery pink 'Sweet Surrender'. The grandiflora 'Love' has scarlet petals with a silvery white underside. The elaborately cupped English rose 'Heritage' is a clear shell pink, the miniature 'Debut' deep crimson with a creamy white base. 'Rosa Mundi', an old garden rose, has flaring petals striped with vivid red, pink, and white.

Gardeners can choose from dozens of exquisite rhododendrons in pink and red hues. Just a few are 'Mrs. Furnival', clear pink with light brown blotches on the upper petals; 'Lem's Cameo', a blending of luminous pink, cream, and apricot; 'Scintillation', a gold-throated pink; and 'President Roosevelt', cherry red merging to a white center.

Peonies offer myriad selections, among them 'America', brilliant scarlet with a tuft of golden stamens; 'Best Man', deep rich red; 'Pink Parfait', vivid pink with a silvery edge; and 'Chiffon Parfait', soft salmon pink.

Tulips are available in many gradations, from palest pink to flamboyant red. Two lovely selections are 'Ice Follies', a combination of crimson, pink, and ivory, and 'Beauty of Volendam', clear white with crimson streaks.

Among the delights of springtime are pink- and rosy red–blossomed trees, including flower-

Clockwise from top: Burning bush (Euonymus alata) turns flaming red in fall; a pink-flowered geranium and a magenta-blossomed one are beautifully paired; and 'Oodnadatta' daylily (Hemerocallis) is an elegant wine red with a yellow throat.

	Height	Season of Color* Sp	Su	F	W	Sun or Shade
Acer palmatum 'Bloodgood' (Japanese maple)	15'		■	■		☼ ◐
Alcea rosea (hollyhock)	2½'–9'		■			☼
Amaranthus caudatus (love-lies-bleeding)	2'–4'		■			☼ ◐
Antirrhinum majus (snapdragon)	8"–3'	■	■			☼
Arbutus unedo (strawberry tree)	5'–25'			■	■	☼ ◐
Aster	1'–6'		■	■		☼ ◐
Astilbe	1½'–5'		■			☼ ◐
Berberis thunbergii 'Rose Glow' (Japanese barberry)	4'–6'	■	■	■		☼
Bergenia	1'–1½'	■			■	◐ ●
Brassica oleracea (flowering cabbage)	8"–1'			■	■	☼
Calluna vulgaris (heather)	6"–3'		■	■		☼
Camellia	6'–20'	■			■	◐ ●
Campsis 'Crimson Trumpet' (trumpet vine)	climbing		■	■		☼
Celosia (cockscomb)	1'–3'		■			☼
Cercis (redbud)	15'–30'	■				☼ ◐
Chaenomeles (flowering quince)	2'–10'	■			■	☼
Clematis 'Nelly Moser'	climbing	■	■			◐
Colchicum autumnale (meadow saffron)	6"–8"			■		☼ ◐
Cornus alba 'Sibirica' (Siberian dogwood)	7'				■	☼ ◐
Cosmos bipinnatus	2'–6'		■	■		☼ ◐
Cotoneaster	8"–20'			■	■	☼
Crataegus laevigata 'Paul's Scarlet' (hawthorn)	25'	■				☼
Dahlia	1'–7'		■	■		☼
Daphne x burkwoodii 'Somerset'	4½'	■				☼ ◐
Dianthus (pink)	6"–1½'	■	■			☼
Dicentra spectabilis (bleeding heart)	2'–3'	■				◐
Dictamnus albus (gas plant)	2½'–3'		■			☼ ◐
Digitalis purpurea (foxglove)	3'–6'	■	■			◐

*Peak season of color shown is an average: it may start earlier or last longer in mild-winter climates, and start later or be briefer in cold-winter regions.

A Rainbow of Garden Colors **63**

ing cherry (Prunus), redbud (Cercis), 'Paul's Scarlet' hawthorn (Crataegus laevigata), and saucer magnolia (Magnolia × soulangiana). The clouds of velvety soft petals produced by crabapples (Malus) are charming, though they may last only a week before falling.

Red foliage adds richness and charm to a garden. Some red-leafed plants work their magic throughout the growing season—for example, the new growth on Fraser's photinia (Photinia × fraseri) spurts up bronzy red, and Japanese blood grass (Imperata cylindrica 'Rubra') has rich red blades that look even more vivid when the sun shines through them. Other plants, such as burning bush (Euonymus alata) and Boston ivy (Parthenocissus tricuspidata), wait until autumn to produce a blaze of color.

The brilliant red fruits of cotoneaster, holly (Ilex), mountain ash (Sorbus), and many forms of firethorn (Pyracantha) provide other surefire ways to brighten the fall and winter garden. And there's no more spectacular winter accent than the coral red shoots of Siberian dogwood (Cornus alba 'Sibirica').

	Height	Season of Color				Sun or Shade
		Sp	Su	F	W	
Echinacea purpurea (purple coneflower)	2½'–4'		●			☼
Erica carnea (heath)	6"–1½'	●			●	☼
Euonymus alata 'Compacta' (burning bush)	7'–10'		●			☼
Filipendula rubra (queen-of-the-prairie)	6'–8'		●			☼ ◐
Geranium (cranesbill)	6"–3'	●	●			☼ ◐
Gomphrena globosa (globe amaranth)	10"–2'		●			☼
Helianthemum nummularium (sunrose)	8"	●	●			☼
Helleborus orientalis (Lenten rose)	1½'	●			●	◐ ●
Heuchera (coral bells)	1'–2½'	●				☼ ◐
Ilex (holly)	1'–40'			●		☼ ◐
Impatiens wallerana	8"–2'		●			◐ ●
Imperata cylindrica 'Rubra' (Japanese blood grass)	1'–2'		●			☼ ◐
Kalmia latifolia (mountain laurel)	8'		●			◐
Kolkwitzia amabilis (beauty bush)	10'		●			☼ ◐
Lathyrus odoratus (sweet pea)	1'–8'	●				☼
Lavatera trimestris 'Silver Cup' (annual mallow)	2'		●			☼

	Height	Season of Color				Sun or Shade
		Sp	Su	F	W	
Liatris spicata 'Kobold' (gayfeather)	2'		●			☼
Lobelia cardinalis (cardinal flower)	3'–4'		●			☼ ◐
Lupinus (lupine)	1½'–5'	●	●			☼
Lychnis coronaria (crown-pink)	2'–3'		●			☼
Lycoris (spider lily)	1½'–2'		●	●		☼ ◐
Magnolia x soulangiana (saucer magnolia)	20'–25'	●				☼ ◐
Malus (crabapple)	8'–30'	●				☼
Matthiola (stock)	1'–2½'	●	●			☼
Monarda didyma (bee balm)	2½'–4'		●			☼ ◐
Nerium oleander (oleander)	6'–12'		●			☼
Oenothera berlandieri (Mexican evening primrose)	1'		●			☼
Paeonia (peony)	2'–6'	●				☼
Papaver orientale (Oriental poppy)	2'–4'	●	●			☼ ◐
Parthenocissus tricuspidata (Boston ivy)	climbing			●		☼ ◐
Pelargonium (geranium)	8"–3'		●			☼ ◐
Penstemon	1½'–3'		●			☼ ◐
Petunia x hybrida	8"–2½'		●			☼

	Height	Season of Color				Sun or Shade
		Sp	Su	F	W	
Phlox	6"–4'					☼ ◑
Photinia x fraseri (Fraser's photinia)	5'–15'					☼
Physostegia virginiana (obedient plant)	1½'–3'					☼ ◑
Primula (primrose)	9"–3'					◑
Prunus sargentii (Sargent cherry)	40'					☼
Pyracantha (firethorn)	2½'–15'					☼
Rhododendron	2'–20'					☼ ◑
Rosa (rose)	1'–15'					☼ ◑
Salvia splendens (scarlet sage)	10"–2'					☼
Scabiosa atropurpurea (pincushion flower)	2½'					☼

	Height	Season of Color				Sun or Shade
		Sp	Su	F	W	
Sedum 'Autumn Joy' (stonecrop)	2'					☼
Senecio x hybridus (cineraria)	1'					◑ ●
Sorbus (mountain ash)	20'–40'					☼
Spiraea x bumalda	2'–4'					☼
Syringa (lilac)	4'–15'					☼
Tulipa (tulip)	6"–3'					☼ ◑
Verbena x hybrida	6"–1'					☼
Viburnum opulus (cranberry bush viburnum)	10'–20'					☼ ◑
Viola x wittrockiana (pansy)	8"					☼ ◑
Weigela florida	5'–10'					☼
Zinnia elegans	6"–3'					☼

Right: The purplish red foliage of 'Atropurpurea' Japanese barberry (Berberis thunbergii) makes a colorful backdrop for a variegated hosta.
  Below: The muted pinks of zinnias and hollyhock (Alcea rosea) mix with pale lavenders and creams in a harmonious scheme.

Yellows & Oranges

Along with scarlet, these are the warm hues found in glowing sunsets, crackling fires, and brilliant fall foliage. Clear yellow reminds us of bright summer sunshine; in fact, the botanical names of some yellow-flowering plants begin with *heli,* from the Greek word *helios* ("sun"). Full-strength orange—an eye-popping blend of red and yellow—evokes crisp autumn images of pumpkins and Halloween.

But not all yellows and oranges are cheery or dazzling. Depending on their value, they can be delicate, sophisticated, or even somber. The many variations of yellow include creamy yellow, clear light lemon, bright egg-yolk gold, and yellow-brown honey. Goldenrod and saffron are bright medium yellows tinged with orange; amber is a darker version. Some yellows, such as sulfur, have a greenish cast.

Gradations of orange include clear bright pumpkin, reddish tangerine, and earthy terra-cotta. Some tints, such as pale peach, are so soft that they seem like genteel distant relatives of orange—if you connect them with that usually blatant hue at all. Yellow-infused orange tones that are muddied or grayed are more commonly called brown.

Clockwise from top left: An exquisite woodland border includes clear yellow daylilies (Hemerocallis) and ligularia; the yellow petal tips of bicolored 'Goblin' blanket flower (Gaillardia × grandiflora) echo the radiant hue of 'Early Sunrise' coreopsis; and the fiery spikes of red-hot poker (Kniphofia uvaria) show a subtle gradation from yellowish orange at the bottom to red-orange at the top.

The distinction between yellow and orange is often blurred. Peach and apricot are seen by some people as pinkish yellow, by others as light to medium orange. Golden is variously described as vivid yellow, sometimes tending toward brown, or lustrous yellow-orange. When you look at California poppy *(Eschscholzia californica)* or black-eyed Susan vine *(Thunbergia alata)*, you may be hard-pressed to say whether the flowers are yellow or orange. Some forms of red-hot poker *(Kniphofia uvaria)* contain both colors, their flower spikes shading from pale yellow at the base up to bright reddish orange.

On overcast or misty days, yellow and orange add an appealing glow to the garden—the next best thing to full sunshine. Take advantage of that fact and use clear yellow, the next lightest color after white, to illuminate shady spots.

Some plants are almost aggressive in their coloration. Geum has radiant yellow and fiery orange-red roselike blooms; montbretia *(Crocosmia × crocosmiiflora)* bears brilliant reddish orange tubular flowers; and marigold *(Tagetes)* is known for its vibrant yellow, gold, and glow-in-the-dark orange blossoms. Keep in mind that

such intense yellows and oranges must be treated carefully: hot-colored plants can overpower or look garish if overused or placed injudiciously. Soft tints, though, mix well with other hues, especially with whites and grays. Clear yellow is an effective accent, but remember that a large amount is difficult to focus on—it's like looking into the sun. Use this luminous hue sparingly to add zest to monochromatic and harmonious planting schemes.

Many plants offer both yellow- and orange-flowering selections. The nuances of the range are evident in daffodils *(Narcissus),* which come in a wide variety of delicate tints and bolder hues in solids and bicolors. Among the many possibilities are blooms with yellow petals and orange cups and all-white flowers with flares of orange inside the cups.

Show-stopping tall bearded irises come in a broad palette of subtle and electric hues in solids, bicolors, and blends. The coloration is generally exquisite—for example, 'Piping Hot' is a combination of tangerine and lighter peachy orange, and 'Early Light' has lemon-tinged cream standards with slightly darker falls and a yellow beard.

When it comes to flamboyance, few plants surpass goldenchain tree (Laburnum × watereri) at the peak of bloom. Long, pendent, wisteria-like racemes of rich yellow blossoms cloak the branches.

It's the rare garden that can't be improved by daylilies (Hemerocallis). Their color range, once limited to bright orange and yellow, now includes many soft pastels. Yellow is still favored, though: 'Stella de Oro', which bears golden yellow flowers over an exceptionally long period, is so popular that breeders have developed versions with smaller and larger blooms.

Many yellow- and orange-flowering plants produce gaily colored daisies, often zoned, banded, or centered with a darker shade. Dark-centered blanket flower (Gaillardia) typically has red petals tipped in yellow; gazania's cream, yellow, or orange blossoms may be solid-colored or ringed with bronze around the center. All forms of sunflower (Helianthus)—from types a couple of feet high to towering 12-footers with enormous, nodding heads—have sunny yellow ray flowers. Yarrows (Achillea) may not look like daisies, but each individual pale yellow to bright sulfur flower in the flattish clusters is in fact a tiny daisy.

Austrian Copper rose (Rosa foetida bicolor), a species rose whose petals are reddish orange on top and yellow underneath, is the source of modern roses in this color range. Among hybrid teas, the many possibilities include golden apricot 'Brandy', pink-edged yellow 'Peace', and yellow and red-orange bicolor 'Flaming Beauty'. Among floribundas, 'Amber Queen' is golden yellow tinged with apricot; 'Prominent' is hot orange. The climber 'Golden Showers' is clear yellow. There are only a few old garden roses in these warm hues, but the elegantly cupped and ruffled English roses make up for the lack. The delightful 'Graham Thomas', for example, produces apricot buds opening to rich yellow.

Although yellow and orange are thought of as summer and autumn hues, they also provide color in winter and early spring. The bare greenish yellow twigs of yellowtwig dogwood (Cornus stolonifera 'Flaviramea') add a sculptural element to the winter garden. In cold-winter regions, witch hazel (Hamamelis) is the earliest

Clockwise from top left: 'Flaviramea' dogwood (Cornus stolonifera) bares yellow twigs late in the year; a hot-color border includes cockscomb (Celosia), coneflower (Rudbeckia), marigolds (Tagetes), and creeping zinnia (Sanvitalia procumbens); and the yellow garden at Hadspen House, England.

	Height	Season of Color* Sp	Su	F	W	Sun or Shade
Acacia baileyana (golden mimosa)	20'–30'				■	☼
Achillea (yarrow)	10"–5'		■	■		☼
Allium moly (golden garlic)	1'–1½'		■			☼
Alstroemeria	1½'–5'		■			☼ ◐
Anthemis tinctoria (golden marguerite)	2'–3'		■			☼
Antirrhinum majus (snapdragon)	8"–3'	■	■			☼
Aquilegia chrysantha (golden columbine)	3'–4'	■	■			☼ ◐
Asclepias tuberosa (butterfly weed)	2'–3'		■			☼
Aurinia saxatilis (basket-of-gold)	1'	■				☼
Belamcanda chinensis (blackberry lily)	3'		■			☼ ◐
Berberis darwinii (Darwin barberry)	5'–10'				■	☼ ◐
Berberis thunbergii 'Aurea' (Japanese barberry)	2'	■	■	■		☼
Calceolaria crenatiflora (pocketbook plant)	1'–1½'		■			◐
Calendula officinalis (pot marigold)	1'–2½'	■	■			☼
Campsis radicans (trumpet vine)	climbing		■	■		☼
Canna	1½'–6'		■	■		☼
Chrysanthemum x morifolium	1'–4'			■		☼
Coreopsis	6"–3'		■			☼
Cornus stolonifera 'Flaviramea' (yellowtwig dogwood)	6'				■	☼ ◐
Cosmos sulphureus	1'–7'		■	■		☼ ◐
Crocosmia x crocosmiiflora (montbretia)	3'–4'		■			☼ ◐
Dahlia	1'–7'		■	■		☼
Digitalis grandiflora (yellow foxglove)	2½'–3'		■			◐
Diospyros kaki (Japanese persimmon)	30'			■		☼
Doronicum (leopard's bane)	1½'–3'	■				◐
Eranthis hyemalis (winter aconite)	2"–8"				■	☼ ◐

*Peak season of color shown is an average: it may start earlier or last longer in mild-winter climates, and start later or be briefer in cold-winter regions.

A Rainbow of Garden Colors   **71**

shrub to bloom. Ribbonlike petals of golden yellow (orange or coppery red in some selections) decorate the bare branches, bringing cheer to bleak landscapes. The bright yellow blossoms of forsythia, also borne on leafless branches and clothing the entire plant, declare that spring is even nearer. Another harbinger of the new season is winter aconite (*Eranthis hyemalis*), with each cheerful yellow stalkless blossom perched on a ruff of bright green bracts.

Brilliant leaves—for example, the spectacular golds, yellows, and reds of various witch hazels or the bright yellow of ginkgo—are one of the great joys of autumn, but colorful foliage is not restricted to that season. Many golden-leafed plants sparkle all year long; some have solid yellow foliage, others yellow-edged or variegated leaves. Among the myriad choices are 'Aurea', a lovely yellow form of Japanese barberry (*Berberis thunbergii*), and 'Emerald and Gold' euonymus, whose glossy bright yellow leaves are centered with a splotch of green.

Yellow and orange fruit add to the year-end spectacle. One of the most picturesque choices is Chinese lantern plant (*Physalis alkekengi*), named for the bright orange-red inflated "lanterns" it bears as the year wanes. The large, edible reddish orange fruit of Japanese persimmon (*Diospyros kaki*), dangling from bare branches, puts on a show for weeks. Firethorn (*Pyracantha*) produces a profusion of long-lasting berries; good selections include yellow-orange 'Teton', orange 'Yukon Belle', and orange-red 'Monrovia'.

	Height	Season of Color				Sun or Shade
		Sp	Su	F	W	
Erysimum cheiri (English wallflower)	8"–2½'					☀ ◐
Eschscholzia californica (California poppy)	1'–2'					☀
Euonymus fortunei 'Emerald and Gold'	1½'					☀ ◐
Euphorbia epithymoides (cushion spurge)	1½'					☀
Forsythia	3'–10'					☀
Fritillaria imperialis (crown imperial)	3'–4'					☀
Gaillardia (blanket flower)	10"–3'					☀
Gazania	6"–1'					☀
Geum	1'–2'					☀ ◐
Ginkgo biloba 'Autumn Gold'	60'–80'					☀
Gladiolus	3'–6'					☀
Hamamelis (witch hazel)	10'–15'					☀ ◐
Helenium (sneezeweed)	2'–4'					☀
Helianthus (sunflower)	2'–12'					☀
Helichrysum bracteatum (strawflower)	1'–3'					☀
Heliopsis helianthoides (false sunflower)	2'–5'					☀

	Height	Season of Color				Sun or Shade
		Sp	Su	F	W	
Hemerocallis (daylily)	1'–6'					☀ ◐
Hyacinthus (Dutch hyacinth)	6"–1'					☀ ◐
Hypericum (St. Johnswort)	1'–6'					☀ ◐
Impatiens wallerana	8"–2'					◐ ●
Iris (tall bearded iris)	2½'–4'					☀ ◐
Jasminum nudiflorum (winter jasmine)	10'					☀ ◐
Kerria japonica	8'					☀ ◐
Kniphofia uvaria (red-hot poker)	1½'–6'					☀
Laburnum x watereri (goldenchain tree)	15'–25'					☀
Lantana camara	2'–6'					☀
Ligularia	2'–6'					◐
Lilium (lily)	1'–8'					☀ ◐
Mahonia	2'–15'					☀ ◐
Mimulus x hybridus (monkey flower)	1'–1½'					◐ ●
Narcissus (daffodil)	6"–1½'					☀ ◐
Nemesia strumosa	8"–1½'					☀ ◐
Oenothera (sundrops)	9"–2'					☀
Paeonia (tree peony)	3'–6'					☀
Papaver orientale (Oriental poppy)	2'–4'					☀ ◐

	Height	Season of Color Sp	Su	F	W	Sun or Shade
Physalis alkekengi (Chinese lantern plant)	2'			■		☼ ◐
Potentilla (cinquefoil)	4"–5'		■	■		☼
Primula (primrose)	9"–3'	■			■	◐
Pyracantha (firethorn)	2½'–15'			■	■	☼
Rhododendron	2'–20'	■			■	☼ ◐
Rosa (rose)	1'–15'		■	■		☼ ◐
Rudbeckia (coneflower)	8"–6'		■	■		☼
Sanvitalia procumbens (creeping zinnia)	8"		■	■		☼
Solidago (goldenrod)	1'–3'		■	■		☼ ◐

	Height	Season of Color Sp	Su	F	W	Sun or Shade
Tagetes (marigold)	6"–4'		■			☼
Thunbergia alata (black-eyed Susan vine)	climbing		■	■		☼
Tithonia rotundifolia (Mexican sunflower)	3'–6'		■	■		☼
Trollius (globeflower)	2'–3'	■	■			☼ ◐
Tropaeolum majus (nasturtium)	8"–15"		■	■		☼
Tulipa (tulip)	6"–3'	■			■	☼ ◐
Verbascum (mullein)	1'–6'		■			☼
Viola x wittrockiana (pansy)	8"	■	■			☼ ◐
Zinnia elegans	6"–3'		■	■		☼

Right: Golden-petaled daisies like coneflower are at home in a prairie garden.

Below: Behind the greenish yellow bracts of cushion spurge (Euphorbia epithymoides) is the russet-orange springtime foliage of 'Goldflame' spiraea.

Greens

Clockwise from top left: The green- and yellow-marbled leaves of 'Icterina' culinary sage (Salvia officinalis) complement the soft purple ones of another sage cultivar, 'Purpurascens'; the feathery chartreuse foliage of 'Frisia' golden locust (Robinia pseudoacacia) stands out beautifully against a dark green background; and the tubular pale green blossoms of this flowering tobacco (Nicotiana) contrast delicately with bright red zinnias.

Often we hear people complain that there's no color in their garden, when the space is actually filled with many gradations of green—a calming hue so taken for granted in nature that its contribution is sometimes overlooked.

The argument can be made, in fact, that green is the most important garden color. A framework of green acts as a backdrop for other hues and provides the main color show during the year's quiet periods.

The various greens may be clear, pale, muddied, or tinged with yellow or blue. Emerald is a pure bright green, apple green a clear light tint. Jade averages a medium bluish green. Of the yellow-greens, chartreuse is lighter and brighter than lime; pea green is dull. Bottle green is the deep green of old-fashioned glass, and avocado a grayish green typical of the fruit's flesh. Greens variegated with white, yellow, or paler green expand the color range. When new leaves unfurl in spring, they're often yellowish, reddish, or coppery, adding still more variety.

Mixing warm and cool, light and dark greens makes for a dynamic garden. Imagine, for example, a combination of the luminous yellow-green leaves of 'Frisia' golden locust *(Robinia pseudoacacia)*, the dark green glossy foliage of many hollies *(Ilex)*, and the smooth medium green leaves of bigleaf hydrangea *(Hydrangea macrophylla)*.

To create a feeling of depth, mass plants with varying green hues and different shapes, heights, and textures at the periphery of the garden. Placing light or variegated greens in front of dark ones expands the space, while doing the reverse closes it up.

Many plants are prized for their attractive greenery. Even if camellias didn't bear exquisite blooms, their rich green, glossy foliage would earn them a place in gardens. Boxwood *(Buxus)*, with its tidy little leaves, is lovely natural or sheared into hedges. The shiny, deep green lobed leaves of fatshedera impart a lush, tropical look to the landscape. Few foliage plants are more striking than hosta, available in greens of every gradation, often with spectacular variegation. And for sheer grace in a woodland setting, nothing can outdo ferns.

Instead of planting ordinary culinary sage *(Salvia officinalis)*, try the more decorative 'Icterina'—its gray-green leaves are elegantly marbled with pale green and yellow. 'Pictum', a cultivar of Italian arum, differs from the straight species in that its handsome arrow-shaped foliage is veined with cream.

A surprising number of plants have greenish flowers. Breeders have produced green-flowering selections of familiar favorites such as tulip and zinnia, but other plants come by their verdant blooms naturally. Angelica's towering stems are topped by airy lime flower clusters. Corsican hellebore *(Helleborus argutifolius)* produces nodding, pale green blossoms. The apple green, bell-shaped "flowers" borne by bells-of-Ireland *(Moluccella laevis)* are actually calyxes, the outer leaves found at the base of most blossoms; tiny purplish or white flowers are hidden inside the bells. Billowing heads of chartreuse blossoms are only part of the charm of lady's mantle *(Alchemilla mollis)*: its large, grayish green, lobed—almost cupped—leaves collect beads of moisture that sparkle in the sun.

Clockwise from top left: A medley of greens includes chartreuse blooms of lady's mantle (Alchemilla mollis) as well as various foliage plants with yellow, blue, and gray overtones; a variegated vining form of euonymus scrambles up a tree, while 'Gold Standard' hostas with bright yellowish green leaves edged in blue-green stand at its base; and a curving grass path is bordered on both sides by plantings in various green shades.

GREENS

	Height	Season of Color*				Sun or Shade
		Sp	Su	F	W	
Alchemilla mollis (lady's mantle)	1½'		■			☽
Amaranthus caudatus 'Viridis' (love-lies-bleeding)	2'		■	■		☀ ☽
Angelica archangelica	6'		■			☽
Arum italicum 'Pictum' (Italian arum)	1'	■		■	■	☽ ●
Buxus (boxwood)	2'–20'	■	■	■	■	☀ ☽ ●
Camellia	6'–20'	■	■	■	■	☽ ●
Cotoneaster	8"–20'	■	■	■	■	☀
Dryopteris (wood fern)	1½'–4'	■	■	■		☀ ☽ ●

	Height	Season of Color*				Sun or Shade
		Sp	Su	F	W	
Euphorbia characias	4'	■				☀
x Fatshedera lizei	8'	■	■	■	■	☽ ●
Hedera helix (English ivy)	climbing	■	■	■	■	☀ ☽ ●
Helleborus argutifolius (Corsican hellebore)	3'	■			■	☽ ●
Hosta	6"–5'	■	■	■	■	☽ ●
Hydrangea	2'–15'		■	■		☀ ☽
Ilex (holly)	1'–40'	■	■	■	■	☀ ☽
Juniperus (juniper)	6"–60'	■	■	■	■	☀
Kochia scoparia (summer cypress)	3'		■	■		☀

Left: An irregular-shaped, closely cropped lawn forms a luxuriant carpet of refreshing bright green. A mixed bed juts into the green expanse, while other plantings encircle it.

Below: Lawn traces a zigzag path through verdant plantings.

Facing page: Big domes of chartreuse bracts are this euphorbia's crowning glory.

	Height	Season of Color				Sun or Shade
		Sp	Su	F	W	
Moluccella laevis (bells-of-Ireland)	2'		▨			☀
Nicotiana 'Lime Green' (flowering tobacco)	2'	▨	▨	▨		☀ ◐
Osmunda regalis (royal fern)	4'–6'	▨	▨	▨		☀ ◐ ●
Pachysandra terminalis (Japanese spurge)	6"–10"	▨	▨	▨	▨	◐ ●
Pieris japonica (lily-of-the-valley shrub)	6'–10'	▨	▨	▨	▨	◐
Prunus laurocerasus (English laurel)	4'–15'	▨	▨	▨	▨	☀ ◐

	Height	Season of Color				Sun or Shade
		Sp	Su	F	W	
Robinia pseudoacacia 'Frisia' (golden locust)	30'	▨	▨	▨		☀
Salvia officinalis 'Icterina' (culinary sage)	2½'	▨	▨	▨	▨	☀
Sarcococca (sweet box)	1½'–4'					◐ ●
Tulipa 'Spring Green' (tulip)	20"	▨				☀ ◐
Vinca (periwinkle)	6"–2'	▨	▨	▨	▨	◐ ●
Zinnia 'Envy'	2'		▨	▨		☀

*Peak season of color shown is an average: it may start earlier or last longer

Silvers & Grays

Gray, the neutral color between black and white, can be light or dark, achromatic or tinged with a hue, hard-edged or soft, muted or shimmering. Silvers are the luminaries of the family; these are the whitish grays that light up the garden on dull days and shine magically in the moonlight.

Besides silver, other grays taking their names from metals they resemble are steel, a dark bluish gray; gunmetal, a medium neutral gray; and pewter, a dull whitish gray. You'll also encounter soft, pale dove gray, light bluish pearl gray, and almost-white powder gray.

The terms just listed are reserved for foliage that is predominantly gray. If a plant is referred to as gray-green or grayish green, it generally appears more green than gray, although it can serve the same function as a more neutral-colored plant—especially if its grayness is emphasized by placing it near a truer green.

Many gray-leafed plants are attractive enough to win a place in the garden on their own merits, but they're most often chosen for their effect on other colors. When grays and pale pastels keep company, the pastels look

Clockwise from top left: Gray-leafed plants including 'Silver Carpet' lamb's ears (Stachys byzantina) and white-blossomed snow-in-summer (Cerastium tomentosum) blanket the soil around stepping stones; the leaves of weeping willowleaf pear (Pyrus salicifolia 'Pendula'), at the end of the walkway, emerge silvery, then turn silvered green; and the woolly gray-white leaves of silver sage (Salvia argentea) are striking in a border.

brighter. Vivid contrasts, on the other hand, are moderated by gray—in the presence of gray plants, bright orange zinnias and electric blue lobelia seem somewhat subdued, almost white-washed. Gray creates harmonious transitions between clashing colors such as rosy pink and orange; it also has a well-deserved reputation as a unifier, tying all parts of a potentially discordant garden into a pleasing whole.

Most plants with silver or gray foliage are native to arid parts of the world, such as the Mediterranean region and similar areas with mild winters and little or no summer rainfall. The foliage owes its color to a covering of small

hairs that provide insulation from heat and slow down water loss. The precise coloration depends on the length, density, and slant of the hairs. Just as they do in their native habitats, gray-leafed plants grow best in full sun; in shade, they often become greener and lankier. Some may lose their downy covering after setting seed to ensure their survival.

Probably the best-known garden gray is dusty miller. Several plants go by this common name, including *Centaurea cineraria*, *Artemisia stellerana* (also called beach wormwood), and *Senecio cineraria*, all of which have lobed, felted whitish gray leaves. The yellow daisies (more

Far left and left: Grays and silvers have the ability to punctuate plantings and unify mixed borders.

Below from top to bottom: Whitish gray, lobed leaves of dusty miller (Centaurea cineraria) are handsome with white-flowering plants; 'Silver Mound' artemisia (Artemisia schmidtiana) forms a low, feathery hummock.

often purple on *Centaurea*) detract from the effect and are best pinched off. Also called dusty miller are crown-pink (*Lychnis coronaria*), better known for its magenta blossoms than its fuzzy gray-white foliage, and silver lace (*Chrysanthemum ptarmiciflorum*), which has finely cut silver leaves and white daisies.

Other silvery plants have white flowers that add to the shimmering effect of the foliage. Silver-leafed *Artemisia ludoviciana albula* bears grayish white flowers; *Achillea clavennae* is a silvery yarrow with pale cream blossoms; and snow-in-summer (*Cerastium tomentosum*) produces pristine white blooms.

The leaves of elaeagnus, a group of shrubs and trees grown for their foliage, are either silver-tinted or stippled with silvery dots that reflect the sun. The silvery white foliage of weeping willowleaf pear (*Pyrus salicifolia* 'Pendula') slowly turns silvery green as the season progresses.

Some lovely small-scale ground covers include velvety 'Silver Carpet' lamb's ears (*Stachys byzantina*); green-edged, silvery white 'Beacon Silver' dead nettle (*Lamium maculatum*), which seems to glow; and fuzzy gray woolly thyme (*Thymus pseudolanuginosis*), charming between stepping stones and in wall crannies.

SILVERS & GRAYS

	Height	Season of Color*				Sun or Shade
		Sp	Su	F	W	
Achillea clavennae (yarrow)	10"	▓	▓			☼
Anaphalis (pearly everlasting)	2'–2½'	▓	▓			☼ ◑
Artemisia ludoviciana albula	3'	▓	▓	▓		☼
Artemisia schmidtiana	1'–2'	▓	▓	▓		☼
Artemisia stellerana (beach wormwood)	2½'	▓	▓	▓		☼
Ballota pseudodictamnus	2'	▓	▓	▓		☼
Centaurea cineraria (dusty miller)	1'–1½'	▓	▓	▓	▓	☼

	Height	Season of Color				Sun or Shade
		Sp	Su	F	W	
Cerastium tomentosum (snow-in-summer)	8"	▓	▓	▓	▓	☼
Chrysanthemum ptarmiciflorum (silver lace)	8"		▓	▓		☼
Convolvulus cneorum (bush morning glory)	2'–4'		▓	▓		☼
Cynara cardunculus (cardoon)	6'–8'	▓	▓	▓		☼
Elaeagnus	8'–20'	▓	▓	▓		☼
Lamium maculatum 'Beacon Silver' (dead nettle)	6"	▓	▓	▓	▓	◑ ●

	Height	Season of Color				Sun or Shade
		Sp	Su	F	W	
Lavandula angustifolia (English lavender)	1'–4'	▨	▨	▨	▨	☼
Lychnis coronaria (crown-pink)	2'–3'	▨	▨	▨	▨	☼
Origanum dictamnus (Crete dittany)	1'	▨	▨	▨	▨	☼
Pyrus salicifolia 'Pendula' (weeping willowleaf pear)	15'–25'		▨	▨		☼
Salvia argentea (silver sage)	2'–3'		▨			☼
Santolina chamaecyparissus (lavender cotton)	2'	▨	▨	▨	▨	☼

	Height	Season of Color				Sun or Shade
		Sp	Su	F	W	
Senecio cineraria (dusty miller)	2'		▨			☼
Stachys byzantina 'Silver Carpet' (lamb's ears)	8"		▨	▨		☼ ☽
Teucrium fruticans (bush germander)	4'–8'	▨	▨	▨	▨	☼
Thymus pseudolanuginosus (woolly thyme)	2"–3"		▨	▨		☼
Verbascum olympicum (mullein)	6'		▨			☼

*Peak season of color shown is an average: it may start earlier or last longer in mild-winter climates, and start later or be briefer in cold-winter regions.

Above and on facing page: A judicious use of silver and gray adds nuance and interest to a predominantly green scheme. Since many of the plants in the silver-and-gray category have velvety, fuzzy, or woolly leaves, they also contribute pleasing textures to a planting.

Planning A Colorful Garden

*Close your eyes and visualize an exquisitely
arranged garden awash in color: mounds
of gaily hued flowers compete for attention,
clusters of brilliant fruit sparkle, greenery
glows against richly mottled bark, and
colorful foliage plants punctuate the
scene. How do you convert that image
into reality? This chapter offers practical
advice, from scheduling a long-lasting show to
creating drifts to planning on paper. You'll also find
eight professional plans; use them as a source of
ideas, or copy one (or more) in your own garden.*

*A springtime planting of purple
primroses (Primula) follows
the gentle curves of a brick-
edged lawn.*

87

The rosy pinks, lavenders, and creamy whites in this border were chosen to harmonize with the pale blue house trim.

Design Basics

You don't actually *have* to design your garden before planting, but the results are bound to be more satisfying if you formulate a plan before you set to work. In choosing a specific design, you'll be forced to think through your ideas and give them shape.

Designing a colorful garden means addressing several issues. First, choose your colors; you can heed the principles we've discussed on pages 29–39 or rely on your intuition. Second, think about timing—do you want to build up to a crescendo of color or spread interest more evenly over the entire growing season? Third, plan your layout, either by working out the design on paper or, if you prefer, by tracing planting areas in the soil.

As you create your garden, do only as much as you can handle comfortably. If designing the whole garden at once is too taxing, do the job in stages. Or complete the entire design but implement it piecemeal. Gradual installation lets you see if your plan really works and offers a chance for revisions if you're disappointed.

Remember that, for most nonprofessionals, a design is just a starting point. If the garden turns out perfectly on your first try, consider yourself lucky! Expect to shift plants and make substitutions.

Committing to a Color Scheme

Your design will take shape more smoothly if you decide on a color scheme from the start. See pages 34–36 for information on four standard schemes: harmonious, complementary, monochromatic, and kaleidoscopic.

Before making a firm decision on a set of colors, remember to consider garden paving, the facade of your house, and any other conspicuous features. If there are existing plants you want to keep, take those into account as well. For example, perhaps you have several mature camellias bearing pinkish coral blossoms in late winter. If you don't favor that tint, just work around it. Compatible colors need only be in evidence when the camellias are in bloom; the rest of the year, don't worry about conflicts.

There's nothing wrong with having more than one color arrangement at a time in the garden. You might choose one set of colors for an entryway planting and another for a mixed border in the backyard. It's fine to set up conflicting schemes within sight of each other; they won't clash if you separate them with enough green or gray.

Orchestrating a different color scheme for each season is more difficult than planning concurrent schemes, since you're at the mercy of nature, which may cause untimely blooming

At top, a walled garden seen in July also contains spring and fall bloomers for a progression of color. Above, the creamy white bark of paper birch (Betula papyrifera) is a focal point in fall and winter.

or fruiting. Miss the mark by just a little and the results could be frightful. Save this type of arrangement until you feel experienced in gardening with color.

Getting the Timing Right

Timing is everything in color gardening. You want appeal throughout the year, not just a single brief, spectacular burst (or even several) followed by a long dearth. To keep the show going, choose as much long-lasting color as possible and fill in with a progression of more fleeting color.

Enduring color often comes in the form of foliage and fruit. Yellow-edged 'Emerald and Gold' euonymus and 'Silver Carpet' lamb's ears (*Stachys byzantina*) are excellent choices for year-round foliage color; many forms of firethorn (*Pyracantha*) and cotoneaster produce bright red or orange berries that can hang on for months.

Some plants with all-year appeal show off something different in each season. For example, Cornelian cherry (*Cornus mas*) begins its show with billows of tiny yellow blossoms on bare twigs; these are followed by lustrous green leaves, large scarlet fruit, and red fall foliage. The tree's mottled gray-and-tan bark, especially noticeable in winter when the branches are leafless, is a bonus.

Some plants bloom briefly, while others produce a prolonged display. But not all long-lasting bloomers will return on their own the next year—annuals like cosmos and marigold (*Tagetes*) are colorful for months, but the plants are short-lived and must be replaced the following year. Flowering perennials, shrubs, and other permanent plants typically bloom for shorter periods, but they can be counted on year after year. To create a succession of color, choose a mix of plants that flower at different times. If all goes according to plan, one group will come into bloom as another fades.

Unfortunately, it's difficult to be precise about blooming and fruiting times, since they vary with the climate. The color charts in this book (beginning on page 47) are averaged for the country; you may well have to advance the timing if you live in a mild-winter area or delay it if your climate is very cold. Even within a given region, the timing may differ from year to

year. For instance, if winter weather turns out to be especially mild, spring blooming will commence earlier.

To make your timetable reflect local conditions, note when the plants in nearby gardens begin and end their seasons of color. Don't rely on what happens in nurseries, since plants there have been forced into early growth under artificial conditions. And remember—whatever your area's color timetable, nature is bound to throw the schedule out of whack occasionally. For this reason, it's wise not to plan so rigidly that the odd fluctuation ruins the scheme.

Building Good Structure

When some gardeners plan color, they think only of gaily blooming annuals, perennials, and bulbs. But flower beds alone make for a flat, two-dimensional display. A well-designed garden needs a framework of hardscape and permanent woody plantings to sustain interest when herbaceous plants are past their peak or have died to the ground. Even a traditional cottage garden, largely just a tangle of flowers, usually has a stone wall or an evergreen hedge to give it structure.

An easy way to build structure is to position the largest elements first, then work down in size. Only when the basic "bones" are in place—trees, shrub groupings, walls, fences, vines, and ground covers—do you fill in with annuals, perennials, and bulbs.

Choose permanent plants for the berries, bark, or other colorful features they contribute to the scene. And don't forget the key role of green: the other colors need a verdant background for maximum impact.

Herbaceous plants can be confined to clearly delineated beds or, for a more flowing look, grouped in drifts (see page 93). To double your color (and to camouflage any dying foliage), interplant perennials, bulbs, and other brief bloomers with flowering ground covers.

As you build the garden, remember that your goal is to choose and combine various elements so there's always something to draw the eye. If it's properly structured, the garden will retain its identity even during lulls in blooming and other quiet periods.

Colorful foliage plants contribute to a long-lasting show. This red-leafed Norway maple (Acer platanoides) maintains its hue throughout the growing season.

Making the Most of Fall Color

Many deciduous trees, shrubs, and vines dramatically change color in autumn, transforming the landscape with the fiery reds, glowing oranges, and vivid yellows of their foliage.

This color change occurs because the plants stop manufacturing chlorophyll, a green pigment involved in plant growth and nutrition, as they approach winter dormancy. As the amount of chlorophyll decreases, other pigments previously masked by green begin to show. For example, carotenoids turn ginkgo and summersweet *(Clethra alnifolia)* bright yellow; anthocyanins produce the bright scarlets and purples of Japanese maple *(Acer palmatum)*, burning bush *(Euonymus alata)*, and Boston ivy *(Parthenocissus tricuspidata)*.

The hue and intensity of fall colors are genetically determined. A plant propagated asexually (by a method other than seeding) will inherit the colorful characteristics of its parent. Seed-grown plants, on the other hand, can be extremely variable: one oakleaf hydrangea *(Hydrangea quercifolia)* may turn an intense crimson, while another is a disappointing yellow-brown. To make sure you know what you're getting, purchase such plants when they're changing color.

It's also important to buy locally, so you can be certain how the plant behaves in your region. If you don't know whether a particular plant is or is not seed-grown, ask the supplier for information. Keep in mind, too, that buying named cultivars will help guarantee good color and performance.

Even in plants renowned for outstanding fall color, the annual display depends on weather and growing conditions. If nighttime temperatures stay warm through autumn, leaves may turn yellow, but the show of purples and reds will be inhibited. The typical autumn chill in cold-winter climates explains why spectacular fall color is prevalent in those areas. Some plants, however, color quite well even in milder regions; check with local nurseries or plant societies for the best bets.

Other factors may conspire to spoil the show. Leaves won't get a chance to color if an early killing frost withers them or strong winds blow them away. Severe drought stress can put the brakes on color, while milder stress can actually enhance it. Overly wet soil has the effect of delaying color development; soil tending toward acidity usually produces better color than alkaline soil does.

To increase your chances of a dazzling display, locate plants where they receive sun for most of the day, or at least from noon on. Choose a site with well-drained soil and keep it on the dry side in fall.

For the most spectacular effect, group several types of trees that display a range of fall colors. An assortment of trees will provide a prolonged show by coloring up at slightly different times and holding leaves for varying periods.

Vary plant forms for maximum interest. This border contains an agreeable combination of sprawling, spiky, and ground-hugging specimens.

Combining Plants Well

The way you arrange your plants can make or break the garden. Don't be afraid to try out different plans—after all, one of the most exciting aspects of color gardening is the opportunity it provides for experimentation. Keep in mind, though, that your main goal is to achieve the most pleasing, longest-lasting color show.

Of course, color shouldn't be the only criterion in placing plants. The right growing conditions are essential, and a plant's color may even depend on them. For example, silver- and gray-foliaged plants require full sun and quick drainage, while golden-leafed types do better in shade. Variegated plants may turn green when overfertilized, so they shouldn't be placed next to heavy feeders. Plants with colorful stems usually look their brightest in full sun.

To save yourself headaches, group together plants with the same soil, water, and fertilizer needs: it's much easier to treat the whole group alike than to try isolating growing conditions in a close planting.

Also consider each plant's appearance. Is it rounded, columnar, spiky, or weeping? Are the leaves or flowers big and bold or small and delicate? Varying shapes and textures is a good way to create interest: when the plants all look the same, the result is bland and monotonous. Just make sure that the differences are compatible and that you don't clutter the planting with too much variety.

Planning a Bed

You may find it easier to organize your space if you include some beds in the lawn (though this will complicate mowing) or other parts of the garden. A narrow bed placed at the edge of the property or against a structure and accessible from only one side is usually called a border.

The first ornamental beds were filled with blazes of annual color. In perennial borders, popularized by the influential garden designer Gertrude Jekyll, perennials traditionally hold sway but are augmented by annuals, bulbs, and small trees and shrubs. Jekyll even used potted plants to plug in seasonal color gaps. Nowadays, the mixed bed relies even more heavily on permanent plants to provide more color with less work. Modern beds often contain small specimen trees, shrub groupings, ground covers, vines, and ornamental grasses in addition to the familiar annuals, perennials, and bulbs.

For your bed, choose a shape that fits the style of your garden and the space you wish to fill. Squares and rectangles are suited to formal gardens, ovals and irregular shapes to more casual designs. Stretch the perimeter for a wide area or compress it for a smaller space.

Designing Drifts

Drifts are casual, free-form groupings of plants—a welcome departure from traditional blocks, in which plants are lined up in a regular pattern like soldiers at attention. Annuals, perennials, and bulbs look most natural when arranged in drifts, and shrubs can also be massed effectively in this way.

The garden designer Gertrude Jekyll arranged her perennial borders in drifts. An artist as well as a landscaper, Jekyll used drifts to create the same impact in the garden as great washes of color did in her paintings.

The individual plants in a drift merge into a pleasing whole when viewed from a distance. For this rea-son, drifts are best suited to open areas or large island beds. For narrow borders in front of a structure, it's preferable to arrange plants in rows according to height—with an occasional taller plant spilling toward the front for added interest.

Creating a drift of bulbs is easy: just toss handfuls of bulbs into the air and plant them where they fall. This method works best with species that naturalize, such as crocus, squill *(Scilla),* and grape hyacinth *(Muscari).* The original planting will increase and spread on its own over the years.

With other kinds of plants, you'll have better results if you design the drifts. As the drawings below show, drifts are based on triangles, though they don't actually resemble that shape once they're in place.

Each drift should contain a single type of plant, preferably in a single color. Enclose the drifts in a bed as shown, or allow them to meander unbounded. Adjoining drifts should fit together like the pieces of a jigsaw puzzle, although not as snugly. If you want to keep the various plant types from intermingling, make the spacing between drifts roughly twice that between plants. Use harmonious colors in adjacent drifts so that the plantings flow together gracefully rather than standing out in stark contrast.

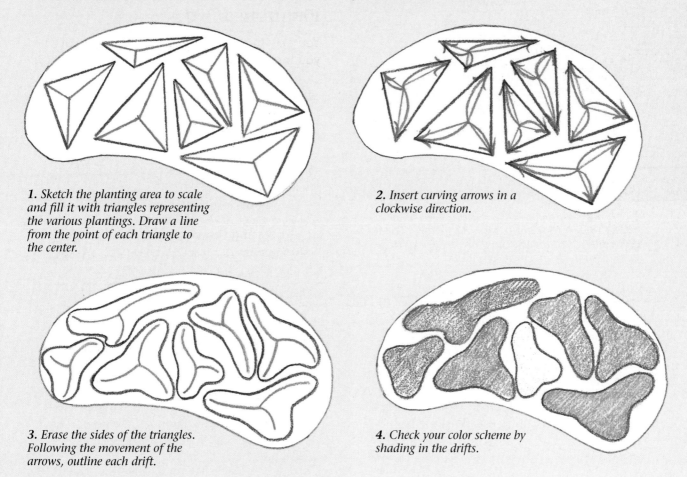

1. Sketch the planting area to scale and fill it with triangles representing the various plantings. Draw a line from the point of each triangle to the center.

2. Insert curving arrows in a clockwise direction.

3. Erase the sides of the triangles. Following the movement of the arrows, outline each drift.

4. Check your color scheme by shading in the drifts.

The formal garden, at top, is characterized by straight lines, clipped hedges, and topiary. The informal garden, above, contains flowing lines and a more casual arrangement of plants.

uniformly wide; it can be broadened at various points to handle the larger plants.

In an island bed, arrange the tallest plants in the middle and stair-step down in all directions. Since a border is viewed head on, it's best to arrange the plants according to height, with the shortest in front and the tallest in back. Don't line the plants up rigidly, though.

All parts of a bed should be accessible for plant care and weeding. Incorporate stepping stones or mulched paths in deep beds. Borders are easier to tend if you leave a clearance of a few feet at the back.

Compiling a Plant List

Even if you consider just one category at a time, the prospect of sifting through a seemingly endless inventory of plants may seem daunting. To speed things up, start with the largest plants and work your way down in size: you'll doubtless need fewer trees and large shrubs than you will smaller plants. Besides, you'll find that ultimate size is a criterion that will eliminate many candidates. Remember, too, that your color scheme and the limitations of your climate and growing conditions will drastically reduce the possibilities. Special considerations, such as drought tolerance or ease of care, further cut down the number of choices.

The encyclopedia on pages 113–205 gives the particulars about many of the best choices available to home gardeners. For other possibilities suited to your area, consult local garden societies and nurseries.

Before deciding in favor of a plant, note when and for how long it will brighten the garden. Be sure you can live with the plant's looks when its season of color is over. As you add each selection to your list, jot down its color, main season of show, and size. Then use the finished, detailed list to lay out your design.

Planning on Paper

Putting your design on paper isn't absolutely necessary, but doing so will help you refine your ideas and provide a road map for installation. Just as a house floor plan does, a garden plan depicts the overall space and shows what goes where.

Although size is arbitrary, any bed should be big enough to accommodate the largest plants without being overpowered by them. A bed looks best when it's about twice as wide as its tallest plants are high, but you can get by with narrower dimensions if need be: just make sure the tallest plant's height isn't more than about one and a half times the width of the bed. That is, if the bed is 4 feet wide, the tallest plant shouldn't exceed 6 feet. A bed needn't be

Instant Color

There may be times when you and your garden are out of synch: you need color *now* for a party or other event, but your plants aren't cooperating. They're looking subdued just when you need fireworks.

A quick trip to the nursery will save the day. There you'll find showy annuals and perennials in full flower, ready to be plugged into beds and containers. Augment these with flowering shrubs, which may be in bloom unseasonably because of artificial conditions in the nursery. Also look for pots of blooming vines with growth long enough to twine up a trellis or along a fence.

It doesn't matter whether the plants chosen for an immediate color display will thrive in your garden at that time of year, since you need them only for short duty. Of course, those you can press into longer service will give you more value for your gardening dollar.

A gala needn't be in the works for you to crave bursts of color close to the house, where they can lift your spirits daily as you come and go. These spots of color make a home cheery and inviting, as real estate agents will affirm. They know the value of "escrow flowers"—pots of brightly blooming annuals that often disappear once the sale is final.

Impatiens, zinnia, lobelia, scarlet sage (Salvia splendens), and geranium (Pelargonium) are among the potted plants brightening this entryway.

Start by measuring the planting area and drawing it to scale. It's easiest to use graph paper, making each square equal to a foot or a fraction of a foot. Once your original drawing is complete, make copies of it; keep the original for future reference and use the copies to work out the design. First, sketch in the hardscape: fences, patios, arbors, paths, and so on. Next, decide where to place all the plants you listed, starting with the largest ones and working your way down in size. Use circles to indicate individual plants, hatch marks or other symbols to represent large plantings of ground covers and bulbs. To indicate drifts, see page 93. As you arrange the plants, remember that masses of color are more effective than scattered dots.

You may not be able to work in every plant on your list: some choices may turn out to be incompatible with the design, or they may so closely resemble other plants in form and color that you can easily eliminate them. Don't try to squeeze in leftovers just to use them up!

Space your plants far enough apart to prevent overcrowding later on—this will save you the trouble of cutting back or moving plants as they grow. In your calculations, use the mature size for all plants except slow-growing trees; ask the supplier how much room to allot for these. Another approach is to use what landscape architects refer to as "design size" for shrubs and trees—the size the plant will be in 5, 10, or even 15 years. Again, consult the supplier.

Use colored pencils to indicate the various hues. You may want to color a separate copy for each season so you can see how the garden will look throughout the year. Keep modifying the plan until you're satisfied with it.

On the following pages, you'll find eight professionally designed plans featuring a variety of color schemes. If they fit your needs, incorporate one or more in your garden; or simply use them as a source of inspiration.

olorful Foliage Garden

anset head gardener Rick LaFrentz designed this private, multihued foliage garden, where homeowners can relax in peaceful seclusion. Shown here in summer, the garden features six different heathers, hardy plants that retain their colorful, scaly leaves all year. When temperatures drop in autumn, some of these heathers change hues, as do the Japanese maple and burning bush.

Plant List

A Acer palmatum 'Sango Kaku' (Japanese maple) **(2)**
B Ajuga reptans 'Purpurea' (carpet bugle) **(4 flats)**
C Berberis thunbergii 'Atropurpurea' (Japanese barberry) **(2)**
D Berberis thunbergii 'Aurea' (Japanese barberry) **(1)**
E Calluna vulgaris 'Aurea' (heather) **(1)**
F Calluna vulgaris 'Beoley Gold' (heather) **(1)**
G Calluna vulgaris 'Cuprea' (heather) **(1)**
H Calluna vulgaris 'Hugh Nicholson' (heather) **(1)**
I Calluna vulgaris 'Orange Queen' (heather) **(2)**
J Calluna vulgaris 'White Mite' (heather) **(3)**
K Elaeagnus pungens 'Fruitlandii' (silverberry) **(2)**
L Euonymus alata 'Compacta' (burning bush) **(2)**
M Euonymus fortunei 'Emerald and Gold' **(1)**
N Hosta 'Thomas Hogg' **(18)**
O Imperata cylindrica 'Rubra' (Japanese blood grass) **(6)**
P Photinia × fraseri (Fraser's photinia) **(3)** (trained as a tall hedge)
Q Prunus cerasifera 'Atropurpurea' (purple-leaf plum) **(1)**
R Santolina chamaecyparissus (lavender cotton) **(2)**
S Teucrium fruticans (bush germander) **(2)**

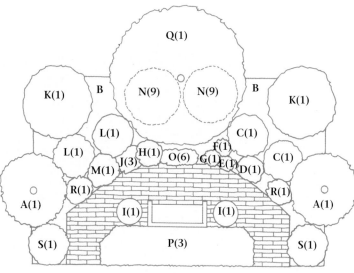

Scale: ½ inch equals 4 feet

Cool-color Garden

Shown in midsummer, this sunny island bed from designer Phil Edinger contains a delightfully cool mix of blue, lavender, purple, pink, and white. When blooming wanes, colored and variegated foliage keeps the planting interesting. Laid out to look lovely from every angle, the bed is especially effective in a large lawn or ground-cover planting.

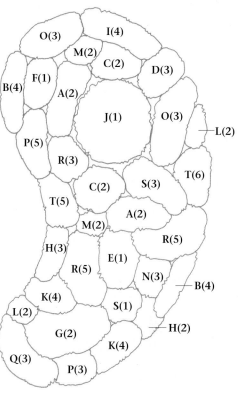

Scale: ½ inch equals 3 feet

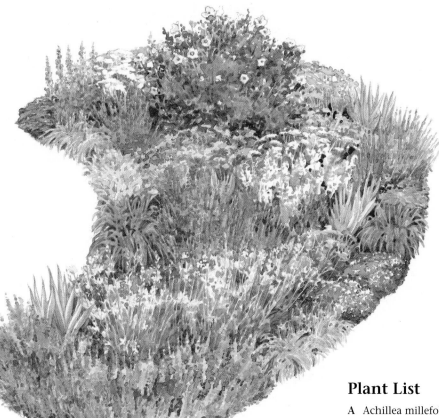

Plant List

A Achillea millefolium 'White Beauty' (yarrow) **(4)**
B Ajuga reptans 'Purpurea' (carpet bugle) **(8)**
C Aster × frikartii 'Mönch' **(4)**
D Cerastium tomentosum (snow-in-summer) **(3)**
E Dictamnus albus 'Albiflorus' (gas plant) **(1)**
F Dictamnus albus 'Purpureus' (gas plant) **(1)**
G Gaura lindheimeri **(2)**
H Hemerocallis 'Little Grapette' (daylily) **(5)**
I Heuchera 'Palace Purple' (coral bells) **(4)**
J Hibiscus syriacus 'Diana' (rose of Sharon) **(1)**
K Iberis sempervirens 'Snowflake' (evergreen candytuft) **(8)**
L Iris 'Pallida Variegata' ('Zebra') (tall bearded iris) **(4)**
M Iris 'Titan's Glory' (tall bearded iris) **(4)**
N Iris 'Stepping Out' (tall bearded iris) **(3)**
O Limonium latifolium (sea lavender) **(6)**
P Liriope muscari 'Silvery Sunproof' (big blue lily turf) **(8)**
Q Nepeta × faassenii (catmint) **(3)**
R Salvia × superba 'East Friesland' (sage) **(13)**
S Scabiosa caucasica (pincushion flower) **(4)**
T Stachys byzantina 'Silver Carpet' (lamb's ears) **(11)**

White Garden

In this corner bed, shown in mid to late spring, garden designer and artist Joni Prittie painted a picture of serenity with a loose blend of whites, creams, and greens—and a touch of pale peach as a gentle accent. To create a rich, layered effect, she arranged the garden so that some plants with strong, dense forms are viewed through slightly taller ones with airier, more open habits.

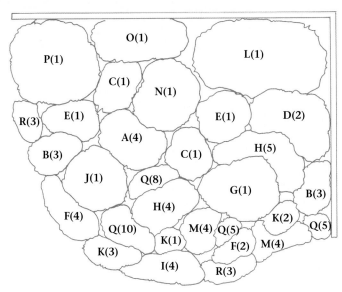

Scale: ½ inch equals 2 feet

Plant List

A Anemone × hybrida 'Honorine Jobert' (Japanese anemone) **(4)**
B Artemisia schmidtiana 'Silver Mound' **(6)**
C Astilbe × arendsii 'Deutschland' **(2)**
D Chrysanthemum × morifolium, white selection (garden chrysanthemum) **(2)**
E Cosmos 'Purity' **(2)**
F Dianthus plumarius 'Pheasant's Eye' (cottage pink) **(6)**
G Gypsophila paniculata 'Bristol Fairy' (baby's breath) **(1)**
H Iris 'Apple Blossom Pink' (intermediate bearded iris) **(9)**

I Lamium maculatum 'White Nancy' (dead nettle) **(4)**
J Papaver orientale 'White King' (Oriental poppy) **(1)**
K Petunia × hybrida, white selection **(6)**
L Philadelphus coronarius (mock orange) **(1)**
M Primula × polyantha, white selection (primrose) **(8)**
N Rosa 'Iceberg' (rose) **(1)**
O Spiraea prunifolia **(1)**
P Syringa 'Mme Lemoine' (lilac) **(1)**
Q Tulipa 'Menton' (tulip) **(28)**
R Viola × wittrockiana, white selection (pansy) **(6)**

Shade Garden

Designer Phil Edinger created this enchanting garden for the dappled light beneath a dogwood and a golden locust, though the plan would work just as well under any trees with airy canopies. Shown in early to mid-summer, the garden features a pleasing mix of soft hues that glow in low light. Plants were also chosen for striking foliage that holds up throughout the growing season.

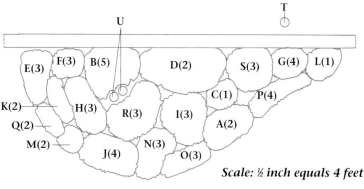

Scale: ½ inch equals 4 feet

Plant List

A Alchemilla mollis (lady's mantle) **(2)**
B Anemone × hybrida 'Honorine Jobert' (Japanese anemone) **(5)**
C Arrhenatherum elatius 'Variegatum' (false oatgrass) **(1)**
D Berberis thunbergii 'Atropurpurea' (Japanese barberry) **(2)**
E Bergenia crassifolia (winter-blooming bergenia) **(3)**
F Digitalis grandiflora (yellow foxglove) **(3)**

G Digitalis purpurea (foxglove) **(4)**
H Helleborus argutifolius (Corsican hellebore) **(3)**
I Helleborus orientalis (Lenten rose) **(3)**
J Hosta 'Chinese Sunrise' **(4)**
K Hosta 'Royal Standard' **(2)**
L Hosta sieboldiana 'Elegans' **(1)**
M Iris foetidissima (Gladwin iris) **(2)**
N Lamium maculatum 'White Nancy' (dead nettle) **(3)**
O Liriope muscari (big blue lily turf) **(3)**
P Liriope muscari 'Variegata' (big blue lily turf) **(4)**

Q Pulmonaria saccharata 'Highdown' (Bethlehem sage) **(2)**
R Thalictrum aquilegifolium (meadow rue) **(3)**
S Thalictrum rochebrunianum 'Lavender Mist' (meadow rue) **(3)**

Existing Trees

T Cornus × rutgersensis 'Aurora' (dogwood)
U Robinia pseudoacacia 'Frisia' (golden locust, multitrunked)

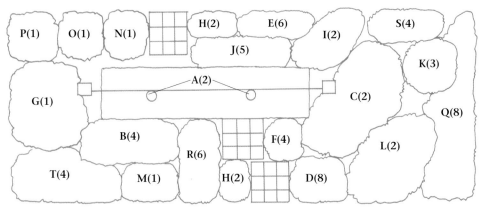

Scale: ½ inch equals 2 feet

Plant List

A   Apple, dwarf   **(2)**
B   Asparagus   **(4)**
C   Blueberry   **(2)**
D   Calendula officinalis (pot marigold)   **(8)**
E   Chives   **(6)**
F   French sorrel   **(4)**
G   Lavandula angustifolia (English lavender)   **(1)**
H   Lemon thyme 'Aureus'   **(4)**
I   Monarda didyma 'Cambridge Scarlet' (bee balm)   **(2)**
J   Peppers   **(5)**
K   Pineapple mint   **(3)**
L   Rhubarb   **(2)**
M   Rosmarinus officinalis 'Prostratus' (rosemary)   **(1)**
N   Salvia officinalis 'Icterina' (culinary sage)   **(1)**
O   Salvia officinalis 'Purpurascens' (culinary sage)   **(1)**
P   Salvia officinalis 'Tricolor' (culinary sage)   **(1)**
Q   Strawberry   **(8)**
R   Sweet basil 'Dark Opal'   **(6)**
S   Swiss chard 'Rhubarb' ('Ruby')   **(4)**
T   Tropaeolum majus (nasturtium)   **(4)**

Note: Most edibles are sold by common name. Those found in the encyclopedia (see pages 113–205) are listed here by botanical name.

Edible Garden

Espaliered apple trees are the focal point of this colorful, richly textured garden from landscape designer Gary Patterson. Though the selections are all edible, this planting is first and foremost an attractive grouping of good-looking plants—each of which happens to have a culinary use. The kaleidoscope of herbs, vegetables, fruits, and edible flowers is shown in late spring.

Cottage Garden

Garden designer and artist Joni Prittie's cottage garden is an impressionistic blend of soft pinks, blues, and creams, punctuated by the hot colors of California poppies. The garden is shown in June or July, and many of these plants will continue to bloom well into late summer. Like all true cottage gardens, this one contains self-sowers (some of which may revert to surprising forms) and provides a good source of cut, dried, and pressed flowers.

Plant List

A Achillea ptarmica 'The Pearl' (yarrow) **(2)**
B Aquilegia caerulea (Rocky Mountain columbine) **(6)**
C Buddleia 'Lochinch' (butterfly bush) **(1)**
D Campanula glomerata 'Alba' (bellflower) **(7)**
E Catananche caerulea (cupid's dart) **(3)**
F Clematis 'Comtesse de Bouchard' **(2)**
G Convallaria majalis (lily-of-the-valley) **(30 pips)**
H Delphinium elatum, 9 each of 'Summer Skies' and 'Galahad' **(18)**
I Digitalis purpurea 'Excelsior Hybrid Mixed' (foxglove) **(12)**
J Eschscholzia californica 'Monarch Mixed' (California poppy) **(11)**
K Filipendula rubra 'Venusta' (queen-of-the-prairie) **(1)**
L Gypsophila paniculata 'Bristol Fairy' (baby's breath) **(2)**
M Lavandula angustifolia 'Hidcote' (English lavender) **(17)**
N Lilium 'Sterling Star' (lily) **(1)**
O Linum perenne (flax) **(18)**
P Monarda didyma 'Croftway Pink' (bee balm) **(2)**
Q Nigella damascena 'Persian Jewels' (love-in-a-mist) **(16)**
R Rosa gallica versicolor ('Rosa Mundi') (French rose) **(1)**
S Rosa centifolia 'Cristata' (crested moss rose) **(1)**
T Viola × wittrockiana 'Imperial Antique Shades' (pansy) **(14)**

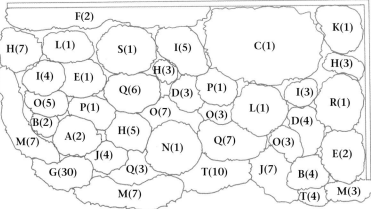

Scale: ½ inch equals 2 feet

Mixed Border

"Quietly colorful" is the description designer Phil Edinger uses for this mixed border of shrubs, vines, ground covers, perennials, and bulbs, shown in early summer. The scheme consists primarily of pinks, rosy purples, and lavenders, accented by white and a dab of yellow. A multitrunked crape myrtle provides height, while flowering vines trained on the fence create colorful backdrops.

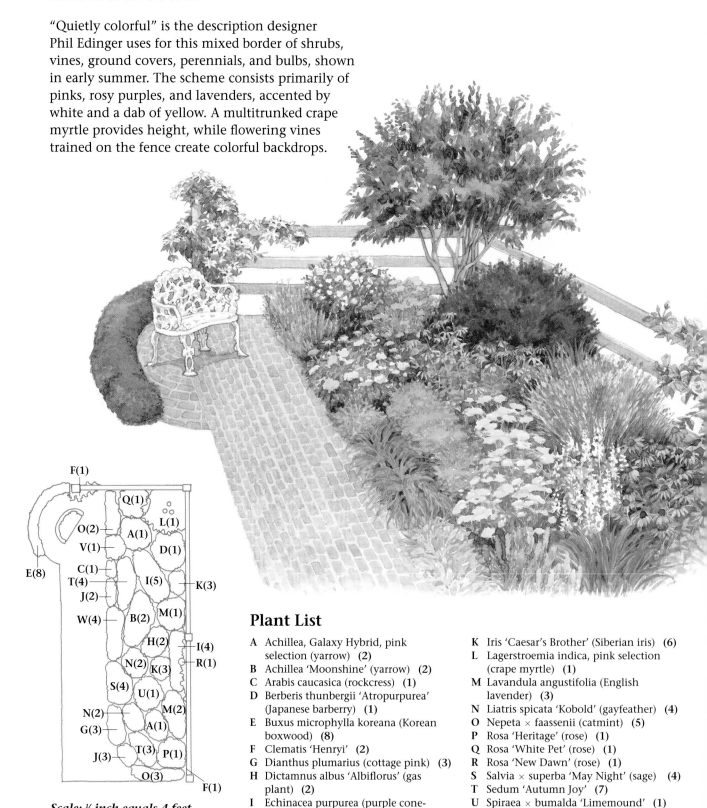

Scale: ½ inch equals 4 feet

Plant List

A Achillea, Galaxy Hybrid, pink selection (yarrow) **(2)**
B Achillea 'Moonshine' (yarrow) **(2)**
C Arabis caucasica (rockcress) **(1)**
D Berberis thunbergii 'Atropurpurea' (Japanese barberry) **(1)**
E Buxus microphylla koreana (Korean boxwood) **(8)**
F Clematis 'Henryi' **(2)**
G Dianthus plumarius (cottage pink) **(3)**
H Dictamnus albus 'Albiflorus' (gas plant) **(2)**
I Echinacea purpurea (purple cone-flower) **(9)**
J Hemerocallis 'Little Grapette' (daylily) **(5)**

K Iris 'Caesar's Brother' (Siberian iris) **(6)**
L Lagerstroemia indica, pink selection (crape myrtle) **(1)**
M Lavandula angustifolia (English lavender) **(3)**
N Liatris spicata 'Kobold' (gayfeather) **(4)**
O Nepeta × faassenii (catmint) **(5)**
P Rosa 'Heritage' (rose) **(1)**
Q Rosa 'White Pet' (rose) **(1)**
R Rosa 'New Dawn' (rose) **(1)**
S Salvia × superba 'May Night' (sage) **(4)**
T Sedum 'Autumn Joy' **(7)**
U Spiraea × bumalda 'Limemound' **(1)**
V Spiraea japonica 'Little Princess' **(1)**
W Stachys byzantina 'Silver Carpet' (lamb's ears) **(4)**

Hot-color Garden

Garden designer and artist Joni Prittie advises wearing sunglasses when tending—or just admiring—this fiery-hued garden! Packed with brilliant reds, scarlets, oranges, and yellows, with touches of magenta for contrast, the planting is shown here in early summer—but it remains vibrant all summer long. Cutting the flowers regularly will give you colorful bouquets and help prolong bloom as well.

Plant List

A Achillea millefolium 'Cerise Queen' (yarrow) **(5)**
B Asclepias tuberosa (butterfly weed) **(2)**
C Calendula officinalis, mixed colors (pot marigold) **(6)**
D Celosia, scarlet selection (plumed cockscomb) **(5)**
E Coreopsis grandiflora 'Sunburst' **(3)**
F Coreopsis auriculata 'Nana' **(12)**
G Dianthus barbatus 'Summer Beauty' (sweet William) **(3)**
H Geum quellyon 'Fire Opal' **(8)**
I Gladiolus hortulanus, 5 each of red, pink, and magenta **(15)**
J Lavatera trimestris 'Mont Rose' (annual mallow) **(3)**
K Lobelia cardinalis (cardinal flower) **(4)**
L Penstemon barbatus 'Prairie Dusk' **(2)**
M Petunia × hybrida, magenta selection **(10)**
N Tagetes patula 'Scarlet Sophie' (French marigold) **(4)**
O Verbena × hybrida 'Showtime' **(4)**
P Zinnia elegans 'Rose Pinwheel' **(6)**

Scale: ½ inch equals 2 feet

Choosing Plants

SHOPPING FOR SEEDS & TRANSPLANTS

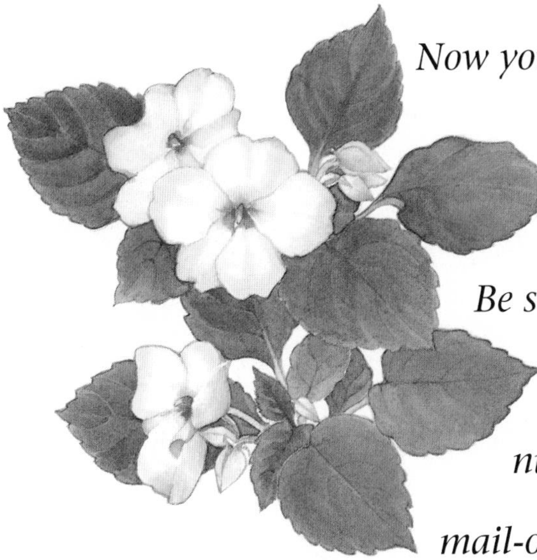

Now you're ready to scout around for just the right plants to transform your garden design into reality. Be sure to keep your plan firmly in mind as you explore local nurseries and thumb through mail-order catalogs—it's all too easy to fall for every pretty flower you see! To help you wade through the tremendous variety you'll encounter, this chapter briefs you on basic plant types and offers hints for making good choices.

A well-stocked local nursery can provide an assortment of colorful plants as well as helpful advice.

Look to local nurseries for plants suited to your locale. This Southern California yard is blanketed with colorful specimens that are both drought-tolerant and fire-resistant.

Types of Plants

The plants available to home gardeners are remarkably diverse. Inspect a few well-stocked nurseries or major seed catalogs and you'll probably encounter more than you could grow in a lifetime of gardening—and the selection expands yearly. Some plants are monochromatic, while others are available in hues to fit every color scheme. Some are grown for flowers,

others for foliage or fruit. Sizes range from ground-hugging to skyscraping, shapes from weeping to rigidly upright. There are woody types that stand duty all year, and herbaceous (soft-stemmed) ones that may disappear during winter. There are evergreen plants, clad in foliage all year round, and deciduous sorts, which abruptly drop their leaves and expose their branches in autumn. Some types live for less than a year, while others survive their owners.

Suppliers usually group plants in the following categories.

Annuals. These herbaceous plants live out their entire lives in a single growing season. They're prolific bloomers, producing flowers literally for months while the weather is favorable. Some annuals, such as zinnias, need warmth, while others—stock *(Matthiola),* for example—prefer cool conditions.

Biennials. Though these herbaceous plants live for 2 years—they grow leaves the first year, then bloom, set seed, and die the second— they're often grouped with annuals in nurseries and catalogs. Garden centers usually sell biennials when they're about to flower, so they should be removed along with annuals when blooming is finished at the end of the season. Foxglove *(Digitalis)* and sweet William *(Dianthus barbatus)* are two popular biennials.

Perennials. These herbaceous plants live for at least 3 years, but their bloom period is usually shorter than that of annuals, typically 1 week to 1 month. In cold-winter areas, most perennials die to the ground when the growing season ends, then regrow from the roots when the weather warms. In milder climates, however, many types are evergreen. Some tender perennials, such as petunias and impatiens, are treated as annuals and replaced yearly even in warm regions.

Bulbs. Growing from underground structures that store food during dormancy, these herbaceous plants comprise not only true bulbs, but also corms, tubers, rhizomes, and tuberous roots. Many appear for a brief show, then disappear until the following year. Some types must be dug up and protected from winter cold or summer moisture. In mild climates, many bulbs that need winter chill—hybrid tulips, for example—flower beautifully the first year if refrigerated before planting, but fizzle out by the next season.

Ground covers. The term "ground cover" refers to any spreading or sprawling herbaceous perennial or low shrub that's typically used to blanket the soil. The most common ground cover is lawn; many other choices produce colorful flowers, fruit, or foliage.

Vines. These plants, which include herbaceous and woody types, may climb on their own—by twining or by attaching suction disks, for example—or by being tied to a structure. Some vines, such as English ivy *(Hedera helix)* and bougainvillea, can also be grown as ground covers, adorning expanses of soil with their foliage or flowers.

Shrubs. These woody, multistemmed plants live from year to year and include evergreen and deciduous types. At maturity, they are generally under 15 feet tall. Very low types are sometimes called subshrubs. In the garden, taller sorts are often used as a green backdrop for other colors.

Trees. The shortest of these long-lived woody plants is typically just over 15 feet tall, while the tallest types reach heights of hundreds of feet. Most trees have a single stem, although some are multitrunked. Like shrubs, they may be evergreen or deciduous, and—again like shrubs—may have colorful fruit, flowers, or foliage.

Sources

It's possible to obtain plants from all over the country and from many parts of the world, but buying locally offers advantages. Not only will you find selections suited to your area, but you can see the plants before you make your purchase. Checking the color of the plant itself— not of a photograph—is important when you're choosing a Japanese maple for fall foliage or a camellia or rhododendron for just the right flower hue.

Your garden is bound to have more zest if you deal with outlets that carry a varied and interesting stock rather than a predictable selection of old standbys. Try to find an establishment with knowledgeable employees, too: a well-informed staff can help with both plant selection and design problems. Experienced personnel are invaluable when you can't track down certain plants and need to make suitable substitutions.

For rare plants or new varieties, you may have to search specialty nurseries or attend sales held by garden clubs, plant societies, botanical gardens, or college horticulture departments. If you're lucky, friends will share treasures from their gardens.

Mail-order companies can probably fill any voids in your list. These firms offer enormous variety, including many unusual and hard-to-find plants, so be sure what you choose is suitable for your climate and growing conditions. Large national companies tend to stock items that do pretty well in most locales, while regional suppliers often carry types more appropriate to the areas they serve.

A Wisconsin prairie garden features carefree perennials, including the native wildflower black-eyed Susan (Rudbeckia hirta).

Deciphering Catalogs

Staggering variety, novelty plants, and extravagant descriptions are all part of that special mail-order allure. Try to keep your head as you read and look: it's easy to succumb to temptation, ordering items that don't really fit your planting scheme or won't grow well for you!

Some catalogs use symbols to convey information about each plant—for instance, whether it needs sun, part shade, or shade; whether it's considered easy to grow; or whether it blooms the first year from seed. Most catalogs use United States Department of Agriculture zones to indicate a plant's hardiness; you'll usually find a zone map in the catalog, but if you still aren't sure which zone you live in, inquire at a nearby USDA office, Cooperative Extension office, or nursery.

Some catalogs identify plants by a common name alone—a confusing practice, since a single plant may have several common names, and the same common name often applies to more than one plant. Far more valuable is a listing of the plant's botanical name. Because each plant has just one such name, knowing it gives you a firm identification, allowing you to look for details in a plant encyclopedia like the one starting on page 113 of this book. The names crown-pink, mullein-pink, campion, rose campion, and catchfly, for example, all refer to the magenta-flowered perennial *Lychnis coronaria*. The first part of a botanical name (here, *Lychnis*) is the genus, identifying the plant as belonging to a general grouping; the second (here, *coronaria*) is the species, identifying the plant more precisely. A third name, also in italics—as in *Hydrangea anomala petiolaris,* for instance—signifies a naturally occurring variety, as opposed to one produced by breeders.

Botanical names are changed from time to time, although growers and catalog firms are

Astilbe × arendsii is a group of hybrids between 2 and 4 feet tall, bearing white, pink, or red plumes. Each has its own cultivar name, such as 'Fanal' or 'Glow'.

often slow to adjust. Ideally, when the old name is still widely used, it is shown in parentheses after the new name.

Though not all companies use the symbol, you'll often see an "×" in botanical names (as in *Clematis × jackmanii*). This signifies that the plant is a hybrid—a cross between different types of plants, usually within a genus. Knowing whether you have a hybrid is important if you like to propagate new plants from those already growing in your garden. To produce plants that look like the hybrid, you must take cuttings or use other vegetative methods; plants grown from seeds you harvest may not even have the same leaf or flower color as the parent.

Many plants sold through catalogs are cultivars (an abbreviation of "cultivated varieties"), breeder-produced plants that differ in some way from the plain species and retain this distinction when reproduced. For example, *Salvia officinalis* 'Icterina' is a form of culinary sage with pale green and yellow marbling on its gray-green leaves. When the parentage is complicated or unclear, the cultivar name directly follows the genus (*Rosa* 'Peace').

To replicate cultivars, growers start new plants vegetatively or breed selected plants to produce seeds with the desired characteristics. You'll notice that some plants, especially annuals, are described as F_1 hybrids: uniform plants produced by crossing inbred lines of cultivars. The offspring of F_1 hybrids, called F_2 hybrids, are more variable.

Thanks to breeders, numerous plants are now available in an astonishing range of color and flower size. Related cultivars are often organized into series: for example, the Short Stuff series of dwarf zinnias comprises plants that are identical except for flower color.

Other terms you may come across in catalogs are "tetraploid" and "triploid." These tell you that breeders have manipulated the number of chromosomes in order to produce certain qualities. For example, tetraploid daylilies (*Hemerocallis*) have four sets of chromosomes instead of the usual two, resulting in larger flowers with stiffer petals. Triploid marigolds (*Tagetes*) bloom prolifically, since their odd number of chromosomes—three sets—prevents them from setting seed.

Primetime is the name of a series of petunias that differ only in blossom color. Choices include solid shades as well as bicolors and versions with prominent veining on the petals.

You'll also notice that some plants are labeled "All-America winner" or "AAS winner." These have been singled out by All-America Selections, an organization that tests and rates new cultivars. The winners are grown in display gardens across the country, including the one at Sunset Publishing in Menlo Park, California. To find out if such a garden is located in your area, check with a local plant society or botanical garden.

Choosing Plants

When you're gardening for color, hue is obviously the key consideration. If you're looking for a particular shade, it's best to see the plant during its season of color. Don't rely on plant labels or catalog photographs: labels are often too vague ("yellow flowers") to be helpful, and photographs can be wildly inaccurate. A botanical garden is likely to display a broad selection of plants, and local plant societies may be able to direct you to other public or private gardens where you can track down your quarry.

Consider the amount of color on a plant. A particular choice may be described as producing yellow flowers or red berries, but that doesn't mean it's showy. A thick blanket of golden blooms makes a bigger splash than a sparse scattering of the same hue; similarly, dense clusters of scarlet berries are more conspicuous than a sprinkling of small, solitary fruits.

The duration of color is also critical, since you want the garden to be dynamic for as long as possible. Breeders are sensitive to the demand for lasting color, so keep an eye out for new cultivars bred for extra-long blooming or fruiting. But remember: even if a plant puts on a spectacular display for months, don't allow it into your garden unless its appearance is acceptable the rest of the year as well.

Don't get so carried away with color that you ignore a plant's basic needs. Your selection should be compatible with your climate and growing conditions. It's also wise to favor choices that help you overcome regional problems. In Minnesota, for example, look for cultivars bred for extra hardiness; in Arizona, seek out those developed for resistance to heat and drought.

Mature size is another important factor. A plant should fit its designated spot without constant cutting back. Drastic pruning not only butchers a plant, but also eliminates flower buds and curtails the color show.

Consider whether the plant's shape—its overall profile as well as the contour of its leaves or flowers—is appropriate. A tall, rigidly upright cultivar may have just the right color, but who will notice if the plant sticks out like a sore thumb among more graceful, arching forms? If you're thinking of juxtaposing a bold-leafed plant with one bearing tiny, delicate foliage, check out the idea by pairing the two in the nursery. An obvious mismatch only detracts from the color display.

Some plants require more care than others, so be realistic about how much effort you're prepared to put in. To lessen the workload, choose plants that do well on their own: annuals that reseed themselves; perennials that don't demand staking or division; flowering plants that keep blooming without pinching; bulbs that naturalize; and shrubs and trees that look good with little pruning.

Seeds versus Transplants

Starting from seed takes more time and effort than buying already growing plants, but it costs less and offers you greater variety. On the other hand, nursery transplants present you with a ready-made garden.

Some plants, including most annuals and certain perennials, develop rapidly from seed (see "Quick Color from Seeds," facing page). Hard-to-start or very slow-growing plants are easier to raise from well-rooted transplants.

When you're looking for a specific blue, red, or other hue, visit a local nursery or public garden to see the plants in question during their season of color. The rhododendrons shown here include, clockwise from top left: rosy pink 'Antoon Van Welie', pink-tinged white 'Mrs. Tom Lowinsky', pink 'Lady Clementine', scarlet 'Jean Marie de Montague', and lavender 'Anah Kruschke'.

Quick Color from Seeds

From just a few seed packets, you can easily produce an entire bed brimming with vivid flowers. Look to annuals first: they're unsurpassed for the speed with which they make the transformation from seed to full bloom.

Most perennials blossom the second year after seeding, but breeders have developed some types that burst into vibrant, long-lasting flower the first season you sow them. Among the best are Debutante and Summer Pastels yarrow (*Achillea*), 'Early Sunrise' coreopsis (*C. grandiflora*), and Disco Belle hibiscus.

Many annuals can be sown directly in the garden because they sprout quickly, but you can't just scatter seeds on unprepared ground and expect good results. Work in organic matter such as compost to a foot deep and smooth the surface; then sow according to packet directions. Maintain moisture so the seeds never dry out. For maximum bloom once plants are growing, mulch the bed, water as needed, fertilize monthly, and pick off dead flowers.

Seeds that are slow to germinate or need careful handling should be started indoors in small containers. You can start other types that way as well, to get a jump on the season or produce plants large enough to pop into a border.

Hybrids must usually be obtained as plants if they are to grow true to type, although special seed is available for many hybrid annuals.

Seeds are widely sold; the instructions on the packet tell you where and how to sow and what kind of care to provide. You can also collect seeds from plants, but keep in mind that those harvested from your garden won't give predictable results: even if a plant is not a hybrid itself, it may still hybridize with plants from neighboring gardens.

Transplants are available in many sizes, from flats containing masses of small plants to huge boxes holding individual, well-developed trees. Herbaceous plants usually come in plugs, cell packs and small pots, woody plants in larger cans. Many trees and shrubs are sold balled-and-burlapped in cold-winter climates, and some deciduous types come bare-root during the dormant season.

You can obtain seeds any time, but it's best to buy transplants only when you're ready for them: many plants languish and die in containers before their owners get around to putting them into the ground. Most mail-order outlets try to ship during the optimum planting time for your region.

When buying plants in person, you may be drawn to those laden with flowers or fruit. Unless your goal is instant color (see page 95), however, you're better off choosing not-yet-blooming plants with lots of buds; they'll establish more readily and give you a lusher, longer-lived display.

Large plants are also tempting, since they make an immediate impact, but younger ones in smaller containers tend to transplant better. In fact, in time they'll catch up with and often surpass the bigger, older ones.

To figure out how many plants to get, consult your design (see "Planning on Paper," page 94). Most of the larger plants will be represented by individual circles, so just count these. Your supplier should be able to advise you on the quantities you'll need to buy for mass plantings and drifts.

An Encyclopedia of Plants

The following pages offer photographs and descriptions of hundreds of colorful plants of all types and sizes. You'll find options for every conceivable color need, including good greens and grays, and for every season. Displays range from subtle to dazzling, from fleeting to long-lasting.

Most of these plants grow well in a broad geographical area; any limitations are spelled out. Of course, there are many possibilities besides the choices listed here; rely on reputable local nurseries to suggest additional plants that will excel in your region.

A white-flowered wisteria trained on a wood arbor invites visitors to proceed along the gravel path.

113

Using This Encyclopedia

Plants are organized alphabetically by botanical name. If an entry covers only a single plant, the heading lists both genus and species (Zinnia elegans). An "×" appears if the plant is a hybrid (Anemone × hybrida). An entry covering several species is headed simply by the genus (Iris).

The common name or names follow the botanical name. If you know a plant only by its common name, refer to the index on pages 206–208.

The plant category, such as "perennial" or "deciduous tree," is listed next. Then come five points of information: color; peak season of color (averaged for the country); hardiness to cold (not listed for annuals, since they don't have to survive winter); preferred exposure (sun, part shade, or shade); and moisture needs, expressed as watering frequency (regular, moderate, or little).

Finally, the text gives a brief description of the plant, including its mature size and growth habit, and discusses the color display more fully. Any especially colorful varieties are also mentioned.

Acacia baileyana

ACACIA BAILEYANA
Golden mimosa
Evergreen tree

Color: *Yellow*
Season: *Winter*
Hardy to: *15°F/–9°C; for Western United States only*
Exposure: *Sun*
Water: *Moderate to little*

The most breathtaking of the acacias when in bloom, golden mimosa is blanketed with clusters of brilliant yellow blossoms in January. It's a good looker the rest of the year, too. Graceful, arching branches bear feathery blue-green foliage; 'Purpurea' has lavender to purple new growth fading to gray-blue.

Golden mimosa reaches a height of 20 to 30 feet. Like most acacias, it grows so rapidly that it wears itself out after a few decades. It also self-sows prolifically, so pull seedlings if you don't want new trees popping up.

ACER
Maple
Deciduous trees and shrubs

Color: *Red, orange, purple, yellow*
Season: *Varies*
Hardy to: *Varies*
Exposure: *Sun, part shade*
Water: *Regular to moderate*

Many maples are valued for their brilliant foliage, and a few contribute ornamental bark or stems. No matter where you live, you'll probably find at least one or a few types suitable for your region; heat, dryness, and lack of winter chill are the limiting factors.

For a good fall leaf display, look for a maple that colors well in your area. The best tactic is to visit local nurseries while the trees are changing hue.

Myriad cultivars of Japanese maple, *A. palmatum* (–10°F/–23°C), put on a vibrant show throughout the growing season. Among the best are upright, 15-foot 'Bloodgood', with deep reddish purple leaves that turn scarlet in fall; and sprawling, 6-foot 'Dissectum Atropurpureum', with finely divided purplish foliage that turns to crimson as the year wanes. Another lovely choice is 20-foot-tall 'Sango Kaku', whose bright coral shoots light up the winter garden. Its foliage is colorful as well: yellow-orange in spring, green in summer, and yellow tinted with rose in fall.

Fewer trees boast more spectacular bark than 20- to 40-foot paperbark maple, *A. griseum* (–20°F/–29°C): the purplish brown outer layer peels off in papery sheets to expose cinnamon-orange patches. Vivid orange and red fall foliage is a bonus.

Acer palmatum 'Bloodgood'

Achillea, **Galaxy Hybrids**

ACHILLEA
Yarrow
Perennial

Color: *Yellow, cream, white, lilac, pink, red*
Season: *Summer*
Hardy to: *–30°F/–34°C*
Exposure: *Sun*
Water: *Moderate*

Prolific bloomers all, the yarrows bear flattened blossom clusters rising above aromatic, finely divided gray or green foliage. Flower colors range from pastels to intensely vivid hues.

Fernleaf yarrow, *A. filipendulina,* the tallest species at 4 to 5 feet, has bright yellow blossoms. The popular 2-foot hybrid *A.* 'Moonshine' bears pale yellow blooms. White-flowered, 3-foot-tall common yarrow, *A. millefolium,* has several cultivars, among them the bright red 'Fire King'.

Perhaps common yarrow's greatest contribution to the garden lies in its offspring. Breeders have crossed it with *A. taygetea* to produce hybrids—the Galaxy, Summer Pastels, and Debutante series—with blooms in subtle, exquisite hues including creamy yellow, lilac, pink, salmon, and rusty red. Both Summer Pastels and Debutante bloom in only 4 months from seed. When buying plants, expect some color variation, since many growers make their own selections from seedlings.

The airy white sprays of *A. ptarmica* 'The Pearl' look a bit like

baby's breath *(Gypsophila).* The 10-inch-tall *A. clavennae* (also sold as *A. argentea*) is grown for its shimmering silver foliage; pale cream blossoms are a welcome extra.

Yarrows are excellent cut flowers that dry well, though pinks and reds tend to be more fragile than other colors. For the most abundant flower show, trim the plants after blooming (cut above the ferny leaves where flower buds form) and divide clumps when they become crowded. Once established, the plants will tolerate drought, but they'll look better with watering.

ACONITUM
Monkshood
Perennial

Color: *Blue, purple, bicolor*
Season: *Summer, fall*
Hardy to: *–30°F/–34°C; needs some winter chill*
Exposure: *Sun, part shade*
Water: *Regular*

Monkshood's long-lasting, vivid blue or purple flower spikes are made up of individual blossoms shaped like little hoods or helmets. The taller types resemble delphiniums and can substitute for them in shady gardens.

Aconitum

Growing to about 4 feet, *A.* × *bicolor* bears blooms that are half purplish, half white. Its most widely available cultivar, 3-foot-tall 'Bressingham Blue', flowers early in summer. Blooming a little later are deep blue *A. napellus,* about 4 feet tall, and *A. variegatum,* a 5-footer bearing blue blossoms tipped with creamy yellow. Last to flower is intense blue *A. carmichaelii;* it's about 4 feet tall, though some forms, such as 'Wilsonii', reach 6 feet.

Monkshood thrives in areas where summers are cool and winter temperatures remain below freezing. Divide clumps every few years. All plant parts are poisonous.

AGAPANTHUS
Lily-of-the-Nile
Perennial

Color: *Blue, white*
Season: *Summer*
Hardy to: *Varies*
Exposure: *Sun, part shade*
Water: *Regular to moderate*

A hardy landscape plant in California and Florida, lily-of-the-Nile is typically grown in containers in other parts of the country. Its tall blossom

Agapanthus, **Headbourne Hybrids**

stalks, capped by spherical flower heads, rise above fountainlike clumps of strap-shaped foliage; in bloom, plants range from about 1 to 5 feet tall. Flower color is blue—ranging from deep purplish to pale ice blue—or white.

Among large evergreen types, the most commonly sold is *A. orientalis* (sometimes labeled *A. africanus* or *A. umbellatus*), bearing huge flower clusters 8 to 12 inches wide atop 4- to 5-foot stems. The true *A. africanus* (sometimes sold as *A. umbellatus*) is a smaller-scale plant. Evergreen dwarf varieties, such as 1½-foot-high 'Peter Pan', make good foreground plantings or ground covers.

The deciduous Headbourne Hybrids are about 2½ feet tall, with 6-inch-wide flower clusters and narrowish, fairly upright leaves. *A. inapertus,* another deciduous type, reaches almost 5 feet tall and bears drooping, deep blue clusters.

All types survive outdoors to about 10°F/–12°C; deciduous kinds are hardier, perhaps to –10°F/–23°C. A thick mulch greatly improves winter survival in borderline areas.

AGERATUM HOUSTONIANUM
Floss flower
Annual

Color: Purplish blue, white, pink
Season: Summer, fall
Exposure: Sun
Water: Regular

Ageratum houstonianum

Floss flower blooms from summer until frost, bearing dense clusters of fluffy, powder-puff flowers above dark green, hairy leaves. The blossoms are usually purplish blue, although some white and pink forms are available.

Plants range from 6 inches to 2½ feet tall. Dwarf types, including 'Blue Puffs' and 'Blue Blazer', are useful for edging. Taller sorts, such as 'Blue Horizon', make good cut flowers.

AJUGA REPTANS
Carpet bugle
Perennial

Color: Blue, purple, red, cream, white
Season: Varies
Hardy to: –30°F/–34°C
Exposure: Sun, part shade, shade
Water: Regular

There's more to this neat little ground cover than deep blue flower spikes in spring and early summer; handsome foliage contributes color all season long. The standard species has dark green leaves, but many of its cultivars are more flamboyant. These include 'Purpurea' ('Atropurpurea'), bronzy purplish; 'Multicolor' ('Rainbow'), green marbled with cream and pink; 'Variegata', green with creamy yellow

Ajuga reptans 'Burgundy Lace'

blotches and leaf edges; and 'Burgundy Lace' ('Burgundy Glow'), reddish purple variegated with white and pink.

Carpet bugle's usual height is about 6 inches. Cultivars with "giant" or "jungle" in their names are bigger plants with larger leaves and taller flower spikes; many of these reach about 1½ feet high.

Mow plantings after flowering to tidy their appearance. Divide and replant when bare patches appear.

ALCEA ROSEA
Hollyhock
Biennial

Color: Pink, red, purple, yellow, apricot, cream, white
Season: Summer
Hardy to: –20°F/–29°C
Exposure: Sun
Water: Regular

An old-fashioned plant for a cottage garden or the back of a border, hollyhock typically bears saucer-shaped, 4-inch-wide blossoms on spikes up to 9 feet tall. Hybrids now include shorter types as low as 2½ feet, often with semidouble or double flowers, in almost every soft color but blue.

Annual strains, such as the double-flowered Summer Carnival series, bloom the first year from seed if started indoors in winter or early spring.

After the plants have flowered, cut the blossom stalks just above the ground to force new growth for a second bloom late in the season.

Alcea rosea

Alchemilla mollis

Allium moly

ALCHEMILLA MOLLIS
Lady's mantle
Perennial

Color: *Chartreuse*
Season: *Late spring, summer*
Hardy to: *–40°F/–40°C; needs some winter chill*
Exposure: *Part shade*
Water: *Regular*

Billowing sprays of tiny chartreuse flowers arch above clumps of nearly circular, scallop-edged, gray-green leaves, creating a frothy mass about 1½ feet tall and 2 feet wide. The leaves catch and hold dew, giving the whole plant a sparkling look in sunlight.

Lady's mantle is unsuited to regions with long, hot, dry summers. Elsewhere, if given moist, well-drained soil, it's attractive all season—and tends to self-sow freely. Clumps never need dividing.

ALLIUM
Ornamental allium
Deciduous bulb

Color: *Blue, violet, red, pink, yellow, white*
Season: *Spring, summer*
Hardy to: *–30°F/–34°C, except where noted*
Exposure: *Sun*
Water: *Regular*

Relatives of the edible onion, these ornamental species range from 6 inches to about 6 feet tall. The spherical flower clusters are carried at the ends of leafless stems; some types have loose, open clusters, while others bear dense balls. Many are fragrant; only a few smell like onions.

Summer-blooming *A. giganteum* produces spectacular softball-size clusters of lavender blossoms on 5- to 6-foot stems. The spring bloomer *A. aflatunense* looks much the same, but has slightly shorter stems and smaller, lavender-pink flower heads.

Among attractive alliums of middling size—about 2 to 2½ feet tall—is *A. sphaerocephalum,* which bears very tight 2-inch balls of purplish red blossoms in early summer.

Some of the best choices for naturalizing are *A. neapolitanum* (hardy to about –5°F/–21°C), with loose, white 3-inch clusters; *A. moly* (golden garlic), with loose, yellow 2-inch clusters; and *A. caeruleum,* with blue 2-inch balls. All three of these bloom in spring and grow 1 to 1½ feet tall.

ALSTROEMERIA
Alstroemeria, Peruvian lily
Perennial

Color: *Orange, red, pink, lilac, purple, yellow, cream, white, bicolors*
Season: *Late spring, summer*
Hardy to: *0°F/–18°C*
Exposure: *Sun, part shade*
Water: *Regular*

From tuberous roots, alstroemeria forms a spreading clump of upright stems 1½ to 5 feet tall, topped by long-lasting clusters of trumpet-shaped, azalealike blossoms.

Once the standard form, the 3-foot-tall, orange-flowered *A. aurantiaca* and its yellow ('Lutea') and red ('Splendens') cultivars have largely been supplanted by hybrid strains with more compact growth and a greater color range. Today's palette includes both solid colors and bicolor combinations, often with contrasting dark spots or streaks.

The summer-dormant Ligtu Hybrids, the first popular hybrid strain, have now been bettered by more recent strains such as the Cordu Hybrids, which keep their leaves when temperatures remain above freezing and have a much longer blooming season.

Since alstroemeria establishes slowly after transplanting, clumps are best left undisturbed.

Alstroemeria

Amelanchier

Amsonia tabernaemontana

Amaranthus tricolor

AMARANTHUS
Love-lies-bleeding
Annual

Color: *Crimson, lime, gold*
Season: *Summer, fall*
Exposure: *Sun, part shade*
Water: *Regular*

These bold, attention-grabbing 2- to 4-foot plants are grown for their vivid flowers or foliage and unusual forms.

A. caudatus produces crimson, tassel-like flower spikes that spill out from all over the plant. A less dramatic version with lime spikes is sold as 'Green Form' or 'Viridis'.

The leaves of *A. tricolor* are brilliantly multihued. 'Joseph's Coat' is blotched yellow, green, and crimson; 'Illumination' is crowned with crimson and gold; and 'Molten Fire' is crimson, bronze, and purple.

AMELANCHIER
Serviceberry
Deciduous shrubs and small trees

Color: *White, pink*
Season: *Early spring*
Hardy to: *Varies; needs a definite period of winter chill*
Exposure: *Sun*
Water: *Regular to moderate*

Ranging from 6 to 30 feet tall, these delicate-looking, typically multi-trunked woody plants bear a profusion of white flowers in early spring.

Their beauty isn't limited to that season, though: they also offer small edible summer fruit (quickly devoured by birds), glowing fall foliage, and a graceful winter silhouette. And because serviceberries have noninvasive roots and canopies that cast only light shade, you can successfully garden beneath them.

One of the best tree forms is the hybrid *A. × grandiflora* (–20°F/–29°C), which bears larger flowers than its parents—*A. canadensis* and *A. laevis*—on a smaller tree reaching 20 to 25 feet tall. Its bronzy red new growth matures to green, then turns orange to red in fall. Cultivars include 'Robin Hill', pink in bud, and 'Rubescens', with purplish pink buds and pink-tinged flowers.

Another outstanding choice is *A. arborea* (–40°F/–40°C)—sometimes a shrubby 6-footer, sometimes as tall as 20 feet. Ideal for small-space gardens or patio plantings, it can also be interplanted in a grove of larger deciduous trees for a "second story" effect. The leaves turn fiery shades of yellow, gold, orange, and red in autumn.

AMSONIA TABERNAEMONTANA
Blue star
Perennial

Color: *Pale blue*
Season: *Late spring*
Hardy to: *–35°F/–37°C*
Exposure: *Sun, part shade*
Water: *Regular to moderate*

Though this undemanding native of the southeastern United States doesn't put on a big or long-lasting flower show, it's worth growing for its subtle grace.

The plant resembles a shrubby willow 2 to 3 feet tall, but each stem is tipped with a cluster of tiny, star-shaped pale blue flowers. After blossoming is over, the glossy foliage remains attractive through summer, then turns clear yellow in fall.

ANAPHALIS
Pearly everlasting
Perennial

Color: *Silver, white, yellow*
Season: *Spring, summer, fall*
Hardy to: *Varies*
Exposure: *Sun, part shade*
Water: *Regular to moderate*

Grown for its woolly gray foliage, pearly everlasting is hardier and more shade-tolerant than most similarly hued plants. Because it needs moisture, it's ideal for irrigated borders, where most gray-leafed plants fail. In summer, plants produce papery, yellow-eyed white daisies that can be dried for arrangements.

A. margaritacea, about 2½ feet tall, is hardy to –40°F/–40°C. Both the compact, 2-foot-tall *A. cinnamonea* (*A. yedoensis*) and the slightly shorter *A. triplinervis* are hardy to –20°F/–29°C. The latter's cultivar 'Sulphur Light' bears pale yellow flowers centered with deeper yellow.

Anaphalis triplinervis

Anchusa azurea

ANCHUSA AZUREA
Italian bugloss
Perennial

Color: *Blue*
Season: *Late spring, summer*
Hardy to: *–30°F/–34°C*
Exposure: *Sun*
Water: *Regular to moderate*

Sometimes sold as *A. italica*, this plant is noteworthy for its brilliant blue flower spikes—similar to those of for-get-me-nots, but larger.

Plants range from 1½ to 5 feet tall; the loftier types tend to become lanky and need staking. At the tall end of the spectrum is 'Dropmore'; a better (and still fairly tall) selection is sturdy 3-foot 'Loddon Royalist'. For the front of the border, try 1½-foot-tall 'Little John'.

Italian bugloss is short-lived. To rejuvenate the plants, divide clumps every 2 to 3 years.

ANEMONE × HYBRIDA
Japanese anemone
Perennial

Color: *White, pink, rose*
Season: *Late summer, fall*
Hardy to: *–20°F/–29°C; not suited to Gulf Coast and Florida*
Exposure: *Sun, part shade*
Water: *Regular*

Prized for its late-season bloom, this graceful perennial bears loose sprays of cupped, golden-hubbed white or pink flowers that resemble wild roses. Up to 3 inches across, the blossoms rise on wiry stems above attractive clumps of dark green, maplelike leaves. The foliage is good-looking from the time it emerges in spring until frost forces it into dormancy.

Many plants sold as *A. japonica, A. hupehensis,* and *A. vitifolia* are ac-tually *A. × hybrida*. One of the best selections—a favorite of gardeners since the mid-1800s—is 'Honorine Jobert', a 5-footer with single white blossoms. Another fine choice is 3-foot-tall 'September Charm', which bears single pink flowers. Numerous cultivars with double or semidouble flowers are also available.

Clumps can grow indefinitely without division, although you may want to divide more vigorous types to curb their spread. Use a mulch in borderline climates, since some se-lections may be more tender than the average.

ANGELICA ARCHANGELICA
Angelica
Biennial

Color: *Lime green*
Season: *Summer*
Hardy to: *–30°F/–34°C*
Exposure: *Part shade*
Water: *Regular to moderate*

This highly decorative herb looks lovely at the back of a semishady border. Grown for medicinal pur-poses in the Middle Ages, it has more recently been used as a flavoring and confection (the candied stems are popular for decorating cakes and other desserts).

A clump of celerylike foliage de-velops during the first year. The fol-lowing year, the plant sends up a thick, hollow 6-foot stem crowned with a branching spray of spherical lime green flower heads, each re-sembling a burst of fireworks. The spent flowers turn straw brown, re-maining ornamental for weeks.

Angelica dies after blooming. If you want more plants, leave the flow-ers in place to self-sow.

Anemone × hybrida

Angelica archangelica

ANTHEMIS TINCTORIA
Golden marguerite
Perennial

Color: *Yellow*
Season: *Summer, early fall*
Hardy to: *–30°F/–34°C; not suited to Gulf Coast and Florida*
Exposure: *Sun*
Water: *Moderate*

Masses of 2-inch-wide, sunny yellow daisies cover this shrubby 2- to 3-foot plant for weeks on end, especially if the stems are lightly cut back after the first bloom to encourage a second flowering.

Anthemis tinctoria

Antirrhinum majus

Varieties include 'Moonlight', soft pale yellow; 'Kelwayi', bright lemon; and 'Beauty of Grallagh', deep golden yellow. All types feature finely cut, aromatic leaves that are light green on the upper surface, felted gray beneath.

Golden marguerite is fairly short-lived, but plantings can be rejuvenated by dividing the clumps.

ANTIRRHINUM MAJUS
Snapdragon
Perennial grown as annual

Color: *Red, lavender, white, yellow, orange, pink, bicolors*
Season: *Spring, summer*
Exposure: *Sun*
Water: *Regular*

The old-fashioned snapdragon of cottage gardens is barely recognizable in some of the forms available today. In place of the familiar hinged "dragon" jaws that snap open and shut when squeezed, many newer types have open bells or azalealike blossoms (double bells). And flowers are often borne in clusters rather than in well-defined spikes that bloom from bottom to top.

Breeders have developed a great selection of colors, including many bicolors; height range has been ex-

panded as well, from as low as 8 inches to as tall as 3 feet. The many series include Madame Butterfly (tall), Sonnet (intermediate), and Little Darling (dwarf).

Snapdragons are excellent cut flowers. Snip the spikes to within several inches of the base to encourage the growth of additional flowering stems.

Although usually treated as an annual, snapdragon is a tender perennial; in mild climates, it will bloom in winter if buds form before night temperatures drop below 50°F/10°C. It can survive for 3 or 4 years if it doesn't fall victim to rust disease. To increase your odds of success, choose rust-resistant varieties and avoid overhead watering.

AQUILEGIA
Columbine
Perennial

Color: *Blue, purple, red, pink, yellow, cream, white, bicolors*
Season: *Spring, early summer*
Hardy to: *Varies; most not suited to Gulf Coast and Florida*
Exposure: *Sun, part shade*
Water: *Regular*

These short-lived perennials are charming, ferny-leafed woodland

plants with showy blooms atop long, slender stems. The traditional flower form consists of five petals forming an upended bell or loose cup; five pointed sepals that form a sort of "saucer" for the cup; and five long, curved spurs, one behind each sepal. Short-spurred and spurless columbines are also available, as are double-flowered types. The range of flower sizes and colors is extensive. Most types self-sow freely.

Among the most common native species are a couple of 2-footers: *A.*

Aquilegia chrysantha

caerulea, Rocky Mountain columbine, with long-spurred flowers of sky blue and white; and *A. canadensis,* a short-spurred type with yellow and red blooms. Another gem is the 3- to 4-foot *A. chrysantha* (golden columbine), which has long-spurred, clear yellow blossoms. The species columbines are generally hardy to –35°F/–37°C.

The many hybrids, available in an extensive range of soft hues and bicolors, are hardy to about –20°F/–29°C. The widely available McKana Giants series has large, long-spurred flowers on stems 2½ to 3 feet tall. For shorter plants—just 1 to 1½ feet tall—try the long-spurred Music series.

ARABIS CAUCASICA
Wall rockcress
Perennial

Color: *White, pink*
Season: *Early spring*
Hardy to: *–10°F/–23°C*
Exposure: *Sun, part shade*
Water: *Moderate*

In early spring, the gray-green leaves of this mustard relative are obscured by small, four-petaled white flowers in the shape of a cross. Just 6 inches high, rockcress is a suitable overplanting for spring-blooming bulbs and a charming choice for wall crannies. 'Variegata' has cream-margined leaves; 'Pink Charm' and 'Rosabella' bear pink flowers.

Arabis caucasica 'Variegata'

Arbutus unedo

ARBUTUS
Strawberry tree, madrone
Evergreen trees and shrubs

Color: *Red*
Season: *Varies*
Hardy to: *Varies*
Exposure: *Sun, part shade*
Water: *Varies*

Strawberry tree, *A. unedo* (5°F/–15°C), takes its name from the ¾-inch, bright red fruits it bears in late fall and winter. The berries are edible as well as decorative, though they're rather dry and bland. Strawberry tree reaches about 25 feet at maturity, but it can easily be kept lower. Naturally shrubby forms include 'Compacta', seldom exceeding 10 feet in height, and 'Elfin King', growing to about half that size and fruiting throughout the year. Plants do well with regular to little water.

The most dramatic feature of madrone, *A. menziesii* (0°F/–18°C), is smooth bark that flakes off to reveal reddish orange patches. Growing anywhere from about 20 to 100 feet tall, this tree is suited only to its native habitat along the Pacific Coast. Though it can be cultivated successfully, it's not as well adapted to garden conditions as *A. unedo.* It does best without supplemental irrigation.

Arrhenatherum elatius 'Variegatum'

ARRHENATHERUM ELATIUS 'VARIEGATUM'
False oatgrass
Deciduous perennial grass

Color: *White*
Season: *Spring, summer, fall*
Hardy to: *–20°F/–29°C*
Exposure: *Sun, part shade*
Water: *Regular*

Neat white edges decorate the gray-green leaves of this pretty perennial grass. The graceful, arching foliage clump grows to about 1½ feet tall; in summer, dainty brown flowering spikelets increase the plant's height to 3 or 4 feet.

A lovely accent plant, false oatgrass performs best in cool seasons and cool climates. Divide and replant the clumps as needed, whenever vigor decreases.

ARTEMISIA
Artemisia
Perennials and small shrubs

Color: *Gray, silver*
Season: *Spring, summer, fall*
Hardy to: *Varies*
Exposure: *Sun*
Water: *Moderate*

Artemisias include both herbaceous and woody plants, all with feathery, aromatic silvery or gray-green leaves. Height varies from just 6 inches to over 5 feet. In mild climates, many types remain attractive all year.

Artemisia 'Powis Castle'

Arum italicum 'Pictum'

Two very hardy (–30°F/–34°C) perennial species are useful as foreground accents everywhere except the Gulf Coast and Florida. The 2½-foot-tall *A. stellerana*, known as beach wormwood or dusty miller, has woolly white leaves and small yellow flowers that can be pinched off to preserve an overall silvery effect. *A. schmidtiana* forms a small, shimmering hillock 2 feet high; its cultivar 'Silver Mound' is half that height.

Other fine artemisias include a couple of 3-footers: the perennial *A. ludoviciana albula* (–20°F/–29°C), with grayish white flowers and leaves, and the shrub *A.* 'Powis Castle' (0°F/–18°C), which has finely divided silvery foliage.

ARUM ITALICUM 'PICTUM'
Italian arum
Perennial

Color: *Cream*
Season: *Fall, winter, spring*
Hardy to: *–10°F/–23°C*
Exposure: *Part shade, shade*
Water: *Regular*

Sometimes sold as 'Variegatum', this perennial is grown for its foliage: large (up to 10-inch-long), glossy, arrow-shaped leaves with cream-colored veins. It's a fine ground cover in a woodland setting, where it can be allowed to spread uncurbed.

The foliage emerges from a tuberous root in fall, then grows about 1 foot tall. In mild regions, the plant continues to increase throughout winter; elsewhere, it may simply sit out the season or die to the ground if exposed to very cold temperatures. In any climate, the leaves die back in spring, soon after the short-stemmed, white or greenish flowers appear. Thick clusters of orange-red fruit follow the blossoms.

Italian arum tolerates drought when dormant. All plant parts are poisonous.

ARUNCUS DIOICUS
Goatsbeard
Perennial

Color: *Cream*
Season: *Summer*
Hardy to: *–35°F/–37°C*
Exposure: *Sun, part shade*
Water: *Regular*

Cream-colored, feathery plumes give this plant the look of a large, shaggy astilbe. The mound of broad, fernlike foliage is about 4 feet tall; the plumes extend the height to 6 feet. 'Kneiffii' is about half the size of the species, with more finely divided leaves.

Goatsbeard needs adequate water for good performance. It will tolerate sun in cool-summer climates, but it doesn't do well in hot, dry regions.

Obtain a female plant (there are separate sexes) if you want green seed pods for dried arrangements. Clumps don't need division, but you can split them to get extra plants.

Aruncus dioicus

ASCLEPIAS TUBEROSA
Butterfly weed
Perennial

Color: *Orange, yellow, red, pink, cream*
Season: *Summer*
Hardy to: *–35°F/–37°C*
Exposure: *Sun*
Water: *Moderate to little*

As the common name suggests, this plant's blossoms attract swarms of butterflies. Monarch caterpillars like butterfly weed, too—they feed on its foliage.

In spring, the dormant root produces many stems that reach 2 to 3 feet tall by the time the plant is ready to bloom. The small, starlike flowers are grouped in broad, flattened clusters atop each stem. The usual blossom color is brilliant orange, but the hybrid seed strain Gay Butterflies also offers yellow, red, pink, and occasionally cream flowers.

Although butterfly weed is drought-tolerant, it performs best when given at least some moisture. The clumps are carefree and never need dividing.

ASTER
Aster, Michaelmas daisy
Perennial

Color: *Blue, purple, red, pink, white*
Season: *Spring, summer, fall*
Hardy to: *Varies; not suited to Gulf Coast and Florida*
Exposure: *Sun, part shade*
Water: *Regular*

Most garden asters produce cool-color daisies from summer into early fall, though a few bloom in spring. Size varies greatly: some types are low and clumping, while others are towering 6-footers.

Michaelmas daisies are the traditional, old-fashioned asters familiar to generations of gardeners. New England aster, *A. novae-angliae*, is a hairy-leafed 6-foot plant with airy sprays of pinkish purple flowers; pink and nearly red selections and dwarf cultivars are available as well. The similar New York aster, *A. novi-belgii*, is a smooth-leafed 3- to 4-foot plant with blue-violet blooms; it, too, has cultivars in other colors. Both New England and New York aster are hardy to –30°F/–34°C.

Many new asters were bred during the past century. Among these, one of the best is *A. × frikartii* (–20°F/ –29°C), a 3-foot-tall, large-flowered plant; it has several excellent cultivars, including 'Mönch' and 'Wonder of Stafa' (both with lavender-blue blossoms).

Vigorous asters like the Michaelmas daisies should be dug up and divided at least every other year. Separate and replant any clump of asters when the center becomes bare and woody.

ASTILBE
Astilbe, false spiraea
Perennial

Color: *White, pink, red*
Season: *Summer*
Hardy to: *–25°F/–32°C; needs some winter chill; not suited to Gulf Coast and Florida*
Exposure: *Sun, part shade*
Water: *Regular*

In summer, astilbe's dark green, fernlike foliage clumps produce spectacular plumes made up of tiny individual flowers. Most astilbes sold today are 1½- to 5-foot-tall hybrids with upright, horizontally branching, or drooping plumes.

Among the finest astilbes are the 2- to 4-foot-tall selections of *A. × arendsii*. These include 'Ostrich Plume', with drooping, brilliant pink plumes, and upright-blooming, creamy white 'Deutschland'. Many of the red bloomers, such as upright-flowering 'Fanal', have attractive bronzy leaves. For an outstanding dwarf, consider *A. simplicifolia* 'Sprite'; growing to just under a foot tall, it bears drooping, shell pink flower clusters.

Astilbe is suited to regions with humid but not extremely hot summers. It takes sun if given ample moisture. Divide clumps when bloom production declines, usually every 4 to 5 years.

Asclepias tuberosa

Aster × frikartii 'Mönch'

Astilbe × arendsii 'Glow'

Aurinia saxatilis

Ballota pseudodictamnus

AURINIA SAXATILIS
Basket-of-gold
Perennial

Color: Yellow, apricot
Season: Spring
Hardy to: –35°F/–37°C; not suited to Gulf Coast and Florida
Exposure: Sun
Water: Moderate

The common name is easy to understand: in spring, clusters of small flowers cloak the spreading mound of grayish green foliage in vivid, startling yellow. Growing to about a foot high, basket-of-gold looks right at home at the front of borders and in rock gardens; its cascading habit also makes it an ideal choice for rock wall crevices.

Some catalogs and nurseries sell the plant under its old name, *Alyssum saxatile*. The various forms include 'Flore Pleno', with double yellow flowers and silvery leaves; 'Citrina' and 'Silver Queen', bearing soft yellow blooms; 'Sunny Border Apricot', with apricot flowers and silvery foliage; and 'Variegata', with bright yellow blossoms and cream-margined leaves.

BALLOTA PSEUDODICTAMNUS
Ballota
Evergreen shrubby perennial

Color: Gray-green
Season: All year
Hardy to: 10°F/–12°C
Exposure: Sun
Water: Moderate to little

Reaching about 2 feet tall, ballota is one of those pretty, gray-leafed, shrubby Mediterranean plants suited to mild-climate, drought-tolerant gardens. Its rounded, woolly gray leaves become grayer as the plant matures. Whorls of flowers appear in summer; enlarged pale green sepals are their most prominent feature.

BAPTISIA AUSTRALIS
False indigo
Perennial

Color: Blue
Season: Late spring, early summer
Hardy to: –35°F/–37°C
Exposure: Sun
Water: Moderate

This extremely long-lived perennial, which thrives for decades with little care, looks like a bushy lupine. Loose spikes of typical pea-family flowers, in colors ranging from pale lavender to dark purple, rise from a shrubby 3- to 4-foot mound of bluish green, cloverlike leaves. Flowers left to fade on the plant are followed by elongated seed capsules, lovely in dried arrangements.

Thanks to its deep taproot, false indigo is drought-tolerant. The root makes division difficult, though, so you'll need to transplant volunteer seedlings or start from seed to get new plants.

Baptisia australis

BELAMCANDA CHINENSIS
Blackberry lily
Perennial

Color: Orange
Season: Summer
Hardy to: –10°F/–23°C
Exposure: Sun, part shade
Water: Regular to moderate

Like its iris relatives, this plant grows from rhizomes and produces fans of sword-shaped leaves. In summer, the slender, zigzagging 3-foot stems bear 2-inch-wide, yellow-shaded orange flowers with reddish brown markings. Each flower lasts for only a day, but new blossoms continue to open for several weeks.

Rounded seed capsules develop as the flowers fade, splitting open at maturity to reveal clusters of glossy seeds that look like blackberries. Cut the seed-bearing stems for dried arrangements.

To increase your planting, divide the clumps or allow volunteer seedlings to grow. Blackberry lily needs some shade in hot-summer areas.

BERBERIS
Barberry
Deciduous and evergreen shrubs

Color: Yellow-orange, yellow, red
Season: Varies
Hardy to: Varies
Exposure: Sun, part shade
Water: Regular to moderate

These tough and thorny plants are more than just good barriers; most types contribute brightly colored flowers, fruit, or foliage to the garden as well.

The showiest bloomer, evergreen *B. darwinii* (10°F/–12°C), has arching branches that reach 5 to 10 feet tall. Brilliant yellow-orange flowers obscure the spiny, hollylike leaves in late winter and early spring; dark blue berries follow the blossoms. The plant spreads by underground runners to form a thicket.

Various cultivars of deciduous Japanese barberry, *B. thunbergii*

Belamcanda chinensis

(–20°F/–29°C), have colorful leaves throughout the growing season—especially when plants are located in full sun. 'Atropurpurea' has purplish red foliage, while 'Rose Glow' is marbled rosy pink and bronze; both plants grow 4 to 6 feet tall. 'Aurea', reaching just 2 feet tall, has bright yellow leaves.

BERGENIA
Bergenia
Perennial

Color: Red, rosy purple, lilac, pink, white
Season: Winter, spring
Hardy to: Varies; not suited to Gulf Coast and Florida
Exposure: Part shade, shade
Water: Regular to moderate

Growing from a woody rhizome, bergenia forms a handsome rosette of cabbagelike leaves up to a foot long; the foliage often takes on a purplish tint in cold weather. Thick stems bearing bell-shaped flowers appear in winter or spring.

The two hardiest species (–30°F/–34°C), both evergreen, are winter-blooming bergenia (*B. crassifolia*) and heartleaf bergenia (*B. cordifolia*). The former species bears lilac, pink, or rosy purple flowers any time from midwinter until early spring, while the latter produces dark pink blooms in spring.

A more tender plant is *B. ciliata* (–10°F/–23°C), a spring bloomer with light pink or white flowers. This species is distinguished by its hairy leaves, which are damaged in hard frosts and die down completely in the coldest areas.

Hybrids with flower colors ranging from magenta through various pink shades to white are available. Generally, the hybrids withstand as much cold as the hardier species mentioned above.

Reaching 1 to 1½ feet tall, bergenia is best grown in small clusters or as a ground cover. When plantings become crowded or leggy, divide and replant. Though all types endure neglect, they respond well to regular watering.

Berberis thunbergii 'Aurea'

Bergenia cordifolia

Betula papyrifera

BETULA
Birch
Deciduous trees

Color: *White, pinkish*
Season: *All year*
Hardy to: *Varies; most need some winter chill*
Exposure: *Sun, part shade*
Water: *Regular*

Although birches have yellow fall foliage, their real splendor is their beautiful bark—all the more striking because of the trees' graceful branching patterns. Usually taller than they are wide, birches are often multitrunked. Heights mentioned here are typical for garden specimens.

The most common species is 30- to 40-foot European white birch, *B. pendula* (–40°F/–40°C), with white bark marked by black clefts. 'Purpurea' has purplish leaves and nearly black twigs.

Heat-tolerant river birch, *B. nigra* (–20°F/–29°C), grows 40 to 70 feet tall. Young trees have apricot to pinkish white bark that peels off in shaggy strips; with age, it turns dark silvery gray to black and peels less. The bark of 'Heritage' has white, tan, cream, and peach tones.

Growing 50 to 70 feet tall, paper birch (*B. papyrifera*, –40°F/–40°C) has creamy white bark. Harder to find is Chinese paper birch, *B. albo-sinensis* (–10°F/–23°C). Reaching about 60 feet tall, this species has gorgeous pinkish brown bark covered with a gray, powdery bloom. Even lovelier is *B. a. septentrionalis;* its silky skin is coppery orange, gray, and pink.

Birches perform best with a steady supply of moisture. When you make your selections, keep in mind that most types are susceptible to insect pests, so look for the sorts least likely to have a problem in your area.

BOUGAINVILLEA
Bougainvillea
Evergreen vine

Color: *Red, violet, lavender, purple, pink, yellow, orange, white*
Season: *Spring, summer*
Hardy to: *25°F/–4°C*
Exposure: *Sun*
Water: *Regular to moderate*

Bougainvillea is prized for its spectacular floral bracts (actually modified leaves at the base of the inconspicuous true flowers), which are often so plentiful they conceal the heart-shaped leaves. Older types of bougainvillea have vibrant red or violet bracts; newer hybrids come in a greater range of colors.

These plants can be grown vertically as vines or horizontally as ground covers. In areas that get some frost, choose a warm planting location—against a south-facing wall, for example. Vines should be tied to a support, though the stems do have thorns that help prop the plant up. A plant that survives the first winter or two will be big enough to take some frost damage and recover.

In moderately cold climates, shrubby hybrids can be grown in containers (pot-bound plants seem to bloom better) and moved to a protected spot in winter. In very cold climates, plants already in bloom can serve as summer annuals.

Bougainvillea

BRACHYCOME
Swan River daisy
Annual and perennial

Color: *Blue, pink, white*
Season: *Spring, summer*
Hardy to: *10°F/–12°C*
Exposure: *Sun*
Water: *Moderate*

Mounding and slightly spreading, these little foot-tall plants bear a mass of jaunty daisies in spring and summer. The annual *B. iberidifolia* blooms in blue, white, or pink. Similar in appearance is the perennial *B. multifida*, which usually has purplish blue blossoms.

Use these delicate, ferny-leafed plants for edgings, at the front of borders, or in containers or hanging baskets.

Brachycome iberidifolia

BRASSICA OLERACEA
Flowering cabbage and kale
Annual

Color: *White, pink, rose, purple*
Season: *Early spring, fall*
Exposure: *Sun*
Water: *Regular*

Developed from edible varieties, these ornamental plants are cultivated for their colorful leaf rosettes. Some types turn bright purple or rose when temperatures fall below 40°F/4°C; others are variegated with white or cream. The color usually intensifies toward the middle of the plant, with the outer leaves remaining bluish green.

Ornamental cabbages are wavy-leafed and 8 to 12 inches tall. Kales may be compact and fringy-leafed, or they may be taller plants (to 1½ feet) with deeply serrated foliage. Many cultivars of each type are commonly available.

Set out both cabbage and kale in late summer or early fall for a show of color in cool weather. Sturdy and frost-resistant, the plants will keep growing into winter in mild climates. As temperatures rise, though, they'll quickly go to seed—so remove them when the weather warms. Spring plantings seldom give satisfactory results.

Browallia speciosa

BROWALLIA SPECIOSA
Amethyst flower
Perennial grown as annual

Color: *Blue, violet, white*
Season: *Late spring, summer*
Exposure: *Part shade*
Water: *Regular*

Initially popular as a house plant, amethyst flower is now grown as a summer annual for beds and hanging baskets. During warm weather, the 1- to 2-foot-tall plant is covered with 2-inch, tubular blooms resembling those of its relative, flowering tobacco (*Nicotiana*).

Flowers are blue, violet, or white; blue types have a contrasting white throat. The compact 'Blue Bells Improved' has lavender-blue blossoms, the trailing 'Silver Bells' pure white ones. The Troll series includes blue and white forms and produces compact, bushy plants ideal for containers. Pinch all types to promote blooms.

BRUNNERA MACROPHYLLA
Siberian bugloss
Perennial

Color: *Blue, white*
Season: *Spring*
Hardy to: *–35°F/–37°C; not suited to Gulf Coast and Florida*
Exposure: *Sun, part shade*
Water: *Regular*

A clumping plant about 1½ feet tall, Siberian bugloss sends up delicate sprays of bright blue forget-me-not flowers in spring. After bloom is over, the handsome foliage keeps the plant attractive. Leaves are large, heart-shaped, and deep green; 'Hadspen Cream' has irregular creamy white borders, 'Langtrees' silvery white spots.

Because Siberian bugloss self-sows, it's a good ground cover or naturalizer in woodland gardens. It takes sun only in cool-summer regions.

Brassica oleracea

Brunnera macrophylla

Buddleia alternifolia

BUDDLEIA
Butterfly bush
Deciduous shrubs

Color: *Purple, lavender, pink, red, white*
Season: *Spring, summer*
Hardy to: *–20°F/–29°C*
Exposure: *Sun*
Water: *Regular to moderate*

Common butterfly bush, *B. davidii*, reaches about 15 feet tall; its slightly arching stems end in long, foxtail-like clusters of fragrant, orange-centered lavender flowers. Cultivar colors range from purple (including deep and pale shades) through wine red, violet, and rosy lavender to white.

The common species blooms in summer on new wood produced the same season, so cut back plants severely during late winter or early spring to promote abundant flowering. Plants may freeze to the ground but will regrow from the roots.

Fountain butterfly bush, *B. alternifolia*, a billowy spring bloomer at least 10 feet tall, produces clusters of mildly fragrant lavender blossoms all along its slender, arching branches. This species forms its flower buds on the previous year's growth, so prune only after blossoms have faded.

Remove the oldest stems annually to encourage strong new growth for the next year's blooms.

BUXUS
Boxwood
Evergreen shrubs

Color: *Green*
Season: *All year*
Hardy to: *Varies*
Exposure: *Sun, part shade, shade*
Water: *Regular*

Grown for their small, tidy, glossy green leaves, these handsome evergreen plants are easily sheared into formal hedges and topiary sculpture. Left unclipped, they have a soft, billowing appearance.

B. sempervirens (–10°F/–23°C) can eventually reach 15 to 20 feet tall. The most widely grown selection is 'Suffruticosa', the classic boxwood of European formal gardens, which grows slowly to 4 or 5 feet. Slightly hardier cultivars are also available.

The best boxwood for dry-summer regions is *B. microphylla japonica* (0°F/–18°C); though it naturally grows to 4 to 6 feet tall, it can be kept trimmed to under a foot. In many areas, its bright green leaves turn a disagreeable bronze during winter—but it does have cultivars that remain green all season, as well as some that are hardier than the species.

B. microphylla koreana (–18°F/–28°C) is a naturally low plant, growing slowly to about 2 feet.

Buxus microphylla japonica

Caladium bicolor 'Fannie Munson'

CALADIUM BICOLOR
Fancy-leafed caladium
Tuberous-rooted perennial

Color: *Red, pink, white, green, silver, bronze*
Season: *Summer*
Hardy to: *55°F/13°C*
Exposure: *Part shade, shade*
Water: *Regular*

Also known as *C. × hortulanum*, the many caladium cultivars, ranging from 1 to 3 feet tall, are grown for their spectacularly patterned foliage. Arrow-shaped, nearly translucent leaves up to 1½ feet long are variegated, veined, spotted, or edged in various combinations of colors, including reds and pinks, white, cream, and bronzy shades. If you see flowers, simply snip them off; they divert energy from leaf production.

These plants need a warm, moist, shady place to grow. In Florida and some areas of the Gulf Coast, caladium tubers can successfully stay in the ground all year long; they go dormant during the winter months. Gardeners living in other regions should dig and store the tubers after leaf dieback, or grow the plants in containers and move them indoors for winter.

Calceolaria crenatiflora

Calendula officinalis

Calluna vulgaris 'Spring Torch'

CALCEOLARIA CRENATIFLORA
Pocketbook plant
Perennial grown as annual

Color: *Yellow, red, maroon, pink*
Season: *Spring, summer*
Exposure: *Part shade*
Water: *Regular*

Sometimes listed as *C. herbeohybrida*, this 1- to 1½-foot-tall bedding plant produces masses of small, often speckled flowers in yellow, red, maroon, or pink. Plants are best suited to cool coastal and high-altitude gardens, since they suffer in hot weather. The Anytime series is the most heat-tolerant.

Grow pocketbook plant from nursery transplants if you can find them, since the plants are difficult and slow to start from seed.

CALENDULA OFFICINALIS
Pot marigold
Annual

Color: *Yellow, orange, apricot, cream, white*
Season: *Spring, summer*
Exposure: *Sun*
Water: *Moderate*

A bushy, upright annual with pale green, rough foliage, pot marigold yields a profusion of 2- to 4-inch daisies with single or double petals. Flower colors are harmonious: white through cream and lemon to bright yellow, apricot, and orange.

The taller cultivars reach 2 to 2½ feet, while dwarf forms grow about a foot high. Though the main bloom occurs in spring and early summer, pot marigold also graces mild-climate gardens in late fall and winter, when cooler temperatures encourage extra-large blossoms. As the weather warms, plants shoot up in height and flower size decreases.

Pot marigold is attractive massed in beds or planted in containers. To keep the color going for months, remove faded flowers regularly. Cut flowers are long-lasting, though scentless. The petals are edible and can be used in salads.

CALLUNA VULGARIS
Heather
Evergreen shrub

Color: *Pink, red, purple, white*
Season: *Summer, fall*
Hardy to: *−30°F/−34°C*
Exposure: *Sun*
Water: *Regular*

In the wild, heather is a billowy 2- to 3-foot plant with scalelike leaves and one-sided spikes of small, bell-shaped, purplish pink flowers at its branch tips. The hundreds of named selections offer considerably more variety, however. In form, they range from prostrate ground covers just 6 inches high to stiffly upright plants 3 feet tall; the flowers, appearing in summer or fall, may be single or double, in a color selection including white and various shades of pink, red, and purple. Foliage color varies as well, covering green, gray, gold, and bronze. The leaves of some types even change color during cold weather.

Though very similar to heath (*Erica*, see page 145), heather is a hardier plant offering more diverse cultivars. It grows and flowers best in full sun but tolerates part shade— and may even succeed in it in areas with long, hot summers. Most heathers need annual pruning, either after flowering or in early spring.

CAMELLIA
Camellia
Evergreen shrubs and small trees

Color: *Red, pink, white, bicolors*
Season: *Fall, winter, spring*
Hardy to: *Varies*
Exposure: *Part shade, shade*
Water: *Regular to moderate*

The many camellia species and cultivars are grown for their lustrous green leaves and the gorgeous waxy flowers that provide color when little else is blooming. Among red and pink varieties, you'll find clear colors as well as blue- and yellow-based ones. Unfortunately, fragrance is not among the camellia's many virtues.

The most common species is *C. japonica* (10°F/−12°C, though some

Camellia japonica

survive to 0°F/–18°C). Typically 6 to 15 feet tall in gardens, this species is agreeable to being clipped into a hedge. Blooms are generally up to 5 inches across.

Usually sun-tolerant, *C. sasanqua* and *C. hiemalis* (5°F/–15°C) can be somewhat vining (and easy to espalier) or upright and bushy to about 12 feet. These two species are the earliest to bloom, with flowers appearing in fall. The blossoms aren't as large or long-lasting as those of *C. japonica,* but their abundance makes up for those shortcomings.

C. reticulata (10°F/–12°C), growing 10 to 20 feet tall, is more open and treelike in habit than *C. japonica.* It has the largest flowers—up to 9 inches in diameter.

Hybrid camellias, including crosses of the species mentioned above, are generally hardy to about 10°F/–12°C, though some types have greater cold tolerance.

Camellias are fairly easy to grow and even thrive in containers. Their leaves turn yellow where soil or water is alkaline.

CAMPANULA
Bellflower
Annuals, biennials, and perennials

Color: *Blue, purple, white, pink*
Season: *Late spring, summer*
Hardy to: *Varies*
Exposure: *Sun, part shade*
Water: *Regular*

Bellflowers include hundreds of species (mostly perennials), from creeping ground covers only a few inches high to erect types with flowering stems that reach about 5 feet tall. As the common name implies, the late-spring or summer blossoms generally resemble bells, though some members of the group have blooms that are cupped, star-shaped, or round and flat. Prevailing colors are various blues and white, with occasional pink selections.

Low spreaders include a couple of easy-to-grow perennials. The vigorous Serbian bellflower, *C. poscharskyana* (–30°F/–34°C), has soft blue, starlike flowers; the more restrained Dalmatian bellflower, *C. portenschlagiana* (also sold as *C. muralis* and hardy to –20°F/–29°C), bears blue-violet bells.

Perhaps the loveliest upright bellflower is Canterbury bells, *C. medium.* Originally biennial but now available in many annual forms, this species produces 2½-foot-tall spires

Campanula poscharskyana

of large bells in blue, lavender, pink, rose, and white.

True to its common name, the perennial clustered bellflower *(C. glomerata,* hardy to –30°F/–34°C) bears typically blue-violet bells in tight bunches at the ends of 1- to 2-foot stems. Another perennial, *C. lactiflora* (–10°F/–23°C), is one of the tallest bellflowers, reaching 3 to 5 feet. The upright stems carry loose panicles of starry bells in blue shades, pink, or white.

CAMPSIS
Trumpet vine
Deciduous vine

Color: *Orange, red, yellow*
Season: *Summer, fall*
Hardy to: *–10°F/–23°C*
Exposure: *Sun*
Water: *Regular*

This vigorous climber bears clusters of large, trumpet-shaped blossoms at its stem ends. *C. radicans* has vivid orange or scarlet blooms; 'Flava' is a yellow-flowering form. Blossoms of the hybrid *C.* 'Crimson Trumpet' are pure red.

Trumpet vine clings with aerial rootlets, so locate it where you don't mind damage to whatever the plant uses as a climbing surface. These plants also spread by suckering roots.

Though trumpet vine may die to the ground in freezing weather, new stems grow quickly. Where winters are severe, the plants are slow to mature and bloom.

Campsis radicans

Canna

CANNA
Canna
Rhizomatous perennial

Color: *Red, pink, orange, yellow, cream, white, bicolors*
Season: *Late summer, fall*
Hardy to: *10°F/–12°C*
Exposure: *Sun*
Water: *Regular*

For a lush, tropical effect, there's no better choice than exotic-looking canna. The vivid flower spikes come in a wide range of blossom colors, often spotted with contrasting hues; the bold leaves, up to 2 feet long, may be green, bronze, or variegated.

Nearly all nursery cannas are hybrids. The old-fashioned garden favorites grow 4 to 6 feet tall, but compact types as short as 1½ feet are also available. Planting in spring should yield you a nice flowering clump by the end of summer. Cannas can also be grown in pots partially submerged in water.

Cannas are best suited to warm-summer climates, and they tend to naturalize where winter temperatures don't fall below 20°F/–7°C. In colder areas, lift and store the rhizomes after frost kills the foliage.

CATANANCHE CAERULEA
Cupid's dart
Perennial

Color: *Blue, white*
Season: *Summer*
Hardy to: *–30°F/–34°C*
Exposure: *Sun*
Water: *Moderate*

Floating above gray-green, grassy foliage, this wispy plant's wiry, 2-foot stems carry 2-inch daisies clasped in strawlike, shining bracts. Flowers are typically lavender-blue with a darker center; named selections include deep blue-violet 'Major' and white 'Alba'.

A good choice for dried arrangements, cupid's dart is best planted in masses, since individual plants look sparse. If soil is very rich or water too abundant, the plant's already brief life span will be cut even shorter. Divide clumps to rejuvenate them, or let volunteer seedlings grow.

CATHARANTHUS ROSEUS
Madagascar periwinkle
Shrub grown as annual

Color: *Pink, rose, white*
Season: *Late spring, summer, fall*
Exposure: *Sun, part shade*
Water: *Regular*

Previously known as *Vinca rosea*, this shiny-leafed tropical subshrub blooms freely from late spring well into fall. Its single, five-petaled flowers come in pink, rose, or white, often with a contrasting eye. The plant is generally used as an annual—even in frost-free regions, where it can survive from year to year but tends to look ragged in winter. Plants reseed freely in mild climates.

Available forms include low creepers, lovely cascading from window boxes or used as ground covers, as well as upright border plants reaching 2 feet tall.

Madagascar periwinkle is a tough plant. It's very heat-resistant, succeeding even in desert gardens; it withstands big-city air pollution; and it tolerates all but the driest soils, though it prefers regular water. Another virtue: it's among the few summer annuals to bloom equally well in sun or part shade.

Catananche caerulea

Catharanthus roseus 'Blush Cooler'

CEANOTHUS
Wild lilac
Evergreen shrubs and ground covers

Color: *Blue, white*
Season: *Spring*
Hardy to: *0°F/–18°C; for Western United States only*
Exposure: *Sun*
Water: *Varies*

Ceanothus 'Julia Phelps'

Celosia 'Golden Triumph'

Centaurea cyanus

Two deciduous wild lilacs are native to eastern North America, but the real showstoppers are the evergreen Western species. In spring, the plants are clothed in dense clusters of blue flowers, in shades from palest azure to deepest cobalt. A few white-flowered forms do exist, but they aren't nearly as striking as the blue-blossomed types.

The dozens of species and hybrids range from foot-tall ground covers to 20-foot shrubs. Some types sport tiny, hollylike foliage; others have large, crinkly leaves.

Moisture requirements vary. Most wild lilacs demand total summer dryness once established, but some—primarily coastal ground cover types grown away from the fog belt—need occasional irrigation.

CELOSIA
Cockscomb
Annual

Color: *Red, orange, apricot, yellow, pink, purple*
Season: *Summer*
Exposure: *Sun*
Water: *Moderate to little*

Vivid—sometimes bizarre—blossoms are this annual's claim to fame. There are two types of cockscomb; both are derived from *C. argentea*, a species with silvery white flowers.

Plume cockscombs (often sold as *C.* 'Plumosa') typically have feathery flower clusters, though in the case of Chinese woolflower (some-

times called *C.* 'Childsii'), the blooms look like tangled balls of yarn. Colors include orange, red, crimson, gold, and pink.

Crested cockscombs, often sold as *C.* 'Cristata', have velvety heads contorted into an almost grotesque shape that can be variously described as a rooster's comb, a convoluted branch of coral, or just plain brains. Because of this odd appearance, the crested types—available in yellow, orange, crimson, purple, and red—are more difficult to use in the garden than are plume cockscombs.

Both types have the same size range, encompassing dwarf types under a foot high as well as standard forms about 3 feet tall. Cut flowers can be used for fresh or dried bouquets.

CENTAUREA
Bachelor's button, cornflower, dusty miller
Annuals and perennials

Color: *Blue, purple, red, pink, white, silver*
Season: *Varies*
Hardy to: *Varies*
Exposure: *Sun*
Water: *Moderate*

Of the hundreds of *Centaurea* species, only a dozen or so are widely cultivated. Of these, bachelor's button and dusty miller are among the most useful for color gardeners.

The summer annual *C. cyanus*, known as bachelor's button or corn-

flower, produces masses of fringed daisies in blue, purple, pink, red, or white. To keep blooms coming, cut the flowers frequently for bouquets. You'll find a good range of heights, from dwarf forms under a foot high to 3-footers that need staking. Plants self-sow, but seedlings often revert to inferior flower forms.

Often used as an annual in cold-winter regions, the perennial *C. cineraria* (0°F/–18°C) is among the several silver foliage plants known as dusty miller. It usually forms a 1- to 1½-foot-high mound of felty, whitish, divided leaves with roundish lobes. To maintain the overall silvery effect, clip off the purple (occasionally yellow) flowers as they appear.

CERASTIUM TOMENTOSUM
Snow-in-summer
Evergreen perennial

Color: *White, gray*
Season: *Late spring, summer*
Hardy to: *–30°F/–34°C*
Exposure: *Sun*
Water: *Moderate*

In late spring and early summer, pure white, star-shaped flowers up to an inch wide nearly obscure the small, woolly, silvery gray leaves of this lovely little perennial ground cover. After bloom, shear off the faded flower stems or mow the entire planting to neaten it. Snow-in-summer is evergreen, but it may look a bit shabby in winter.

Cerastium tomentosum

Avoid large drifts, since the plants are fairly short-lived. It's best simply to start over every few years—and easy, too, since a single plant spreads 2 to 3 feet in a year. Just 8 inches high, snow-in-summer is ideal as a bulb cover, in rock gardens, between stepping stones, or on a sunny slope. Plants tolerate drought ; they also take regular water if soil is well drained.

CERATOSTIGMA PLUMBAGINOIDES
Dwarf plumbago
Deciduous perennial

Color: *Blue*
Season: *Summer, fall*
Hardy to: *–10°F/–23°C; not suited to Gulf Coast and Florida*
Exposure: *Sun, part shade*
Water: *Moderate*

Where the growing season is long, this small-scale, foot-high ground cover provides dazzling color from

Ceratostigma plumbaginoides

midsummer until frost, bearing loose clusters of electric blue flowers at the tips of wiry, purplish stems. Frost produces additional color, turning the oval leaves bronzy red.

Dwarf plumbago spreads quickly by underground stems to form a dense mat. Cut old stems to the ground sometime between late fall and early spring, before new growth commences. A deciduous perennial, the plant is semievergreen in the warmer parts of its range.

CERCIS
Redbud
Deciduous trees and shrubs

Color: *Pink, red, white*
Season: *Early spring*
Hardy to: *Varies*
Exposure: *Sun, part shade*
Water: *Moderate*

Redbuds put on an exquisite display of small, sweet pea–shaped, purplish pink blossoms before leafing out in spring. Other features that give these trees their year-round interest are handsome, rounded leaves with a heart-shaped base, yellow fall color, and beanlike, reddish brown pods that dangle from the bare branches in winter.

Eastern redbud, *C. canadensis* (–20°F/–29°C), needs some winter chill. At maturity, it reaches about 30 feet tall, with branches growing in horizontal tiers. 'Rubye Atkinson' bears pure pink flowers; 'Forest Pansy' has rosy pink blossoms and purple leaves on reddish branches.

The Southwest equivalent of Eastern redbud, *C. reniformis* (0°F/ –18°C), does not require winter chill. White-flowered *C. r.* 'Alba' ('Texas White') and wine red *C. r.* 'Oklahoma' are sometimes erroneously listed as selections of Eastern redbud.

Two drought-tolerant species, both hardy to –10°F/–23°C, are especially suited to the West. The Judas tree, *C. siliquastrum* , about 25 feet tall, has the typical purplish pink flowers. Western redbud, *C. occidentalis*, a shrub about 15 feet tall, produces brilliant magenta blossoms. Both

Cercis canadensis

these species put on the best display if grown in full sun in regions where winter temperatures drop at least a few degrees below freezing.

CHAENOMELES
Flowering quince
Deciduous shrub

Color: *Pink, red, orange, white*
Season: *Late winter, early spring*
Hardy to: *–30°F/–34°C*
Exposure: *Sun*
Water: *Regular to moderate*

For a few weeks in late winter or early spring, this otherwise bland-looking shrub produces gorgeous blossoms up to 2½ inches across, in soft or vibrant colors.

Nearly all flowering quinces sold in nurseries are hybrids derived from *C. speciosa* and one or more other

Chaenomeles

species. You'll find a wide range of sizes and growth habits. The taller sorts are upright-growing and fall into the 6-foot-or-higher category, with some reaching as high as 10 feet. Low growers are 2 or 3 feet tall, often with a spreading habit. Most flowering quinces are thorny and make good barriers. Some produce a sparse crop of small fruit.

Since this shrub shines so briefly and often defoliates in midsummer, don't give it too prominent a location. To enjoy the flowers close up, cut budded stems and bring them indoors to bloom.

CHRYSANTHEMUM
Chrysanthemum
Perennial

Color: *White, cream, yellow, pink, red, orange, bronze*
Season: *Spring, summer, fall*
Hardy to: *Varies*
Exposure: *Sun*
Water: *Regular*

Chrysanthemum × superbum

One type or another of these prolific bloomers is in flower throughout the growing season, producing modest to spectacular daisylike blossoms in soft to vivid colors. The following species are good bets; both old and new names are cited, since most nurseries haven't kept pace with changes in nomenclature.

The showiest mums are the many hybrids of garden chrysanthemum, *C. × morifolium (Dendranthema × grandiflora)*, hardy to –10°F/–23°C. Mainstays of the late-summer and fall garden, they offer an astounding range of flower sizes and forms—from button-size to softball-size, from flat to ball-shaped—on plants 1 to 4 feet tall. Choose from white or a variety of autumn hues: red, gold, orange, and bronze. Overwintered plants often put on a brief second display in spring. Divide clumps every other year or so.

Painted daisy (–30°F/–34°C) may be listed as *C. coccineum, Tanacetum coccineum,* or *Pyrethrum roseum.* A spring bloomer, it bears large, yellow-eyed white, pink, or red daisies above a ferny foliage clump 1½ to 3 feet tall. If cut back after bloom, it will flower again in late summer. Divide every few years.

Shasta daisy (–20°F/–29°C) may be listed as *C. × superbum, C. maximum,* or *Leucanthemum maximum.* Growing 2 to 4 feet tall, it produces showy, golden-centered white daisies in summer. Divide every other year or so.

Marguerite, *C. frutescens (Argyranthemum frutescens)*, a short-lived perennial to 3 feet tall, bears white, yellow, or pink daisies throughout summer. Hardy to 20°F/–7°C, it tends to get very woody and should be replaced every few years. In cold climates, this species is grown as an annual.

C. ptarmiciflorum (Tanacetum ptarmiciflorum), known as silver lace or dusty miller, forms a mound of finely cut silvery leaves about 8 inches tall. In areas where temperatures remain above 20°F/–7°C, it will establish itself as a perennial, eventually producing white daisies on 1½-foot stems. Elsewhere, it's grown as an annual foliage plant.

Cimicifuga racemosa

CIMICIFUGA RACEMOSA
Bugbane
Perennial

Color: *White*
Season: *Summer*
Hardy to: *–35°F/–37°C; needs some winter chill; not suited to Gulf Coast and Florida*
Exposure: *Part shade*
Water: *Regular*

In mid to late summer, this statuesque woodland plant puts up slim stalks of pure white flowers that tower above the clump of finely divided, delicate foliage. In bloom, the plant can reach a height of 7 feet. Seed clusters follow the blossoms; left to dry on the plant, they'll look ornamental for weeks.

Though bugbane prefers part shade, it will take full sun where summers are cool or mild—or if given ample water. Clumps grow for many years before needing division.

CISTUS
Rockrose
Evergreen shrubs

Color: *White, pink, rose, magenta, yellow, bicolors*
Season: *Spring, early summer*
Hardy to: *15°F/–9°C; suited to dry-summer regions*
Exposure: *Sun*
Water: *Moderate to little*

These attractive evergreen shrubs bear crepe-papery, five-petaled blos-

Cistus

Clematis

Cleome hasslerana

soms that look like wild roses. The bloom season lasts for a month or more—usually in mid and late spring, though a few rockroses put on a show into summer. Flowers come in pure white, yellow-eyed white, white with red or yellow splotches at the petal bases, clear pink, purplish pink, and magenta.

In size, these plants range from low spreaders about 1 foot high to taller types in the 3- to 6-foot range. Typically rough-textured and grayish or dull green, the foliage may be slightly sticky.

In dry-summer climates, rockrose is carefree, requiring no pruning, no fertilizer, and little water. It doesn't take well to relocation, so plant it in a dry, sunny spot and keep it there.

CLEMATIS
Clematis, virgin's bower
Deciduous and evergreen vines

Color: *White, pink, red, lavender, blue-violet, purple, yellow, bicolors*
Season: *Spring, summer, fall*
Hardy to: *Varies*
Exposure: *Sun, part shade*
Water: *Regular*

Though this genus includes a few shrubs and perennials, it's best known for flowering vines. Many are grown for spectacular, richly hued, sometimes enormous (up to 9-inch-wide) blossoms. Others are chosen for their ability to form leafy screens quickly; these vigorous types usually have small but very fragrant flowers, often

in white or pale colors. Most types of clematis are deciduous.

With careful planning, you can have various clematis blooming in your garden throughout the growing season. Hardiness varies, so choose types suited to your climate.

Locate the vines so that the roots are in shade, the tops in sun. To create cooling shade for the root zone, cover the soil with mulch, a ground cover, or flat rocks or bricks.

Prune clematis to promote flowering. Types that bloom on old wood formed the previous year should be lightly thinned after flowering. Those that flower on new wood produced the same year should be cut nearly to the ground when dormant, though some gardeners find the vines easier to train if some part of the older stems remains tied to the support.

CLEOME HASSLERANA
Spider flower
Annual

Color: *White, pink, lavender*
Season: *Summer, fall*
Exposure: *Sun, part shade*
Water: *Regular*

Each stem of this vigorous annual ends in a flower head that elongates from summer until the first frosts, producing a continuous display of spidery-looking white, pink, or lavender blossoms. In bloom, the plant rises 4 to 5 feet tall. The stems are spiny—hence the alternative name *C. spinosa.*

Since spider flower tends to be leggy and leafless at the bottom, locate shorter plants at its base. It's a good back-of-the-border choice and useful for filling empty spots in the garden.

Spider flower's blossoms are long-lasting as cut flowers, and the slender seed capsules are attractive in dried arrangements. The plant self-sows freely.

CLETHRA ALNIFOLIA
Summersweet
Deciduous shrub

Color: *White, pink*
Season: *Late summer, fall*
Hardy to: *–40°F/–40°C*
Exposure: *Part shade*
Water: *Regular*

Slender spires of tiny, gleaming white, spicily perfumed flowers decorate summersweet's branch tips for many weeks late in the season. The white selection 'Paniculata' has longer spires than the species; 'Pinkspire' is deep pink, 'Rosea' pale pink.

Clethra alnifolia

The attractive dark green foliage turns yellow in fall, but the color isn't reliable. Old flower spikes hang on while the leaves are changing.

Typically about 8 feet tall, summersweet grows well in soils where rhododendrons thrive. It prefers part shade but adapts to various light conditions. Plants spread slowly by suckers, eventually forming broad clumps.

COBAEA SCANDENS
Cup-and-saucer vine
Perennial vine grown as annual

Color: *Violet, white*
Season: *Summer*
Exposure: *Sun*
Water: *Regular*

Throughout summer, this vigorous tropical vine produces showy 2-inch bells that open pale green, then turn violet. There's also a white form. The bell-shaped flower forms the "cup"; the green ruffle at the petals' base is the "saucer."

Cobaea scandens

Because the vine grows and flowers in a single season, it's commonly used as an annual—though it must be started early, then set out as a sizable plant. Using its curling tendrils, it can quickly climb a trellis or arbor without support. In the mildest regions (where temperatures remain above 39°F/4°C), the plant winters over as a big woody vine.

COLCHICUM AUTUMNALE
Meadow saffron, autumn crocus
Deciduous corm

Color: *Pinkish lavender, purple, white*
Season: *Fall*
Hardy to: *–20°F/–29°C*
Exposure: *Sun, part shade*
Water: *Regular*

Large, wineglass-shaped blossoms push out of the earth in fall; the foliage emerges after the flowers are gone and disappears in late spring, long before blooming resumes the next autumn. The usual color is pinkish lavender, but white and purplish forms are also sold, as are double-flowered types.

Meadow saffron is most effective in drifts or large clumps. Locate the planting where the 6- to 8-inch-high blooms are plainly visible, but don't give it so much prominence that the dying foliage is on display. Also choose an area that won't be disturbed by digging. Flowering peters out after a couple of seasons in mild-winter regions; at that time, it's best to replant.

Colchicum autumnale

Convallaria majalis

CONVALLARIA MAJALIS
Lily-of-the-valley
Perennial

Color: *White, pink*
Season: *Spring*
Hardy to: *–40°F/–40°C; needs some winter chill*
Exposure: *Part shade, shade*
Water: *Regular*

This charming old favorite is beloved for the curved stems of small, nodding, delightfully sweet-scented white bells that peek through the glossy green leaves in spring. Double and pink-flowered forms are available, as well as a variegated type with cream-striped foliage. Plants grow 6 to 10 inches high.

Though lily-of the-valley's pendent bells last only a few weeks, the broad, bold, deciduous foliage is attractive from spring to fall. Grown from small rootstocks called pips, the plant makes a lovely small-scale ground cover in a woodland garden. All plant parts, including the bright red fall berries, are poisonous.

CONVOLVULUS CNEORUM
Bush morning glory
Evergreen shrub

Color: *White, gray*
Season: *Spring, summer*
Hardy to: *15°F/–9°C*
Exposure: *Sun*
Water: *Moderate*

Growing 2 to 4 feet tall, this evergreen shrub blooms from spring through summer, bearing yellow-throated, white or pink-tinged morning glories that unfurl from pink buds. The narrow, silky-textured leaves are silvery gray.

In full sun, bush morning glory is free-blooming and compact; in shade, it has a looser habit and flowers sparsely. Prune severely to maintain a dense shape and promote bloom. In dry climates, plants perform best if the roots are soaked every couple of weeks.

Convolvulus cneorum

Coreopsis verticillata 'Zagreb'

COREOPSIS
Coreopsis
Annuals and perennials

Color: *Yellow, orange, red, bronze, bicolors*
Season: *Summer*
Hardy to: *Varies*
Exposure: *Sun*
Water: *Moderate*

Most of these easy-to-grow plants, ranging from ankle height to about 3 feet tall, bear sunny yellow daisies over a long season. The primary bloom time is summer, though many begin blossoming in late spring and continue into fall. Shearing the flowers periodically will prolong bloom.

The shortest species is the early-blooming, 6-inch perennial *C. auriculata* 'Nana' (–30°F/–34°C); its yellow-orange daisies rise just above a clump of spoon-shaped leaves.

C. grandiflora (–20°F/–29°C) has many fine selections; one good choice is 'Sunburst', a 2-foot-tall, narrow-leafed plant that bears bright yellow, semidouble blooms all summer long.

Delicate-looking threadleaf coreopsis, *C. verticillata* (–40°F/–40°C), holds its blossoms above a clump of ferny foliage. Depending on the cultivar, flower color ranges from pale yellow to golden, plant height from 1 to about 2½ feet. The 1½- to 2-foot-tall 'Moonbeam' produces soft yellow daisies continuously from early summer into fall.

The showy, lacy-leafed annual *C. tinctoria*, about 2½ feet tall, has wiry stems carrying yellow, orange, maroon, bronze, or reddish flowers. The blossoms are often banded in a contrasting color around the purplish brown center. Dwarf and double forms are also available.

CORNUS
Dogwood
Deciduous shrubs and small trees

Color: *White, pink, red, yellow*
Season: *Varies*
Hardy to: *Varies; needs some winter chill*
Exposure: *Sun, part shade*
Water: *Regular*

Few trees surpass dogwood for exquisite spring bloom and vivid red berries. The lovely white or pink blossoms are actually modified, petal-like leaves called bracts; the true flowers are inconspicuous.

Two of the finest flowering species—Eastern dogwood *(C. florida)* and Pacific dogwood *(C. nuttallii)*—have serious disease problems, but luckily for gardeners, there are beau-

Cornus kousa

tiful alternatives. One such choice is the disease-resistant Kousa dogwood, C. kousa (–10°F/–23°C), a shrubby Asian species that is sold in many forms and can be trained into a 20-foot tree. Its bracts perch above the branches, while the leaves hang below. This species blooms in early summer, a few weeks later than Eastern dogwood.

The newly developed stellar dogwood, C. × rutgersensis (–20°F/–29°C), was bred to withstand the pests and diseases plaguing American dogwoods. A hybrid between C. florida and C. kousa, it's a single-stemmed, low-branching tree about 20 feet tall. It blooms after C. florida but before C. kousa, producing showy bracts after leaf-out. Cultivars include 'Stellar Pink' and the white-blossomed 'Aurora', 'Galaxy', 'Ruth Ellen', and 'Constellation'.

Several shrubby dogwoods are grown for colorful stems that become more vivid in cold weather. Two of the best are vase-shaped plants hardy to –50°F/–46°C. Siberian dogwood, C. alba 'Sibirica', is a 7-footer with bright coral red stems; the slightly smaller yellowtwig dogwood, C. stolonifera 'Flaviramea' (C. sericea), has golden stems.

Cornelian cherry, C. mas (–20°F/–29°C), a shrub or small tree to 20 feet tall, provides a progression of color. First come clouds of tiny yellow blossoms on bare twigs; these are followed by shiny green leaves, then by cherry-size fruits that ripen to scarlet. The foliage turns red in autumn, then drops to showcase flaking bark mottled in gray and tan. Leaves of 'Variegata' are marbled with creamy white.

COSMOS
Cosmos
Annual

Color: *White, pink, red, lavender, yellow, orange, bicolors*
Season: *Summer*
Exposure: *Sun, part shade*
Water: *Moderate*

Lovely massed in borders, these rangy, feathery-leafed annuals bear

Cosmos bipinnatus

big, yellow-eyed daisies with single or double petals in a wide range of colors. The main bloom season is summer, though flowering can continue until frost. All types are wonderful as cut flowers.

C. bipinnatus offers numerous color choices, from white through pink to red and bicolors. Cultivars of this species vary in height from 2 to 6 feet.

The extremely heat-resistant C. sulphureus produces flowers in the yellow-to-scarlet range. The plant grows to 7 feet tall, though forms as low as a foot high are available.

Give cosmos full sun or afternoon shade. If grown in day-long partial shade, the plants tend to stretch up and out, then fall over.

COTINUS COGGYGRIA
Smoke tree
Deciduous shrub or small tree

Color: *Purple, pinkish gray*
Season: *Summer*
Hardy to: *–20°F/–29°C*
Exposure: *Sun*
Water: *Moderate*

Dramatic puffs of "smoke" from fading flowers give smoke tree its name: as the tiny, greenish blooms wither, they send out elongated stalks clothed in fuzzy, pinkish gray hairs.

The most striking color display, though, comes from the foliage of this plant's purple-leafed cultivars (the bluish green–leafed species are less frequently planted). 'Royal Pur-

Cotinus coggygria

ple' and 'Velvet Cloak' remain purple throughout the growing season, while 'Purpureus' fades to green. All types offer gold, orange, or red fall color.

Left to its own inclinations, smoke tree is a billowing, multi-stemmed shrub to 15 feet tall and wide. However, it can be trained to a single-trunked tree up to 25 feet tall.

COTONEASTER
Cotoneaster
Evergreen and deciduous shrubs and ground covers

Color: *Red, orange-red*
Season: *Fall, winter*
Hardy to: *Varies*
Exposure: *Sun*
Water: *Moderate*

This group of easy-care woody plants includes ground covers under a foot high as well as arching shrubs up to 20 feet fall. Though most cotoneasters produce small white or pinkish flowers in spring, their real color contribution is their fruit: pea-size red or orange-red berries that ripen in fall and may last through winter.

Two low-growing deciduous species (both hardy to –20°F/–29°C) have especially showy fruit. Cranberry cotoneaster, C. apiculatus, produces clusters of extra-large scarlet berries on a mound about 3 feet high and 6 feet across; creeping cotoneaster, C. adpressus praecox, bears a profusion of bright red fruit on a 1½-foot-tall plant about 6 feet wide.

Cotoneaster apiculatus

Two evergreen species are noted for bright, long-lasting berries. Parney cotoneaster, *C. lacteus* (5°F/–15°C), forms an 8-foot fountain covered with large clusters of brilliant red fruit; rockspray cotoneaster, *C. microphyllus* (–10°F/–23°C), bears rosy red berries on a tiny-leafed, spreading plant 2 to 3 feet tall.

CRATAEGUS
Hawthorn
Small deciduous trees

Color: *White, pink, red, orange-red*
Season: *Spring, fall, winter*
Hardy to: *–20°F/–29°C; needs some winter chill*
Exposure: *Sun*
Water: *Moderate*

Typically thorny and multitrunked, these densely foliaged, 25- to 30-foot trees bloom profusely after spring leaf-out, then develop pendent clusters of fruit resembling tiny apples. The pomes ripen from summer into fall, often remaining on the branches after leaf drop and providing food for wildlife.

Washington thorn, *C. phaenopyrum,* is considered a fine choice for most areas except the hot-summer lower Midwest. Masses of white flowers are followed by clustered fruits that turn glossy red in fall and hang on through winter. This species is resistant to fireblight, a bacterial disease that sometimes attacks hawthorns.

Green hawthorn, *C. viridis* 'Winter King', has year-round good looks as well as resistance to insects and diseases. After the white flower clusters fade, the branches are decorated with big, showy orange-red fruits that persist through winter. The silver-gray bark, which flakes from older trees to expose orange-brown patches beneath, makes a striking backdrop for the bright fruit.

English hawthorn, *C. laevigata,* is prone to fireblight, but its colorful flowers lure gardeners nonetheless. The basic species has white single blossoms, but cultivars include 'Double Pink'; 'Paul's Scarlet', with rosy red double flowers; and 'Crimson Cloud' ('Superba'), with white-centered, bright red single blooms. Red berries follow the blossoms, though double-flowered types produce little fruit.

CROCOSMIA ×
CROCOSMIIFLORA
Montbretia
Deciduous corm

Color: *Orange, red, yellow, cream*
Season: *Summer*
Hardy to: *0°F/–18°C*
Exposure: *Sun, part shade*
Water: *Moderate to little*

Grown from bulblike corms, montbretia forms big clumps of sword-shaped leaves about 3 feet high. In summer, flat sprays of flowers appear on branched, 3- to 4-foot stems. The blossoms are typically reddish orange marked with dark red, but forms in red, deep orange, yellow, and cream are also available.

Crataegus laevigata

Crocosmia 'Lucifer'

A wonderful accent plant, montbretia naturalizes in mild-winter regions. It provides good cut flowers.

CROCUS
Crocus
Deciduous corm

Color: *Blue, lavender, purple, orange, yellow, cream, white, bicolors*
Season: *Fall, winter, spring*
Hardy to: *Varies; most need some winter chill*
Exposure: *Sun, part shade*
Water: *Regular*

Just 2 to 6 inches high, crocuses are delicate plants noted for their grassy foliage and dainty, cupped or flaring blossoms. Most appear in late winter or early to midspring; a few bloom in

Crocus, Dutch hybrid

fall. These plants are lovely in masses; where they are adapted, most types will naturalize.

The most commonly grown crocuses are Dutch hybrids (most are hardy to –40°F/–40°C), harbingers of spring in cold-winter regions. The large blooms—solid-colored, striped, or mottled—appear with or after the foliage. Colors include white and shades of yellow, lavender, and purple. These crocuses need pronounced cold to come back yearly.

Bulb specialists offer various spring species with smaller flowers. Hardiness varies, so choose types suited to your region.

The earliest and showiest fall bloomer—and the easiest to grow—is *C. speciosus* (–10°F/–23°C), which bears orange-eyed lavender flowers before the leaves emerge.

CYNARA CARDUNCULUS
Cardoon
Perennial

Color: *Silvery gray*
Season: *Spring, summer, fall*
Hardy to: *5°F/–15°C*
Exposure: *Sun*
Water: *Regular*

Related to the artichoke and raised for its edible leafstalks, 6- to 8-foot-tall cardoon also makes a striking gray accent. The leaves are very spiny, so locate the plant where it won't get in your way. The thistlelike violet flowers that appear in summer dry well for everlasting arrangements.

Cardoon is usually cut back in winter in mild climates, where it naturalizes and can become a weed. In cold regions, it's typically treated as an annual.

CYNOGLOSSUM AMABILE
Chinese forget-me-not
Biennial grown as annual

Color: *Blue, white, pink*
Season: *Spring, early summer*
Exposure: *Sun, part shade*
Water: *Regular to moderate*

This upright, densely branching plant bears loose sprays of small, star-shaped flowers, most commonly deep or sky blue, above soft grayish green leaves. 'Firmament' produces a multitude of sky blue blossoms; 'Blue Showers' was bred for cutting. White and pink forms are also available.

Since this 1½- to 2-foot-high plant has a somewhat untidy habit, it looks best in informal plantings and woodsy areas. Pinch off spent blooms to reduce the number of volunteer seedlings and promote flowering on side branches.

DAHLIA
Dahlia
Perennial grown as annual

Color: *Pink, red, lilac, purple, orange, yellow, cream, white, bicolors*
Season: *Summer, fall*
Hardy to: *20°F/–7°C*
Exposure: *Sun*
Water: *Regular*

These Mexican natives provide spectacular color from the start of summer until frost—to keep the show going, just pinch off spent flowers.

The myriad cultivars range from about 1 to 7 feet in height, from 2 to 12 inches in flower diameter. You'll find blossoms in a fantastic array of forms: some are ball-shaped, while others resemble water lilies or cacti. Blooms come in every color but true blue and green, and many are patterned or shaded with a second color.

Most dahlias are planted from tubers. These are usually dug up and stored at the end of the season, but in the mildest climates, they can stay in the ground.

Dwarf dahlias can be grown from seed for bloom the first year. Although far less dramatic in appearance than the taller types, they do not require staking.

Cynoglossum amabile

Dahlia 'Rebecca Lyon'

Cynara cardunculus

DAPHNE
Daphne
Deciduous and evergreen shrubs

Color: *White, pink*
Season: *Winter, spring*
Hardy to: *Varies*
Exposure: *Sun, part shade*
Water: *Moderate*

More than a dozen daphne species are grown for their lovely, tubular white or pink blossoms. The following are the most widely planted.

The 3- to 4-foot *D. × burkwoodii* (−30°F/−34°C) blooms in spring and often again in summer, bearing white blossoms that fade to pink. 'Somerset' is a slightly larger form with pink flowers; 'Carol Mackie' has light pink blooms and cream-edged leaves. In the coldest parts of their range, plants are only partially evergreen.

Reaching 4 to 5 feet tall, evergreen winter daphne, *D. odora* (5°F/−15°C), produces waxy, intensely fragrant blossoms in late winter. The flower buds are crimson, opening to pink-throated white blooms with rosy red petal backs. 'Marginata' has creamy leaf margins.

Garland daphne, *D. cneorum* (−30°F/−34°C), about a foot high and twice as wide, bears pink blossoms in spring and sometimes again in summer. 'Variegata' has cream-bordered foliage.

Daphnes need good drainage, moisture, and protection from wind and intense sun. Most types don't take well to transplanting. All plant parts are poisonous.

Daphne × burkwoodii 'Somerset'

Delphinium Blue Fountains

DELPHINIUM
Delphinium
Perennial

Color: *Blue, purple, pink, white, cream, bicolors*
Season: *Summer*
Hardy to: *−35°F/−37°C; needs some winter chill; not suited to hot-summer regions*
Exposure: *Sun, part shade*
Water: *Regular*

Majestic blossom spires rising from clumps of big, maplelike leaves have made delphiniums a mainstay of summer borders and cottage gardens. Flowers come in a full range of blues and purples, as well as in cool pinks, cream, and white.

Plants with the traditional form—towering, upright growers 5 to 7 feet tall—are hybrids of *D. elatum*. The short-lived Pacific strain (listed variously as Pacific Hybrids, Pacific Coast Hybrids, and Pacific Giants) is available both in separate colors and in bicolors with contrasting center petals (called the "bee"). The longer-lived Blackmore and Langdon strain, developed in England, is usually sold in mixed colors.

Shorter delphiniums grow as low as 2½ feet; these aren't nearly as stately, but they require less staking and are better for windy sites.

Cut spikes of any delphinium just below the lowest flower to get a second bloom late in the season. In hot-summer areas, treat these plants as annuals; set out young plants as early as possible after the danger of frost is past, so they'll bloom before hot weather sets in.

DIANTHUS
Pink, carnation
Annuals, biennials, and perennials

Color: *Red, purple, pink, white, yellow, bicolors*
Season: *Spring, summer*
Hardy to: *Varies*
Exposure: *Sun*
Water: *Moderate*

The hundreds of *Dianthus* species and hybrids produce strikingly pretty, often spicy-scented flowers; you'll find solid colors as well as blooms edged, striped, or blotched in a second color. Perennial types are evergreen or semievergreen, typically hardy to about −30°F/−34°C; all kinds make good cut flowers.

The genus can be divided into three categories: pink, sweet William, and carnation.

Pinks, named for their fringed or "pinked" petals, are the largest group. Typically 1 to 1½ feet tall (though some types are smaller), they bloom in spring and summer, bearing single to double, often bicolored, blooms in the white, pink, red, and purplish range. Old-fashioned pinks produce masses of very fragrant, fringed blossoms in a single flowering period. Modern types, derived from *D. × allwoodii* (a cross between an old-fashioned pink and a carnation), are repeat bloomers; their petals may be smooth-edged or fringed.

The biennial sweet William, *D. barbatus,* resembles an old garden

Dianthus

pink but is often given its own category. Its white, pink, or red blossoms, usually edged in a contrasting color, are borne in tight, flat clusters. Plants bloom the first year if started indoors in late winter; they often reseed.

Carnations make up the final group. The 1- to 3-foot-tall border carnation (originally developed from *D. caryophyllus*) is more compact and smaller-flowered than the greenhouse-grown florists' carnation. It blooms once in summer, producing five or more headily fragrant, semi-double or double blossoms on each stem. Flower colors range from white through pink to purplish and include scarlet and yellow as well. These plants are usually treated as annuals.

DICENTRA SPECTABILIS
Bleeding heart
Perennial

Color: Pink, white
Season: Spring
Hardy to: −35°F/−37°C; not suited to areas with mild winters and hot summers
Exposure: Part shade
Water: Regular

In spring, this showiest of the bleeding hearts is decked with nearly horizontal sprays of dangling, heart-shaped rosy pink blossoms, each with a protruding white tip. The one-sided,

Dicentra spectabilis

arching flower stems are carried in and above the ferny, soft green foliage. 'Alba' ('Pantaloons') has pure white hearts.

Growing 2 to 3 feet high, bleeding heart thrives in the semishady light of woodland gardens, though it can take full sun in cool regions. It dies to the ground in summer, even in mild climates. Plants never need dividing.

DICTAMNUS ALBUS
Gas plant
Perennial

Color: Pink, lilac, white
Season: Late spring, summer
Hardy to: −35°F/−37°C; needs some winter chill; not suited to Gulf Coast and Florida
Exposure: Sun, part shade
Water: Regular to moderate

In late spring or summer, upright spires of pink, narrow-petaled flowers with long stamens form at the branch tips of this bushy 2½- to 3-foot perennial, also sold as *D. fraxinella*. 'Purpureus' has lilac blooms; 'Albi-florus' is white-flowered. For fall interest, leave the seedpods in place—but keep in mind that they, like all other parts of the plant, are poisonous.

Dictamnus albus

Gas plant is so called because it emits a gas that may ignite briefly if a lighted match is held near the flowers. The leaves are lemon-scented. Just brushing against them causes skin irritation in some people.

A long-lived perennial, gas plant can stay in the same spot indefinitely and, in fact, does not take well to division or relocation.

DIGITALIS
Foxglove
Biennials and perennials

Color: Pink, rose, lavender, purple, white, yellow
Season: Spring, summer
Hardy to: Varies
Exposure: Part shade
Water: Regular

The classic cottage-garden foxglove is the biennial *D. purpurea* (−20°F/−29°C); it forms a rosette of large, furry leaves the first year, then sends up great spikes of thimble-shaped, dangling blossoms in mid to late spring of the following year. Flowers come in pink, lavender, purple, or white, usually spotted with a dark color inside. Though the species blooms on only one side of the spike, the blossoms of modern cultivars en-

Digitalis purpurea Foxy

circle the stem. Many strains in heights from 3 to 6 feet are available, including the 3-foot Foxy, which blooms in 5 months from seed.

Perennial foxgloves only reach about 3 feet high. Strawberry foxglove, *D. × mertonensis* (−20°F/−29°C), which grows true from seed, has coppery rose flowers. Yellow foxglove, *D. grandiflora (D. ambigua)*, hardy to −30°F/−34°C, bears pale yellow blossoms with brown spots inside.

Cut the spent spikes of any foxglove to encourage a second bloom. To get more plants, leave a flowering stem or two in place to self-sow. All plant parts are poisonous.

DIOSPYROS KAKI
Japanese persimmon
Deciduous fruit tree

Color: *Orange*
Season: *Fall*
Hardy to: *0°F/−18°C*
Exposure: *Sun*
Water: *Moderate*

This highly ornamental tree reaches about 30 feet tall, forming a rounded canopy with wide-spreading branches. The glossy dark green leaves turn vivid yellow, orange, or red in autumn, even in mild climates. Brilliant orange, 3- to 4-inch-wide fruits appear in fall and hold on until winter, lighting up the bare branches—unless, of course, they're harvested. Besides providing late-season decoration, these persimmons make delicious eating; they're the same fruits sold in markets. Varieties include 'Fuyu', 'Hachiya', and 'Chocolate'.

Unlike many other fruit trees, Japanese persimmon does extremely well on the West Coast and in many areas of the South. Trees can be espaliered.

DORONICUM
Leopard's bane
Perennial

Color: *Yellow*
Season: *Spring*
Hardy to: *−30°F/−34°C*
Exposure: *Part shade*
Water: *Regular*

Summer is the season for most yellow daisies—but leopard's bane flowers in spring, producing a profusion of 2- to 3-inch blooms on slender, branching stems that rise above a low clump of rounded to heart-shaped leaves.

D. cordatum (D. caucasicum, D. columnae, or *D. orientale)* is about 1½ feet tall in bloom; 'Finesse' and 'Magnificum' are a little taller, with bigger blossoms. *D. plantagineum* is a larger, coarser plant 2½ to 3 feet high; the flowering stems of its selection 'Excelsum' ('Harpur Crewe') may exceed that height.

Use leopard's bane in a spring planting scheme, since it dies back by midsummer. Mark the location and provide some moisture during dormancy. This plant prefers part shade, but it will take full sun in cool-summer areas. Divide clumps every few years.

DRYOPTERIS
Wood fern
Deciduous and evergreen ferns

Color: *Green*
Season: *Throughout the growing season*
Hardy to: *Varies*
Exposure: *Sun, part shade, shade*
Water: *Regular to little*

Wood ferns' delicately divided, verdant fronds provide welcome touches of greenery in woodland gardens, and perennial borders.

The stiff, dark evergreen foliage of male fern, *D. filix-mas* (−40°F/−40°C), forms a flattened vase 2 to 3

Diospyros kaki 'Hachiya'

Doronicum cordatum

Dryopteris filix-mas

Echinacea purpurea

ECHINOPS
Globe thistle
Perennial

Color: *Blue*
Season: *Summer*
Hardy to: *−35°F/−37°C*
Exposure: *Sun*
Water: *Regular to moderate*

As the common name suggests, this prickly perennial is indeed related to the thistles. In summer, it produces upright stems topped by golfball-size blooms that resemble pincushions stuck full of steel blue pins. Blooming plants stand about 4 feet tall and are half that wide.

You'll find globe thistles of the above description sold as *E. ritro*, *E. exaltatus*, *E. humilis*, or *E. sphaerocephalus*. One of the most common cultivars, 'Taplow Blue', may be listed as a form of any of these species. The flowers of all types are excellent in dried arrangements.

Given good soil and ample moisture, plants may grow so vigorously that they need staking. Many types will rebloom if cut to the ground immediately after the flowers fade. Clumps can be left in place, undivided, for many years.

Echinops exaltatus

feet tall. The fronds need shade in very warm climates, but they'll succeed in sun or shade elsewhere.

The following species are strictly shade lovers. The evergreen, 1½- to 2-foot autumn fern, *D. erythrosora* (−20°F/-29°C), forms reddish new growth that turns deep green. The deciduous giant wood fern, *D. goldiana* (−30°F/-34°C), has yellowish green fronds that are upright and arching to 3 or 4 feet tall; they turn pale yellow in fall.

ECHINACEA PURPUREA
Purple coneflower
Perennial

Color: *Rosy purple, pink, white*
Season: *Summer*
Hardy to: *−35°F/−37°C*
Exposure: *Sun*
Water: *Moderate*

This coarse-leafed perennial forms a dense clump of stiff, upright stems 2½ to 4 feet tall; these are capped by flashy 4-inch daisies with rosy purple petals that droop slightly from an orange-brown dome. Selections with flatter flowers are available, as are sorts with truer pink or white petals. Summer flowering may last for several months; the bristly seed heads hang on into winter.

Purple coneflower has modest needs: give it a sunny spot and average soil, and it will be productive. In hot-summer regions, the plant also succeeds in part shade. Divide clumps when they become crowded, usually after about 4 years.

ELAEAGNUS
Elaeagnus
*Deciduous and evergreen shrubs
and small trees*

Color: *Silvery gray, yellow, white*
Season: *All year*
Hardy to: *Varies*
Exposure: *Sun*
Water: *Moderate to little*

These tough, often spiny, plants contribute a silvery sheen—or, in some selections, multicolored foliage—to the garden. Fragrance from the inconspicuous blooms is a dividend.

Deciduous Russian olive, *E. angustifolia* (−40°F/-40°C), sports narrow, willowlike silvery gray leaves, handsome against the dark brown, shredding bark. The tree usually reaches about 20 feet high, though it may grow taller; it can also be clipped down into a 4-foot hedge.

Elaeagnus angustifolia

Elaeagnus shrubs have broadly oval leaves, typically silvery gray in deciduous species. Silverberry, *E. commutata* (–50°F/–46°C), an upright grower to 10 to 14 feet, also has silvery branch scales and silver-coated fruits.

The foliage of evergreen elaeagnus shrubs is dappled with silvery (sometimes brown) dots that reflect sunlight. Most commonly planted are cultivars of evergreen silverberry, *E. pungens* (0°F/–18°C), a rounded, 8- to 15-foot shrub with wavy-edged, olive drab leaves and silver-coated red fruits. 'Fruitlandii' has larger leaves than the species, with a more silvery sheen; leaves of 'Maculata' are blotched with gold in the center; 'Marginata' has silvery white margins; and 'Variegata' is edged in yellowish white. Selections with variegated foliage revert to green easily, so snip out branches with leaves that fail to color properly.

ENDYMION
Bluebell, wood hyacinth
Deciduous bulb

Color: Blue, white, pink
Season: Spring
Hardy to: –30°F/–34°C
Exposure: Part shade
Water: Regular

These charming old-fashioned relatives of the hyacinth (see page 158) bear loose spikes of little blue bells in spring. Pink- and white-flowered forms are also available. Finding bluebell shouldn't be too difficult if you look for it under the names *Endymion* or *Scilla;* the new classification *Hyacinthoides* has not yet been adopted by the nursery trade.

Spanish bluebell, *E. hispanicus* (*Scilla campanulata, S. hispanica*), produces upright 20-inch stems with ¾-inch bells. English bluebell, *E. non-scriptus* (*Scilla nonscripta*), bears smaller, narrower, fragrant bells on foot-high stems that arch at the tips. Your climate will determine which species is best for you: Spanish bluebell thrives in warmer regions, while the English species prefers definite winter cold and moderate to cool summers.

Both Spanish and English bluebells are excellent for drifts or naturalizing.

ERANTHIS HYEMALIS
Winter aconite
Deciduous tuber

Color: Yellow
Season: Late winter, early spring
Hardy to: –30°F/–34°C
Exposure: Sun, part shade
Water: Regular

These 2- to 8-inch-high plants are cheerful little harbingers of spring, blooming even earlier than crocuses. Emerging before the foliage, the flowering stems each bear a 1½-inch-wide, buttercuplike golden yellow flower resting on a green ruff. All traces of the plant disappear by the time summer arrives.

Like most early-blooming bulbs, winter aconite prefers full sun during the flowering season and part shade for the remaining months of the year. An easy way to meet that need is to locate the plant beneath deciduous trees or shrubs.

ERICA
Heath
Evergreen shrubs and ground covers

Color: Pink, red, purple, lavender, white
Season: All year
Hardy to: Varies
Exposure: Sun
Water: Regular

Though similar to heather (*Calluna vulgaris,* see page 129), heaths comprise many species from diverse climates and range from low ground covers to shrubs approaching tree size. Their leaves are tiny and needle-like; the small flowers may be bell-shaped, urn-shaped, or tubular. One species or another blooms in each season.

Erica cinerea

Endymion hispanicus

Eranthis hyemalis

145

The hardiest heaths—the types most commonly grown in this country—are low spreaders native to northern Europe. Winter heath (*E. carnea*, hardy to –20°F/–29°C) and its cultivars range from 6 inches to 1½ feet tall, bearing red, pink, or white flowers in winter and early spring. A pair of foot-high summer bloomers are Dorset heath, *E. ciliaris,* with red or white flowers; and twisted heath, *E. cinerea,* with purple or red blossoms. Both are hardy to 0°F/–18°C.

Mediterranean heaths are larger and bushier than the northern kinds; they tolerate more heat and dryness but less cold. The hardiest is upright, 5- to 10-foot Biscay heath, *E. erigena* (*E. mediterranea;* 0°F/–18°C), which bears lilac-pink flowers in winter and spring.

South African species, ranging from low, spreading types to large shrubs, are the least hardy of the heaths. They withstand cold to about 15°F/–9°C.

ERIGERON
Fleabane
Perennial

Color: *Blue, violet, lavender, pink, white*
Season: *Varies*
Hardy to: *Varies*
Exposure: *Sun*
Water: *Moderate to little*

Fleabanes produce a bonanza of daisies with single or double rows of threadlike rays around a button center. Among the most widely sold plants are bushy, 2-foot-tall hybrids that bloom mainly in summer, producing clusters of 1½- to 2-inch blossoms in various soft colors. Three of the best are blue-violet 'Darkest of All', carmine pink 'Förster's Liebling' ('Förster's Darling'), and light violet 'Strahlenmeer'. Plants are hardy to about –20°F/–29°C.

In the West, one of the most valuable species is Santa Barbara daisy, *E. karvinskianus* (0°F/–18°C), a trailing plant 1 to 2 feet high that grows almost anywhere, even in sidewalk cracks. Its little white to pinkish daisies bloom over a long season.

Erigeron 'Dignity'

ERYNGIUM
Sea holly
Perennial

Color: *Blue*
Season: *Summer*
Hardy to: *Varies*
Exposure: *Sun*
Water: *Moderate*

Stiff and prickly, the sea hollies form foliage rosettes from which rise branched stems; these are topped by cone-shaped flower heads of light to dark metallic blue, each sitting on a starburst of spiny bracts. The various species range from about 1½ to 4 feet tall. All dry well for everlasting arrangements.

Probably the most attractive species is *E. amethystinum* (–35°F/–37°C), with steely blue to violet flower heads and blue-gray bracts on plants to 3 feet tall. *E. alpinum,* soft to the touch despite its spiny appearance, is also hardy to –35°F/–37°C. It has the largest flowers—silvery violet blooms set in a 3-inch collar of bracts.

Many of the sea hollies on the market are likely to be the hybrid *E. × tripartitum* (–20°F/–29°C), a 2-foot plant with thimble-size blue flower heads and dark blue bracts.

Eryngium alpinum

ERYSIMUM
Wallflower
Perennial grown as annual or biennial

Color: *Yellow, orange, red, pink, bronze, cream*
Season: *Spring*
Exposure: *Sun, part shade*
Water: *Regular*

Two spring-blooming wallflower species bring bright color and sweet fragrance to cottage gardens and other plantings. Though perennial, both are usually treated as temporary plants.

Erysimum cheiri

English wallflower, *E. cheiri* (*Cheiranthus cheiri*), ranging from under a foot to over 2 feet tall, bears clusters of showy, four-petaled yellow flowers. Double-blossomed sorts and forms in other colors, from cream through orange to dark red, are also available. Hardy to 10°F/–12°C, this wallflower is suited to cool, moist regions like the Pacific Northwest.

Siberian wallflower, *E. hieraciifolium* (*Cheiranthus × allionii*), produces clusters of rich orange blooms on a 2-foot plant. A form with bright yellow flowers exists as well. Hardy to 0°F/–18°C, this species is more often grown in the East than is *E. cheiri*.

ESCHSCHOLZIA CALIFORNICA
California poppy
Annual

Color: *Orange, yellow, red, pink, white*
Season: *Spring, summer*
Exposure: *Sun*
Water: *Moderate to little*

In the wild, California poppy bears single flowers of brilliant orange to yellow—but thanks to plant breeders, gardeners today can choose poppies

Eschscholzia californica

in reds, pinks, and white, some with semidouble and double blooms up to 3 inches across. The satiny petals close at night and on overcast days.

In cold-winter regions, California poppy is treated as a summer annual. In mild climates, the 1- to 2-foot-high plants bloom from spring to summer, reseeding freely; in these areas, the poppies are best suited for informal plantings and for covering hillsides. Keep in mind that the lacy blue-green leaves turn straw-colored once flowering is over—and that cultivars usually revert to orange or yellow when they reseed.

EUONYMUS
Euonymus
Deciduous and evergreen shrubs and ground covers

Color: *Red, white, yellow*
Season: *Varies*
Hardy to: *Varies*
Exposure: *Sun, part shade*
Water: *Moderate*

Deciduous burning bush, *E. alata* (–30°F/–34°C), turns a flaming red in autumn. For a reliable show, choose 7- to 10-foot 'Compacta', since fall color is variable among the larger, seed-grown types. For the most dramatic display, give the plant a full-sun location.

Evergreen *E. fortunei* (–20°F/–29°C) has many cultivars that offer colorful foliage all year. Among them are white-edged 'Silver Queen', 4 to

Euonymus alata

6 feet tall, and yellow-margined 'Emerald and Gold', 1½ feet high.

Evergreen spindle tree, *E. japonica* (–5°F/–21°C), is a narrow, upright grower to about 10 feet tall. Like *E. fortunei*, it's available in variegated forms; some have green leaves with a yellow central blotch, while others have yellow or white leaf margins.

EUPHORBIA
Euphorbia, spurge
Perennial

Color: *Yellow, chartreuse, white*
Season: *Spring*
Hardy to: *Varies*
Exposure: *Sun*
Water: *Moderate*

Though euphorbias are a diverse lot, perennial types suitable for borders tend to be in the 1- to 4-foot range. The stems are encircled, bottlebrush fashion, by narrow leaves that lead up to clusters of typically cupped flowers (actually modified leaves called bracts). All euphorbias have milky sap that can irritate the skin.

The deciduous cushion spurge, *E. epithymoides* (*E. polychroma*), grows in a dense, 1½-foot-high clump; its flattened clusters of greenish yellow bracts last into summer. The foliage turns red in fall. Hardy to –30°F/–34°C, this plant does not thrive in Gulf Coast gardens.

The shrubby evergreen perennial *E. characias* (10°F/–12°C), a rounded plant to 4 feet tall, has narrow

Euphorbia characias wulfenii

blue-green leaves and domed clusters of dark-eyed chartreuse bracts. The subspecies *E. c. wulfenii* has bracts of an even yellower green, without the dark center.

× FATSHEDERA LIZEI
Fatshedera, botanical wonder
Evergreen shrub

Color: *Green, white*
Season: *All year*
Hardy to: *0°F/–18°C*
Exposure: *Part shade, shade*
Water: *Regular*

This lush, tropical-looking hybrid inherited ivylike leaves (albeit giant ones) and trailing stems from its English ivy parent *(Hedera helix)*, shrubbiness from its Japanese aralia parent *(Fatsia japonica)*. 'Variegata' has white leaf margins.

An irregularly shaped plant with a sprawling habit, fatshedera can be used as an 8-foot shrub, trained as a vine (tie new stems to supports before they become brittle and break), or positioned horizontally for growth as a ground cover. If the branching isn't satisfactory, cut the plant to the ground; it will regrow quickly.

*× **Fatshedera lizei***

Felicia amelloides

FELICIA AMELLOIDES
Blue marguerite
Small evergreen shrub

Color: *Blue*
Season: *Spring, summer, fall*
Hardy to: *20°F/–7°C*
Exposure: *Sun*
Water: *Moderate*

This little evergreen subshrub churns out bright blue, yellow-eyed daisies nonstop from spring through fall, with the heaviest bloom early in the season. Dark blue and larger-flowered selections are also available. Plants grow 1½ to 2 feet high and twice as wide.

In mild-winter gardens, blue marguerite is permanent. Pinch it back regularly to maintain compactness; or cut back severely in late summer to rejuvenate. Replant yearly in cold climates and in areas where plants burn out from summer heat.

FESTUCA OVINA GLAUCA
Blue fescue
Evergreen perennial grass

Color: *Blue*
Season: *All year*
Hardy to: *–30°F/–34°C*
Exposure: *Sun, part shade*
Water: *Moderate*

Festuca ovina glauca

Often massed as a small-scale ground cover, blue fescue grows in rounded, 10-inch tufts of steely blue, needle-thin foliage. Straw-colored flower spikelets appear in late spring or early summer; remove them if they seem distracting.

Divide blue fescue clumps if they become bare in the middle. In hot-summer areas, provide some shade.

FILIPENDULA RUBRA
Queen-of-the-prairie
Perennial

Color: Pink
Season: Summer
Hardy to: –40°F/–40°C; not suited to Gulf Coast and Florida
Exposure: Sun, part shade
Water: Regular

Reminiscent of a lofty astilbe, queen-of-the-prairie forms a handsome clump of large, jagged leaves topped by flattish, feathery plumes of tiny, bright pink, early summer flowers. With ample moisture, plants can reach 6 to 8 feet tall when in bloom. 'Venusta' has deeper pink blossoms on 4- to 6-foot stems.

Its size and boldness make queen-of-the-prairie an ideal plant for the rear of borders and other back-ground positions. It's well suited to boggy sites.

Forsythia × intermedia

FORSYTHIA
Forsythia
Deciduous shrubs

Color: Yellow
Season: Late winter, early spring
Hardy to: –20°F/–29°C
Exposure: Sun
Water: Regular to moderate

Forsythia's sudden, profuse burst of yellow blossoms on leafless branch-es trumpets the arrival of spring. The most widely sold types, ranging from about 3 to 10 feet tall, are selections derived from *F. × intermedia*. All have blossoms up to 2 inches across in pale to deep yellow, sometimes tinged with orange. Most are quite upright-

growing plants with arching branch-es, though some have a spreading habit. 'Meadowlark', a somewhat arching plant 6 to 9 feet high, is an extra-hardy selection that survives to –35°F/–37°C.

Since forsythia blooms on the previous year's wood, delay pruning until after the bloom period has ended.

FOTHERGILLA GARDENII
Dwarf witch alder
Deciduous shrub

Color: White, orange-red, yellow
Season: Spring, fall
Hardy to: –20°F/–29°C
Exposure: Sun, part shade
Water: Regular

In spring, this 3-foot-tall Southern native bears fragrant, creamy white flowers shaped like small, round bottlebrushes. The blooms appear before (or sometimes with) the hand-some heart-shaped leaves. Color in-terest picks up again in the autumn, when the foliage turns orange-red and yellow.

'Blue Mist' has bluish leaves in summer; 'Mt. Airy' is taller than the species and boasts larger flower clus-ters and better fall color.

Filipendula rubra

Fothergilla gardenii

Fritallaria imperialis

Gaillardia × *grandiflora* 'Goblin'

Galanthus

FRITILLARIA IMPERIALIS
Crown imperial
Deciduous bulb

Color: Red, orange, yellow
Season: Spring
Hardy to: –20°F/–29°C; needs some
    winter chill
Exposure: Sun
Water: Regular

A big, bold plant, crown imperial sends up thick 3- to 4-foot stalks topped by a circle of large, drooping bells in red, orange, or yellow. A tuft of leaves rests atop the flowers.

Because the plant smells a bit skunky, choose a location where the odor won't be objectionable. Also keep in mind that the plant dies to the ground every summer. Once the foliage is gone, the bulb can go without water until fall.

GAILLARDIA
Blanket flower
Annual and perennial

Color: Yellow, red, orange, bicolors
Season: Summer, fall
Hardy to: –35°F/–37°C
Exposure: Sun
Water: Moderate to little

From early summer into fall, these easy-to-grow plants display flamboyant daisies above their foliage clumps.

G. pulchella, an annual up to 2 feet high, commonly has 2-inch red blooms with yellow petal tips. 'Red Plume' produces brick red single blooms, 'Lollipop' red-and-yellow double blooms; both grow about 1 foot tall.

A short-lived but exceptionally long-blooming perennial, 2- to 3-foot-tall *G.* × *grandiflora* bears flowers typically in warm shades of red and yellow banded with orange or maroon. Many strains and varieties are available, including dwarf forms and types with extra-large blooms.

Blanket flower is a splendid, heat-resistant choice for mass plantings and borders. Removing spent flowers (or cutting the bossoms earlier for bouquets) will prolong the bloom period.

GALANTHUS
Snowdrop
Deciduous bulb

Color: White
Season: Late winter, early spring
Hardy to: –40°F/–40°C; needs some
    winter chill
Exposure: Sun, part shade
Water: Regular

In cold-winter climates, these little woodland plants are among the first bulbs to bloom as winter draws to a close. Each bulb produces a pair of narrow leaves and a stem capped by a nodding white flower with three long outer petals and three short inner ones; the inner petals are usually marked with green.

The 6- to 9-inch-high common snowdrop, *G. nivalis*, has bell-shaped blossoms an inch long. 'Flore Pleno' bears double blooms.

Giant snowdrop, *G. elwesii*, growing to a foot tall, is larger-flowered than the common species and doesn't need as much winter cold. Its blossoms are egg-shaped.

The ideal location for snowdrops is a spot beneath deciduous plants, where they'll receive sun during flowering and light shade for the rest of the year.

GAURA LINDHEIMERI
Gaura
Perennial

Color: White
Season: Late spring, summer
Hardy to: –10°F/–23°C
Exposure: Sun
Water: Moderate

Vase-shaped, wispy gaura puts up slender, branching spikes of rosy buds opening to 1-inch, starry blooms; the flowers are white at first, then fade to pink. Since just a few blossoms on each stem open at a time, a large clump or mass planting makes for the most effective display. In bloom, plants can reach 4 feet high.

Gaura lindheimeri

A Southwestern native, gaura takes heat and drought in stride. To keep the blooms coming, cut back seed-bearing spikes. If you want extra plants, though, leave some spikes to self-sow, since clumps never need dividing.

GAZANIA
Gazania
Perennial

Color: *Yellow, orange, cream, white, maroon, red, pink, bronze, multicolors*
Season: *Spring, summer*
Hardy to: *20°F/–7°C*
Exposure: *Sun*
Water: *Moderate*

These cheery daisies are among the most varied and colorful flowers available to gardeners. Blossoms are usually 2 to 4 inches across; the single petals, centered around a light or dark disk, may be solid-colored or marked with a contrasting band or stripes. The flowers typically open on sunny days, close in late afternoon, and remain closed on overcast days—though some selections stay open all the time.

Most gazanias sold in nurseries are complex hybrids with either clump-forming or trailing habits. Both types grow from about 6 inches to a foot high and can be successfully used as small-scale ground covers. Clumping gazanias offer a wider variety of color combinations

Gazania 'Burgundy'

and tend to have greener foliage than the trailing types do.

Gazanias bloom most heavily from late spring into summer, though flowering occurs sporadically during the rest of the year in frost-free regions. In these areas, the clumps usually need dividing every several years. Gazanias will grow in Gulf Coast states, but they're short-lived there. In cold-winter climates, they can be treated as summer annuals.

GENTIANA ASCLEPIADEA
Willow gentian
Perennial

Color: *Blue*
Season: *Late summer, fall*
Hardy to: *–10°F/–23°C*
Exposure: *Part shade*
Water: *Regular*

This perennial forms a clump of arching stems clothed with willowlike leaves; tubular, vibrant blue blossoms appear amidst the foliage from late summer into fall.

Reaching about 2 feet tall, willow gentian is ideal for moist, shady borders. It doesn't take well to being moved, so be sure you've chosen the right location before you plant.

Gentiana asclepiadea

GERANIUM
Cranesbill, geranium
Perennial

Color: *Pink, magenta, purple, blue, lavender, white*
Season: *Spring, summer*
Hardy to: *Varies; not suited to Gulf Coast and Florida*
Exposure: *Sun, part shade*
Water: *Regular to moderate*

Not to be confused with the tender *Pelargonium* (see page 181) commonly called "geranium," the cranesbills include spreading, mounding, and bushy plants that grow from about 6 inches to 3 feet high. All are beautiful in borders, and low types also make good edgers and small-scale ground covers. Foliage varies from maplelike to finely cut, but all types

Geranium psilostemon and *G. endressii* 'Wargrave Pink'

of cranesbills have similar flowers: 1- to 1½-inch blossoms made up of five equal, overlapping petals.

Among the loveliest of the low spreaders is 6-inch-high *G. cinereum* 'Ballerina' (–20°F/–29°C), which bears crimson-veined, lilac-pink blossoms. *G. sanguineum* (–30°F/–34°C), mounding to about 1½ feet high, produces brilliant magenta blossoms. Among upright types is *G. pratense* (–30°F/–34°C), a 2- to 3-foot-tall border plant with red-veined, violet-blue flowers.

GEUM
Geum, avens
Perennial

Color: *Scarlet, orange, yellow*
Season: *Spring, summer*
Hardy to: *–10°F/–23°C; not suited to Gulf Coast and Florida*
Exposure: *Sun, part shade*
Water: *Regular*

This member of the rose family bears airy clusters of luminous blooms up to an inch across, carried on slender stems above a mound of green, softly hairy foliage. Good for cut flowers, it's a nice choice for front-of-the-border or rock garden plantings.

The tallest and showiest geums are selections of *G. quellyon* (also sold as *G. chiloense* and *G. coccineum*), all growing up to 2 feet tall. Scarlet 'Mrs.

***Geum quellyon* 'Mrs. Bradshaw'**

Ginkgo biloba

Bradshaw' and yellow 'Lady Stratheden', both double-flowered, grow true from seed.

The foot-high *G. × borisii* bears single orange blooms.

GINKGO BILOBA
Ginkgo, maidenhair tree
Deciduous tree

Color: *Yellow*
Season: *Fall*
Hardy to: *–20°F/–29°C*
Exposure: *Sun*
Water: *Regular to moderate*

Long-lived ginkgo's unique fan-shaped leaves turn from bright green to dazzling yellow in autumn. After remaining on the branches for a while, they drop quickly and cleanly, leaving the tree ankle-deep in brilliant gold.

The plain species has an irregular habit but generally grows upright, slowly reaching 60 to 80 feet tall and not quite that wide. Cultivars have more predictable forms: 'Autumn Gold' is broad-spreading, with outstanding fall color; 'Fairmont' is broadly pyramidal; and 'Lakeview' and 'Princeton Sentry' are more columnar.

Ginkgo trees may be male or female; all the cultivars are male. Keep in mind that female trees grown in the vicinity of a male produce messy, foul-smelling fruit.

GLADIOLUS
Gladiolus
Deciduous corm

Color: *White, cream, yellow, orange, apricot, pink, red, lavender, purple, green, multicolors*
Season: *Summer*
Hardy to: *0°F/–18°C*
Exposure: *Sun*
Water: *Regular*

The biggest, most dramatic forms of gladiolus are the summer-blooming hybrids, available in almost every color except true blue as well as in combinations of colors. Generally grouped as *G. × hortulanus*, these hybrids produce attractive clumps of sword-shaped leaves and tall spikes crowded with flaring, funnel-shaped blossoms up to 8 inches across. Some of the newer forms have strong flower stems that don't need staking. When in bloom, selections range from 3 to 6 feet high, making them ideal for the middle and back of borders—though the plants are often grown in special beds or cutting gardens.

Even in mild climates, gladiolus is usually planted yearly. For a succession of bloom—and a plentiful supply of long-lasting cut flowers—set out corms every week or two.

Gladiolus* × *hortulanus

Gomphrena globosa

Gypsophila paniculata

GOMPHRENA GLOBOSA
Globe amaranth
Annual

Color: *Pink, red, purple, lavender, white*
Season: *Spring, summer, fall*
Exposure: *Sun*
Water: *Moderate*

Borne on long stems, this easy-care annual's cloverlike flower heads—round, papery, and 1 to 1½ inches across—make a pretty show in the garden as well as in fresh or dried bouquets. The heat-resistant plants are upright and bushy, with hairy, oval leaves. Selections range in height from 10 inches to 2 feet. Low types, like the deep purple or white Buddy series, are good edgers; taller plants, such as true red 'Strawberry Fields', are better for cutting.

GYPSOPHILA PANICULATA
Baby's breath
Perennial

Color: *White, pink*
Season: *Summer*
Hardy to: *–35°F/–37°C; not suited to Gulf Coast and Florida*
Exposure: *Sun*
Water: *Regular*

An airy border plant, baby's breath produces delicate summertime clouds of little grayish white or pink flow-ers that are lovely in fresh or dried bouquets. The small leaves are hardly noticeable when the plant is in full, billowy bloom.

Several named selections range from about 1½ to 4 feet tall. The 3-foot 'Bristol Fairy' has double white blossoms; pinkish-flowered 'Pink Fairy' is about half that height. The 4-foot 'Perfecta' has double, extra-large white blooms.

If your soil is strongly acid, add lime to it before planting. Ring the plants with a support so they'll maintain a rounded form. Don't disturb established clumps, since they develop long taproots.

HAMAMELIS
Witch hazel
Deciduous shrubs

Color: *Yellow, orange, red*
Season: *Fall, winter*
Hardy to: *–20°F/–29°C, except where noted*
Exposure: *Sun, part shade*
Water: *Moderate*

Witch hazels contribute more than their share of garden color: cheery winter blooms, attractive summer greenery, and bright fall foliage. Angular in their branching pattern, the plants range from about 10 to 15 feet tall—though many will grow taller, becoming treelike in time.

In cold-winter climates, these shrubs are the earliest to bloom, bearing their unusual, spidery flowers in clusters along the bare branches. Most types, including those described below, are fragrant.

H. × intermedia comprises a group of mid- to late-winter-blooming hybrids. Growing to about 15 feet tall, they are the offspring of *H. mollis* and *H. japonica* (see below). Vase-shaped 'Arnold Promise' has bright yellow flowers and orange-red fall foliage; upright 'Ruby Glow' produces coppery red flowers and rusty gold fall color. Broad-spreading 'Diane' has deep coppery red blooms and rich orange-red autumn leaves.

Chinese witch hazel, *H. mollis* (–10°F/–23°C), is a wide-spreading 12-footer. The species bears bright yellow flowers, while its selection 'Pallida' boasts extra-large soft yel-

Hamamelis × intermedia
'Arnold Promise'

low blooms; both have orange-yellow fall foliage. *H. japonica* is shorter than Chinese witch hazel; bright red fall foliage is its chief distinction.

HEDERA HELIX
English ivy
Evergreen vine or ground cover

Color: *Green, white, cream, yellow*
Season: *All year*
Hardy to: *–10°F/–23°C*
Exposure: *Sun, part shade, shade*
Water: *Regular to moderate*

A rugged plant with dark green, leathery, lobed leaves, English ivy makes a fast-spreading ground cover. Grown as a vine, it clings to surfaces by aerial rootlets.

Selections with smaller or elongated leaves and forms with white, cream, or yellow variegation are available. An extra-hardy selection is 'Baltica', a small-leafed type that turns purplish in winter; it survives to about –20°F/–29°C.

Ivy cultivars are often sold as house plants though they can be grown outdoors—where they're usually more restrained than the plain species.

Hedera helix 'Buttercup'

Helenium autumnale 'Moerheim Beauty'

HELENIUM
Sneezeweed
Perennial

Color: *Yellow, orange, rust, mahogany*
Season: *Summer, fall*
Hardy to: *–35°F/–37°C*
Exposure: *Sun*
Water: *Regular*

Despite its common name, this perennial plant is neither a weed nor a sneeze-inducer. Its highly decorative daisies in bright autumn hues appear from midsummer into early fall; each 1- to 2-inch blossom consists of a central knob sitting on a "skirt" of notched petals.

H. autumnale, a yellow-flowered 5-footer, is less commonly grown than the hybrids derived from it. These range in height from about 2 to 4 feet and offer a greater color choice than the species. Three good selections are all-yellow 'Butterpat', mahogany-colored 'Moerheim Beauty', and rusty orange, dark-centered 'Brilliant'.

Although sneezeweed is quite drought-tolerant, it looks better if given regular water. Divide clumps every few years.

Helianthemum nummularium 'Wisley Pink'

HELIANTHEMUM NUMMULARIUM
Sunrose
Evergreen shrub

Color: *Pink, red, orange, yellow, white*
Season: *Spring*
Hardy to: *–20°F/–29°C*
Exposure: *Sun*
Water: *Moderate*

This little Mediterranean shrublet produces clusters of showy, five-petaled single or double flowers; each 1-inch bloom lasts only a day, but new buds keep the display going. Available colors include white and shades of pink, red, orange, and yellow. After spring bloom has ended, shear the plants back to encourage another flowering in fall.

Various forms of *H. nummularium*, as well as hybrids between this species and others, are commonly sold. Most types grow about 8 inches high and spread to about 3 feet wide. Foliage varies from nearly gray to a deep, glossy green.

Use sunrose as a small-scale ground cover, let it tumble over rocks, or tuck it into dry wall crevices. The roots are sensitive, so don't cultivate around them or try to relocate the plants.

HELIANTHUS
Sunflower
Annuals and perennials

Color: *Yellow, orange, cream, maroon, bicolors*
Season: *Summer, fall*
Hardy to: *Varies*
Exposure: *Sun*
Water: *Regular*

Perhaps the best-known *Helianthus* is annual sunflower, *H. annuus,* a towering giant cultivated for its enormous, nodding flower head packed with edible seeds. But other, shorter types are better suited to most gardens and don't need staking. Among these are cultivars of *H. annuus,* which come in heights from 2 to 12 feet and bear single or double blooms from 4 inches to 2 feet across. Though most have yellow rays, you'll also find selections in orange, cream, or maroon, sometimes with a contrasting zone. Seeds develop in the purplish, reddish, or brown central disk. The plants bloom all summer.

Some perennial sunflowers can be invasive, but the following two are well-behaved. Both bloom in late summer and early fall and usually need dividing every few years.

H. × *multiflorus* (–20°F/–29°C), a hybrid between annual sunflower and the perennial *H. decapetalus,* has some choice cultivars. These include 4-foot 'Flore Pleno' and 5-foot 'Loddon Gold', both with double, bright yellow 4-inch blossoms. The late-blooming swamp sunflower, *H. angustifolius* (–10°F/–23°C), is a 6- to 10-footer with dark-centered yellow daisies 2 to 3 inches across.

Helianthus

Helichrysum bracteatum

HELICHRYSUM BRACTEATUM
Strawflower
Perennial grown as annual

Color: Yellow, orange, white, pink, red, purple
Season: Summer
Exposure: Sun
Water: Moderate to little

Strawflower's papery blooms are just as pretty in the garden as they are in everlasting bouquets, where their color stays vivid indefinitely. The stiff, shining "petals," ranging from creamy white through yellow and orange to rosy pink and purple, are actually bracts surrounding the central floral disk.

These heat-resistant plants grow 1 to 3 feet high. The taller types are best planted toward the back of a border, since they become leggy and need staking.

HELIOPSIS HELIANTHOIDES
False sunflower, oxeye
Perennial

Color: Yellow, gold
Season: Summer, fall
Hardy to: –30°F/–34°C
Exposure: Sun
Water: Regular to moderate

This sunflower look-alike offers single to double daisies in yellow shades ranging from pale to orangy. The

Heliopsis helianthoides

bushy, hairy-foliaged plants grow 2 to 5 feet tall.

Selections include semidouble 'Patula', 2 to 3 feet high; double 'Gold Greenheart' and 'Golden Plume' ('Goldgefieder'), to 4 feet tall; and single 'Karat', another 4-footer. These and other cultivars are sometimes listed as selections of *H. h. scabra.*

HELIOTROPIUM ARBORESCENS
Heliotrope
Perennial grown as annual

Color: Purple, lavender
Season: Summer
Exposure: Sun
Water: Regular

An old-fashioned favorite, heliotrope produces dense clusters of rich pur-

Heliotropium arborescens

ple or lavender flowers against rough, deeply veined dark green leaves. There's a white-flowered form, too, but it isn't nearly as effective. Some liken heliotrope's sweet fragrance to vanilla, while others are reminded of freshly baked cherry pie.

Selections range from 8 inches to 2 feet tall. Use them in the front of borders or in containers, where the perfume can be enjoyed up close. In frost-free gardens, heliotrope will live over as a perennial.

HELLEBORUS
Hellebore
Perennial

Color: *Pink, maroon, green, white*
Season: *Winter, early spring*
Hardy to: *Varies; not suited to Gulf Coast and Florida*
Exposure: *Part shade, shade*
Water: *Regular to moderate*

Helleborus orientalis

At a time of year when little else is in bloom, the hellebores produce their nodding, roselike, long-lasting blossoms. All are elegant shade plants with large, leathery, toothed leaflets.

The 2- to 3-inch flowers of Christmas rose, *H. niger* (–30°F/–34°C; needs winter chill), start out creamy white and age to pink. Growing about 1½ feet tall, the plants bloom sometime between December and early spring, depending on the weather.

Lenten rose, *H. orientalis,* is about the same size as Christmas rose; it has the same hardiness, too, but doesn't need freezing weather to succeed. It flowers in late winter and early spring, bearing large blooms in greenish white, pink shades, or maroon, often with dark spots.

Corsican hellebore, *H. argutifolius* (*H. lividus corsicus*), can reach 3 feet tall. In mild-winter areas, its large, pale green flowers often appear in late fall, but in colder climes the blossoms hold off until early spring. Although the roots survive to –5°F/–21°C, the foliage and flower buds are hardy to only 5°F/–15°C. This species tolerates some sun and drought.

HEMEROCALLIS
Daylily
Perennial

Color: *Cream, yellow, orange, red, pink, lavender, purple, bicolors*
Season: *Spring, summer, fall*
Hardy to: *Varies*
Exposure: *Sun, part shade*
Water: *Regular to moderate*

Daylilies flaunt their big, funnel-shaped flowers above a clump of arching, swordlike foliage. Once limited to vivid yellow and orange, blooms now come in a dazzling range of bright colors and soft pastels; pure white is missing, though. Plant height ranges from 1 to 6 feet; blossoms measure from 3 to 8 inches across in the standard hybrids, from 1½ to 3 inches wide in the miniatures.

Thanks to the efforts of breeders, you'll also find double-flowered forms, "spider" types with long, twisted petals, and tetraploids with un-

Hemerocallis 'Raging Tiger'

usually heavy-textured blossoms. Some forms even bear flowers that stay open longer than a day.

For prolonged flowering, plant varieties with early, midseason, and late bloom, and include reblooming types for blossoms from late summer into fall. Deciduous daylilies (hardy to about –35°F/–37°C) do well in colder climates, since they need some chill. Evergreen sorts (hardy to about –20°F/–29°C) are suited to mild-winter areas.

Daylilies are equally beautiful massed or planted as individual clumps in borders. In the hottest climates, the plants prefer light shade. Divide clumps when they become crowded.

HEUCHERA
Coral bells
Perennial

Color: *Red, pink, cream, white*
Season: *Spring, summer*
Hardy to: *–30°F/–34°C; not suited to Gulf Coast and Florida*
Exposure: *Sun, part shade*
Water: *Regular*

Coral bells forms a low clump of roundish, often scallop-edged leaves on long leafstalks. Rising above the foliage are narrow spikes of tiny bells in colors from white through pink to vivid red. In bloom, the plants are 1 to 2½ feet high.

Most of the coral bells sold are selections or hybrids of *H. sanguinea*; the hybrids are collectively called *H. × brizoides*. Among the best are the Bressingham Hybrids, which offer the full range of colors and heights.

Also commonly available are several distinct hybrids—such as 'Palace Purple', derived from *H. micrantha*. This plant is grown not for its white flowers, but for its foot-high clump of wrinkled, maplelike, purplish to bronzy red leaves. Other hybrids with brightly marbled foliage are sold as well.

Give coral bells part shade in hot, dry climates. Divide clumps after a few years.

Heuchera

Hibiscus moscheutos

HIBISCUS
Hibiscus
Deciduous perennials and shrubs

Color: *Red, pink, lavender, purple, white*
Season: *Summer*
Hardy to: *Varies*
Exposure: *Sun, part shade*
Water: *Regular to moderate*

Although many gardeners think of hibiscus as a strictly tropical greenhouse plant, some hardy types flourish outdoors in many parts of the country.

The shrublike perennial rosemallow, *H. moscheutos* (–10°F/–23°C), growing 2 to 8 feet tall, displays huge, saucer-shaped blossoms from 6 to 12 inches across; blooming begins in early summer and often continues until frost. Cultivars are available in red, pink shades, and white, often with a red center. The 2- to 3-foot-tall Disco Belle strain, bearing red-eyed white or rosy red saucers, blooms the first year from seed. Stems of all types die to the ground each winter. Clumps don't need dividing.

The deciduous rose of Sharon, *H. syriacus* (–20°F/–29°C), displays blooms up to 4 inches across from mid- or late summer often until frost. Single-flowered types open wider than double-blossomed sorts, but produce unattractive seed capsules. Triploid hybrids, including 'Aphrodite' (pink with a red eye) and 'Diana' (pure white), are seedless. Growing to about 10 feet tall, these shrubs are

narrowly upright when young, widespreading when mature. Where winter temperatures drop to 10°F/–12°C or lower, provide cold protection until the plants are established.

HOSTA
Hosta, plantain lily
Perennial

Color: *Green, chartreuse, yellow, cream, white, blue*
Season: *Summer*
Hardy to: *–35°F/–37°C; needs some winter chill*
Exposure: *Part shade, shade*
Water: *Regular*

Hosta

Hosta's handsome foliage eclipses its summertime spikes of trumpet-shaped white or lavender flowers. Literally hundreds of hostas are available, from 6-inch dwarfs to 5-foot giants, and the range of leaf types and colors is likewise tremendous. Foliage comes in green shades, chartreuse, gold, and blue, and many types have white, yellow, or cream variegation. Leaves may be lance-shaped, heart-shaped, oval, or nearly round; textures vary from smooth to puckered, margins from uniform to wavy, and surfaces from glossy to dull. In keeping with this enormous variety, there's massive confusion about names—so it's best to buy a hosta in full leaf to make sure you're getting the right one.

Hostas are a must for the shade garden: the smaller types are often used as ground covers and edgers, the larger ones as foliage accents.

All hostas are dormant in winter. Where cold is severe, choose cultivars that emerge late, after the danger of frost is past. In regions where slugs and snails are a problem, provide protection or try reportedly resistant selections. Clumps don't need dividing and, in fact, grow more beautiful as they increase.

HYACINTHUS
Dutch hyacinth
Deciduous bulb

Color: *Blue, purple, red, pink, yellow, cream, white*
Season: *Early spring*
Hardy to: *–30°F/–34°C; needs some winter chill*
Exposure: *Sun, part shade*
Water: *Regular*

The well-known Dutch hybrid hyacinths, derived from *H. orientalis*, put on an early spring show of stout spikes crowded with small, waxy, intensely fragrant blossoms shaped like flaring bells. Since spike size is directly related to bulb size, buy good-size bulbs—but not the very largest ones, since these tend to produce top-heavy plants.

Growing to about a foot high, Dutch hyacinths look beautiful in containers or massed in small drifts. Keep the soil moist until the foliage yellows. Plantings will increase over the years, but the spikes become thinner, with sparser blossoms—a more natural look that many gardeners prefer.

Hyacinthus '**Pink Pearl**'

HYDRANGEA
Hydrangea
Deciduous shrubs and vines

Color: *Blue, pink, red, white*
Season: *Summer*
Hardy to: *Varies*
Exposure: *Sun, part shade*
Water: *Regular*

Famous for their showy flower heads, hydrangeas are good-looking, woody shrubs and vines. The plants produce two types of flowers: large sterile ones and tiny fertile ones. Species

HOUTTUYNIA CORDATA 'VARIEGATA'
Houttuynia
Perennial

Color: *Combination of green, cream, yellow, pink, and red*
Season: *Spring, summer, fall*
Hardy to: *–10°F/–23°C*
Exposure: *Part shade, shade*
Water: *Regular*

Sometimes sold as 'Chameleon', this perennial is a bit like ivy but far more gorgeously colored. The heart-shaped leaves sport a central green blotch surrounded by splashes of cream, yellow, pink, and red.

Deciduous even in mild-winter climates, houttuynia makes a colorful small-scale ground cover reaching about 1½ feet high. It spreads by underground stems and can be invasive in wet soils.

Houttuynia cordata '**Variegata**'

Hydrangea macrophylla

bearing big globes composed entirely of sterile blossoms are called "hortensia"; those with a more subtle arrangement of fertile flowers ringed by sterile ones are known as "lace cap" hydrangeas.

All hydrangeas bloom in summer; some continue into early fall. Sterile blossoms remain attractive for weeks, then fade to dull pink, green, or garnet.

Bigleaf hydrangea, *H. macrophylla* (–10°F/–23°C), produces huge flower heads about a foot across. The many selections, in heights ranging from 3 to 8 feet, include both lace caps and hortensias. Plants growing in acid soil bear blue to purple blooms; those in neutral to alkaline soil show pink to red blossoms. To manipulate the color, add agricultural sulfur to acidify the soil or dig in lime to make it more alkaline.

The following white-flowered selections of *H. arborescens* (–30°F/ –34°C), both growing about 4 feet

high, are showier than the plain species. 'Grandiflora', known as hills-of-snow, has 6-inch balls of sterile flowers; those of 'Annabelle' reach up to a foot across. In both types, the blossoms eventually fade to green.

Oakleaf hydrangea, *H. quercifolia* (–10°F/–23°C), up to 6 feet tall, has handsome lobed leaves and triangular heads of sterile white flowers that age to purplish pink. Bronzy red fall foliage is a bonus.

Climbing hydrangea, *H. anomala petiolaris* (–30°F/–34°C), displays white lace caps up to 10 inches across. The plant uses aerial rootlets to attach itself to vertical supports; without a surface to scale, it's shrubby and sprawling.

In cool-summer regions, hydrangeas can take full sun, but they need some shade in hotter areas. With the exception of *H. arborescens*, the species cited above bloom on old wood and should be pruned immediately after flowering. *H. arborescens* flowers on new wood, so cut its stems back to the ground late in the dormant season.

HYPERICUM
St. Johnswort
Evergreen shrubs and ground covers

Color: *Yellow*
Season: *Summer*
Hardy to: *Varies*
Exposure: *Sun, part shade*
Water: *Moderate*

These low shrubs and ground covers, ranging from 1 to 6 feet tall, produce a bounty of five-petaled, creamy yellow to gold flowers centered with a fluffy burst of stamens. Many types are semievergreen in the colder parts of their range.

Among ground covers, one of the most useful sorts is the foot-high creeping St. Johnswort, *H. calycinum* (–10°F/–23°C), which bears a profusion of 3-inch, bright yellow blossoms in the summer months. This species spreads by underground stems and can be invasive. Mow or shear the planting every few years to rejuvenate it.

An excellent midsize choice is *H.* 'Hidcote', also sold as *H. patulum* 'Hidcote' and hardy to 0°F/–18°C. A rounded shrub reaching 2 to 3 feet tall, it produces 3-inch, egg yolk–yellow flowers.

Among the loveliest tall St. Johnsworts is *H.* 'Rowallane' (10°F/ –12°C), with 3-inch, deep golden yellow blooms. It grows upright to about 6 feet.

IBERIS
Candytuft
Annuals and evergreen shrubs

Color: *White, pink, red, purple*
Season: *Spring, summer*
Hardy to: *–30°F/–34°C; not suited to Gulf Coast and Florida*
Exposure: *Sun, part shade*
Water: *Regular to moderate*

During their bloom time, these small, narrow-leafed plants smother themselves in four-petaled, typically white flowers. They're lovely as edgings and small-scale ground covers, in rock gardens, and in mixed borders.

Two annual species sport showy flower spikes from spring into summer. The more dramatic of these is 1- to 2-foot-tall rocket candytuft, *I. amara*, with dense, hyacinthlike clusters of fragrant blossoms up to an inch across.

The other annual is globe candytuft, *I. umbellata*. As the common name implies, this cottage-garden favorite carries its tiny flowers in flattened globes. Red and pur-

Hypericum calycinum

Iberis sempervirens

ple selections in pale to intense shades are available. Growing about 6 inches to a foot high, globe candytuft is sometimes mistaken for sweet alyssum (*Lobularia maritima*; see page 170).

Evergreen candytuft, *I. sempervirens,* is a hardy subshrub growing about 8 inches to a foot high and twice that wide. Its dark green leaves are handsome throughout the year; sparkling white flowers appear in spring. 'Autumn Snow' blooms again in fall, and 'Snowflake' bears extra-large blooms at intervals all year long where summers and winters are mild.

ILEX
Holly
Evergreen and deciduous shrubs and trees

Color: *Green, red*
Season: *All year*
Hardy to: *Varies; most need some winter chill*
Exposure: *Sun, part shade*
Water: *Regular*

Hollies are generally thought of as evergreen plants with spiny-edged, glossy leaves and bright red berries. But beyond this familiar type, you'll

Ilex cornuta

find many others, including deciduous hollies, species with smooth-edged or dull foliage, and sorts with yellow or black fruit.

If you want a holly for bright fall and winter berries, be sure to get a female plant. Also keep in mind that, though a few types self-pollinate, most require a nearby male of the same species or one that flowers at the same time. Some growers offer female plants with a male branch grafted on.

Hollies contribute handsome greenery for even longer than they do berries. Many types are shrubby by nature, but some reach tree height, with branches that sweep the ground unless pruned up to expose the trunk. The myriad choices, often even within a species, range from dwarf cultivars only a foot high to large plants that can grow to about 40 feet.

Though hollies do fine in part shade, the most compact growth and best berry production occur in full sun. Check local nurseries to find the most suitable selections for your area.

IMPATIENS WALLERANA
Impatiens, busy Lizzie
Perennial grown as annual

Color: *White, pink, magenta, scarlet, orange, lavender, bicolors*
Season: *Summer, fall*
Exposure: *Part shade, shade*
Water: *Regular*

A favorite bedding plant, impatiens is sold in all colors but yellow and true blue. The plants have been so highly bred that many are organized into series; some of these offer up to 20 shades, available singly or in mixes.

The many versions vary from about 8 inches to 2 feet tall, bearing single or double short-stemmed blossoms from dime to silver dollar size. Single-flowered impatiens are showier in masses than those with double blooms, but both blossom types are pleasing against the dark green, pointed leaves.

Buy impatiens by color and size rather than by cultivar names, since different growers often give different names to highly similar plants.

Impatiens wallerana 'Deco Orange'

Shear impatiens to within 6 inches of the ground any time during the growing season; it will flower again in a couple of weeks. The plant reseeds itself in mild-winter climates.

IMPERATA CYLINDRICA 'RUBRA'
Japanese blood grass
Perennial grass

Color: *Red*
Season: *Spring, summer, fall*
Hardy to: *–10°F/–23°C*
Exposure: *Sun, part shade*
Water: *Regular to moderate*

An ornamental grass also sold as 'Red Baron', this plant forms a clump of upright foliage 1 to 2 feet high. From early in the growing season into fall, the upper portion of each leaf blade is a brilliant blood red that glows when sunlight shines through the foliage. The plant develops the most intense color in a full-sun location,

Imperata cylindrica 'Rubra'

though it needs some shade in hot-summer regions.

Japanese blood grass spreads slowly and is not invasive. It's dormant in winter.

IPOMOEA TRICOLOR
Morning glory
Perennial vine grown as annual

Color: *Blue, purple, red, pink, white, bicolors*
Season: *Summer, fall*
Exposure: *Sun*
Water: *Regular to moderate*

Morning glory twines upward as high as 15 feet in a single season, quickly decorating a trellis or arbor with its spectacular blooms and big, heart-shaped leaves. The show continues from summer until frost.

The saucer-shaped 3- to 5-inch flowers come in white and shades of blue, red, and purple, sometimes with contrasting stripes or edges. Most types open early in the morning and fade by midafternoon.

One of the best selections is 'Heavenly Blue', with sky blue blossoms paling to white at the throat. 'Pearly Gates' is all white. The Early Call mix includes white, pink, crimson, lavender-pink, light blue, and violet flowers.

Morning glory reseeds itself, but volunteers are usually inferior. All plant parts are poisonous.

IRIS
Iris
Perennial

Color: *Blue, purple, pink, white, yellow, orange, multicolors*
Season: *Spring, summer, fall*
Hardy to: *Varies*
Exposure: *Sun, part shade*
Water: *Regular*

Irises are a varied group ranging from tiny miniatures to 4-footers, all with either swordlike or grassy, usually deciduous leaves. Regardless of the species, the flowers are remarkably similar in form: each blossom has three upright true petals (standards) and three drooping or horizontal, petal-like sepals (falls). Most types bloom for several weeks in spring and early summer, though a few re-blooming sorts put on a second show later in summer—and sometimes again in fall.

Bearded irises, so named for the ridge of hairs they sport on each fall, come in several sizes (tall, intermediate, and dwarf) and in an astounding range of solid colors and combinations. The most dramatic

are the tall types, which reach 2½ to 4 feet high; their swordlike foliage provides a bold accent even when the flowers are gone. The smaller versions grow as low as a few inches. Bearded irises need protection when the temperature dips below –15°F/ –26°C; none is suited to the Gulf Coast and Florida.

Moisture-loving Japanese irises, derived from *I. ensata* (*I. kaempferi*) and hardy to about –20°F/–29°C, produce the largest flowers of any iris. Flowering stems up to 4 feet high rise above the grassy foliage clumps, each bearing a graceful, rather flat, single or double bloom from 4 inches to a foot across. Flower colors include white and all shades of purple, blue, and pink; pale colors are often marked with a darker hue.

The most widely sold Siberian irises are hybrids derived from *I. sibirica* and *I. sanguinea*. Hardy to about –30°F/–34°C, they form clumps of grassy leaves; at bloom time, each 1- to 4-foot flowering stem carries two to five blossoms in blue, purple, pink, white, or light yellow.

Of the irises that grow from bulbs instead of rhizomes, Dutch hybrids (–10°F/–23°C) are the most commonly planted. Growing 1½ to 2 feet high, they produce yellow, white, blue, or purple flowers in spring; the foliage yellows and dies back short-

Ipomoea tricolor 'Heavenly Blue'

Iris ensata

ly after bloom. The bulbs naturalize more readily in the colder parts of their range.

Among the many other types of irises, the shade-loving evergreen Gladwin iris, *I. foetidissima* (0°F/–18°C), is grown for its seedpods rather than its flowers. The casings split open in winter to reveal brilliant orange seeds.

JACARANDA MIMOSIFOLIA
Jacaranda
Deciduous to semievergreen tree

Color: *Blue*
Season: *Late spring*
Hardy to: *20°F/–7°C*
Exposure: *Sun, part shade*
Water: *Moderate*

At bloom time, jacaranda's airy canopy is transformed into a lavender or purplish haze by big clusters of tubular blossoms that nearly obscure the finely divided, ferny foliage. The trees usually flower in late spring, but blooming can occur at any time until the end of summer.

Also sold as *J. acutifolia*, jacaranda is an irregularly shaped, deciduous to semievergreen tree growing 25 to 40 feet tall. If it does drop all its leaves, it usually does so for a very short period just before flowering.

This spectacular bloomer is strictly for mild climates. Young trees may freeze to the ground at 25°F/–4°C, but will grow back as multistemmed shrubs. Established trees, however,

Jacaranda mimosifolia

can survive lower temperatures with little or no damage.

JASMINUM
Jasmine
Deciduous and evergreen vines and shrubs

Color: *Yellow, white, pink*
Season: *Winter, spring, summer*
Hardy to: *Varies*
Exposure: *Sun, part shade*
Water: *Regular to moderate*

Winter jasmine, *J. nudiflorum* (–10°F/–23°C) is a deciduous, viny shrub grown for its cheerful winter flowers—not for fragrance, since it has none. Its orange-eyed, bright yellow blossoms are borne along bare, arching green shoots before the leaves unfold. Trained on a trellis, it will grow about 10 feet tall; otherwise, it forms a 4-foot mound.

Two twining vines provide both long-lasting color and intense fragrance in areas where they're hardy. Deciduous to semievergreen common jasmine, *J. officinale* (0°F/–18°C), is a summer bloomer with pure white flowers. Evergreen pink jasmine, *J. polyanthum* (10°F/–12°C), produces dense clusters of blossoms that are

Jasminum nudiflorum

white inside, rosy pink outside. It blooms heavily from midwinter into summer in the mildest climates, from midspring into summer elsewhere.

JUNIPERUS
Juniper
Evergreen trees, shrubs, and ground covers

Color: *Green, blue, yellow, cream*
Season: *All year*
Hardy to: *Varies*
Exposure: *Sun*
Water: *Regular to little*

Junipers are grown for their attractive foliage—sometimes an overall deep green, sometimes blued, grayed, or yellowed, sometimes tipped or variegated with gold or cream. The leaves may be small, prickly needles (juvenile stage) or tiny, overlapping scales (mature foliage)—or both may be present on the same plant.

You'll find an astounding number of selections, from ground covers only a few inches high to 60-foot trees. Some junipers are shaped like fountains, globes, cones, or spires; other kinds are broadly spreading or irregular.

Junipers adapt successfully to most growing conditions. They generally perform best in full sun, but will tolerate part shade. All are quite hardy, although the exact degree depends on the selection. Check a well-stocked local nursery for an as-

Juniperus squamata 'Blue Star'

sortment of junipers suited to your growing area.

KALMIA LATIFOLIA
Mountain laurel
Evergreen shrub

Color: *White, pink, red*
Season: *Spring*
Hardy to: *–20°F/–29°C; not suited to dry-summer regions*
Exposure: *Part shade*
Water: *Regular*

In late spring, this elegant shrub is covered with dark pink buds shaped like fluted turbans; these open to unusual cup-shaped blossoms about an inch wide, exquisite against the glossy, dark green, leathery leaves. The typical flower color is medium pink, but selections in white, various pink shades, and red are also available. Some have contrasting spots or bands.

A rounded shrub reaching about 8 feet tall in cultivation, mountain laurel is related to rhododendrons and resembles them in form and foliage. It's lovely planted beneath trees requiring the same moist, rich, organic conditions. The leaves and flower nectar are poisonous.

Kalmia latifolia

Kerria japonica

Kniphofia 'Shining Scepter'

KERRIA JAPONICA
Kerria
Deciduous shrub

Color: *Yellow*
Season: *Spring*
Hardy to: *–20°F/–29°C; needs some winter chill*
Exposure: *Sun, part shade*
Water: *Regular*

In spring after leaf-out, kerria's arching green stems are adorned all along their length with 1- to 2-inch, golden yellow flowers resembling wild roses. 'Picta' has creamy white leaf margins; 'Pleniflora' bears double flowers that resemble little pompoms.

Kerria forms a spreading thicket; the basic species is around 8 feet tall, the cultivars a little smaller. Thin out old stems after flowering ends.

KNIPHOFIA UVARIA
Red-hot poker
Perennial

Color: *Orange, yellow, cream, coral, bicolors*
Season: *Spring, summer*
Hardy to: *–10°F/–23°C*
Exposure: *Sun*
Water: *Regular to moderate*

Torchlike spikes crowded with narrow, drooping, tubular flowers jut from this bold accent plant's fountain of grassy leaves. The plain species is old-fashioned red-hot poker, with a foliage mound up to 3 feet across and blossom spikes 4 to 6 feet tall. Each poker head looks as though it has just been pulled from the fire—yellow at the bottom, glowing reddish orange at the top.

Modern hybrids with smaller foliage mounds and spikes as low as 1½ feet show the same fiery combination as the species, but they come in solid colors and pastel bicolors as well. The exact flowering time depends on the selection. If you choose your plants carefully, you can have red-hot pokers in bloom from late spring into fall.

These plants tolerate heat and drought. Where temperatures fall to 0°F/–18°C or below, tie the foliage over the clump in fall to protect the growing points; in warmer areas, cut it to the ground. Clumps can grow undisturbed for many years.

Kolkwitzia amabilis

KOCHIA SCOPARIA
Summer cypress
Annual

Color: *Green, red*
Season: *Summer, fall*
Exposure: *Sun*
Water: *Regular*

This annual foliage plant is grown for its pleasing colors: light green in summer, turning to luminous purplish red in fall. *K. s. trichophylla* is the form commonly sold.

Left to its own devices, summer cypress forms a dense, feathery 3-foot sphere, though it can be sheared into any shape and used as a temporary hedge or low edging. Allowed to grow naturally, it makes a fine border accent.

Kochia scoparia trichophylla

Laburnum × watereri

KOLKWITZIA AMABILIS
Beauty bush
Deciduous shrub

Color: *Pink*
Season: *Spring*
Hardy to: *–30°F/–34°C; needs some winter chill*
Exposure: *Sun, part shade*
Water: *Regular to moderate*

In mid to late spring, beauty bush bears masses of bell-shaped, yellow-throated, soft pink blossoms among its green leaves. The bristly, pinkish brown fruits that follow the flowers prolong the color display; peeling brown bark provides winter interest.

Beauty bush is a robust, fountainlike shrub reaching about 10 feet. In part shade, it attains its full height and shows a more arching habit; in full sun, it's shorter and denser.

To promote blooming, thin the oldest stems after the flowers have faded. If you want to enjoy the fruit display, however, prune lightly in early spring, removing wood that bloomed the year before.

LABURNUM × WATERERI
Goldenchain tree
Small deciduous tree

Color: *Yellow*
Season: *Spring*
Hardy to: *–20°F/–29°C; best with some winter chill*
Exposure: *Sun*
Water: *Regular*

Goldenchain tree is grown for its magnificent midspring floral display: draped with pendent, brilliant yellow blossom clusters up to 2 feet long, it suggests a tree wisteria. Though blooming occurs after leaf-out, the bright green foliage doesn't detract from the spectacle.

Vase-shaped in form, goldenchain ranges from about 15 to 25

feet high. Trees left multitrunked are at the shorter end of the scale, with broader canopies; those trained to a single stem are taller and more upright. The widely available 'Vossii' has the most graceful form.

Best suited to the Northeast and Pacific Coast states, this tree doesn't thrive in the lower Midwest and lower South. It's weak-wooded and should be protected from strong winds. Remove the brown, beanlike pods that follow the flowers, since they can sap the tree's strength. All plant parts are poisonous.

LAGERSTROEMIA
Crape myrtle
Deciduous shrubs and small trees

Color: *White, purple, lavender, pink, red, orange, yellow; mottled brown or gray*
Season: *All year*
Hardy to: *0°F/–18°C*
Exposure: *Sun*
Water: *Moderate*

Crape myrtles bear their profuse, crinkly blooms in dense, foot-long panicles at the branch tips and in smaller clusters lower on the stems. The dazzling display continues for at least a couple of months during summer, with the best flower production occurring in warm- to hot-weather climates. Bright autumn foliage and exfoliating bark extend the color show.

Common crape myrtle, *L. indica*, has been overshadowed by new

hybrids developed by crossing it with a mildew-resistant Japanese species, *L. fauriei*. While the common species blooms in basic red, pink, lavender, or white, the hybrids feature an expanded palette including blue-reds, peachy tints, and various pinks and purples. They also bloom longer, withstand more cold, and are more mildew-resistant than the common species; and they cover a greater height range, from about 6 to 35 feet tall.

These hybrid crape myrtles bear the names of Native American tribes. Examples include the tree-size selections 'Natchez' (white), 'Biloxi' (pale pink), 'Miami' (red-purple), and 'Muskogee' (light lavender); and the shrubby forms 'Acomi' (white), 'Hopi' (clear pink), and 'Pawhatan' (medium purple).

Both the common species and its hybrids have smooth gray or light brown bark that flakes off to reveal patches of pinkish inner bark. In fall, the small oval leaves turn yellow, orange, or glowing red, the color being more pronounced when the plant is kept on the dry side in late summer.

Though crape myrtles can be trained to a single trunk, they're more attractive multitrunked. Since blossoms form on new wood, cut back branches lightly during the dormant season.

LAMIUM MACULATUM
Dead nettle
Perennial

Color: *White, pink, silver*
Season: *Spring, summer*
Hardy to: *–30°F/–34°C*
Exposure: *Part shade, shade*
Water: *Regular*

This shade-loving plant spreads by runners to form a 6-inch-high blanket of soft, downy, heart-shaped leaves; in late spring or early summer, the foliage is topped by hooded rosy pink or white blossoms.

The cultivars are more attractive and less aggressive than the basic species. 'Beacon Silver' has green-edged, silvery foliage and rosy blooms; 'White Nancy' is similar, but

Lamium maculatum 'White Nancy'

with white flowers. The green leaves of 'Chequers' have a white center stripe, while those of 'Aureum' are yellow-blotched; both bear rosy pink blossoms.

Dead nettle makes a lovely small-scale ground cover for spring bulbs. Selections with variegated foliage maintain interest throughout the growing season.

LANTANA
Lantana
Evergreen shrubs and ground covers

Color: *Lavender, yellow, orange, red, pink, cream, white, multicolors*
Season: *Spring, summer, fall*
Hardy to: *28°F/–2°C*
Exposure: *Sun*
Water: *Moderate*

Lantana

Lagerstroemia

Flowering over a long season, lantana bears small, nosegaylike blossom clusters above its attractive, crinkly dark green leaves. In mild-climate gardens, plants bloom profusely from spring into fall, sporadically the rest of the year. Elsewhere, heat-resistant lantana can be treated as a summer annual.

Trailing lantana, *L. montevidensis,* is a lavender-flowered species growing about 1½ feet high and 3 to 6 feet wide. Its viny stems root as they spread.

L. camara, an upright shrub that can reach 6 feet tall and wide, has bicolored flower clusters: the tiny blossoms in the inner ring of the nosegay are cream to yellow, while those in the outer ring are pink or orange. Nurseries generally don't offer the plain species; instead, you'll find its various forms, as well as hybrids between *L. camara* and *L. montevidensis.* Colors range from white through cream and yellow to orange, plus rosy shades and combinations of hues. Plants vary from the basic size down to 2-footers that may spread twice as wide or more. One of the most colorful is 'Confetti', bearing yellow, pink, and purple nosegays on a low, spreading plant.

LATHYRUS ODORATUS
Sweet pea
Annual

Color: Pink, red, purple, lavender, apricot, cream, white, bicolors
Season: Spring, summer
Exposure: Sun
Water: Regular

This fragrant bloomer, so often grown in cottage gardens, produces long-stemmed flower clusters that are ideal for cutting. The blossoms have the typical pea-family form: one large, upright, roundish petal (the banner or standard), two narrow side petals (the wings), and two united lower petals (the keel).

Bush sweet peas grow 1 to 2½ feet high, while climbers can twine upward 5 to 8 feet. Both types are available in every pastel shade—but unfortunately, fragrance has been

Lathyrus odoratus

sacrificed in many of the newer selections.

Plants are sometimes sold by their bloom time: early-, spring-, and summer-flowering. Early types will bloom during short winter days in the mildest climates; spring and summer sorts need at least 15 hours of daylight. Summer bloomers are the most resistant to heat, though they won't tolerate very warm weather.

Sweet peas are ideally suited to the Pacific Northwest, coastal New England, and other cool, moist regions. In these areas, plants will thrive in summer. Along the Gulf Coast and in Florida, plant sweet peas in autumn for bloom before summer heat arrives. To prolong blooming, cut flowers at least every other day and remove seedpods.

LAVANDULA
Lavender
Small evergreen shrubs

Color: Lavender, purple, pink, gray
Season: Spring, summer
Hardy to: Varies; short-lived in humid Deep South
Exposure: Sun
Water: Moderate to little

These drought-tolerant Mediterranean plants are prized for their typically blue or purple flower spikes and their domes of gray or grayish green foliage. Both leaves and blossoms are aromatic.

The source of the classic scent is English lavender, *L. angustifolia (L. officinalis, L. spica,* or *L. vera),* hardy to –10°F/–23°C. Growing 3 to 4 feet high, it bears slender lavender-blue spikes in late spring or early summer. Purple-flowered 'Twickel Purple' is a bit shorter. For selections in the 1½-foot range, try 'Hidcote' (deep purple); 'Munstead' (deep lavender, blooming a month earlier than the species); 'Jean Davis' (pale pink); and 'Lavender Lady' (deep purple, blooming the first year from seed).

L. × intermedia is a hybrid between English lavender and *L. latifolia.* Known as lavendin, it's about as hardy as its English parent, but it blooms a little later and is more tolerant of warm, humid summers. Selections include the 2-footers 'Provence' and 'Dutch', both bearing pinkish lavender blooms.

Spanish lavender, *L. stoechas* (0°F/–18°C), is a 3-footer flowering in midspring to early summer. It bears fat violet spikes topped by purple bracts; 'Otto Quast' ('Quasti') is especially showy. Flower spikes of French lavender, *L. dentata* (10°F/

Lavandula angustifolia

–12°C), are similar to those of Spanish lavender, but the bracts are less flashy.

Though often restricted to herb gardens, lavenders are pretty enough for mixed borders, low hedges, and edgings. To keep the plants compact, cut them back either after flowering or just as growth begins in early spring.

LAVATERA TRIMESTRIS
Annual mallow
Annual

Color: *White, pink, red*
Season: *Summer, fall*
Exposure: *Sun*
Water: *Regular*

Reaching up to 4 inches across, mallow's big, tropical-looking, satiny blooms are gorgeous against its maplelike dark green leaves. The plant makes a colorful, fast-growing summer hedge or background planting.

Various types are available, including 3- to 4-foot 'Loveliness' (deep rose pink) and the compact 2-footers 'Mont Blanc' (brilliant white), 'Mont Rose' (rosy pink), and 'Silver Cup' (bright pink). Heights range from 2 to 6 feet.

Lavatera trimestris **'Silver Cup'**

Annual mallow performs best in moist, cool-summer climates. In cold-winter regions, it needs at least 4 frost-free months.

LIATRIS SPICATA
Gayfeather
Perennial

Color: *Rosy lilac, white*
Season: *Summer*
Hardy to: *–35°F/–37°C*
Exposure: *Sun*
Water: *Regular to moderate*

Gayfeather's vivid, foxtail-like flower spikes, sometimes said to resemble fireworks sparklers, rise above narrow, almost grassy, green foliage. The upper part of each spike is packed with buds, which open from the top of the spike down—in contrast to the bottom-up blooming of most other plants with terminal spikes. The cut flowers are long-lasting in bouquets.

Wild plants may reach 4 feet tall, but nurseries usually sell 2-foot 'Kobold', which bears spikes of a particularly vibrant rosy lilac. 'Alba', another 2-footer, is a white form. Plants are sometimes listed as *L. callilepis*.

Gayfeather is drought-tolerant, but it will perform better if given at least moderate watering. Clumps can go for many years before needing division.

LIGULARIA
Ligularia
Perennial

Color: *Yellow, orange*
Season: *Summer*
Hardy to: *–30°F/–34°C; not suited to Gulf Coast and Florida or dry-summer regions*
Exposure: *Part shade*
Water: *Regular*

Stately ligularias offer a spectacular summer display of yellow or orange daisies. Foliage is attractive, too: bold, leathery leaves a foot or more across.

The narrow blossom spires of yellow-flowered *L. stenocephala* 'The Rocket' shoot up to 5 feet tall, rising

Liatris spicata **'Kobold'**

Ligularia stenocephala
'The Rocket'

above a clump of bright green, heart-shaped foliage. *L. przewalskii* looks much the same, but with deeply lobed leaves and bloom spires to 6 feet tall.

L. dentata is the only commonly grown ligularia with flattened clusters instead of spires. Its clump of nearly circular, long-stalked leaves sends up 3- to 5-foot stems topped by big, branching heads of orange daisies. 'Desdemona' and 'Othello' have deep purple leafstalks, veins, and leaf undersides.

All types of ligularias, including species less hardy than those described here, require rich soil, ample moisture, and some shade. Protection from slugs and snails is essential in the regions where those pests are a problem.

LILIUM
Lily
Deciduous bulb

Color: *Yellow, orange, red, pink, cream, white, lavender, purple, green, multicolors*
Season: *Spring, summer, fall*
Hardy to: *Varies*
Exposure: *Sun, part shade*
Water: *Regular*

Each lily bulb produces a leafy stem from 1 to 8 feet tall, bearing from a few to almost two dozen blossoms. All types have six-petaled flowers, which may be recurved or shaped like trumpets, bells, or bowls. For continuous bloom from midspring to early fall, make a careful selection of early, midseason, and late-flowering types.

Hybrids are now more commonly planted than species lilies. Perhaps the easiest to grow are the early-blooming, 1½- to 6-foot-tall Asiatic hybrids (–40°F/–40°C), with 4- to 6-inch flat or recurved blossoms facing up, out, or down, depending on the type. They come in a full range of colors; flowers generally are not fragrant.

As their common name implies, the midseason trumpet hybrids (–20°F/–29°C) bear trumpet-shaped blossoms. The 6- to 10-inch, often very fragrant flowers come in white and shades of pink, yellow, and orange. Stems reach 4 to 6 feet or even higher, each holding as many as 20 flowers. This category also includes sunbursts, whose blossoms open wider than trumpets do.

The late-blooming Oriental hybrids (–20°F/–29°C) produce 10-inch, recurved or bowl-shaped blooms in colors from white through yellow to pink and deep red, many with dark shading on the outer surfaces. Each stem grows 3 to 6 feet tall (or taller), carrying up to 20 richly perfumed flowers.

The early-blooming Madonna lily, *L. candidum* (–30°F/–34°C), is among the finest species lilies. Its flower stems reach 3 to 4 feet, bearing fragrant, outward-facing pure white trumpets with golden stamens. Unlike other lilies, this one dies down

***Lilium* 'Enchantment'**

soon after flowering, then overwinters as a low clump of leaves. 'Cascade' is an improved, disease-resistant selection.

Lilies look lovely clustered in border plantings and equally beautiful in drifts in woodland gardens. Unlike many hardy bulbs, they can be planted in spring or fall; be sure to purchase them fresh and plant them promptly, since their fleshy scales have a short shelf life. These plants thrive in sun except in the hottest climates, where they need part shade. Divide clumps when they become crowded.

LIMONIUM LATIFOLIUM
Sea lavender, statice
Perennial

Color: *Lavender*
Season: *Summer*
Hardy to: *–35°F/–37°C; not suited to Gulf Coast and Florida*
Exposure: *Sun*
Water: *Moderate*

This attractive perennial forms a misty cloud of lavender-blue flowers over a rosette of big, leathery green leaves. Carried at the ends of wiry, branched stems, the long-lasting blossoms, each held in a papery base, are favorites for everlasting bouquets. In

bloom, the plant is about 2 feet tall and 3 feet wide.

Though sea lavender is drought-tolerant, it produces better flowers if it receives some water.

Limonium latifolium

Linum perenne

Liriope muscari

LINUM
Flax
Perennials and annuals

Color: Blue, yellow, red
Season: Spring, summer
Hardy to: −10°F/−23°C; not suited to Gulf Coast and Florida
Exposure: Sun
Water: Moderate

The various flaxes are upright, narrow-leafed plants with branching stems ending in five-petaled, shallow-cupped blossoms. Though each flower lasts just a day, new buds keep the display going. Fairly short-lived, the plants are charming in borders and glades.

Among species suitable for the garden, the airy, 1½- to 2-foot perennial *L. perenne* comes closest to duplicating the beautiful sky blue blossoms of the field crop, which blooms only briefly each year. *L. perenne* bears the same silky flowers but blooms over a longer period, from spring through late summer. It's the most vigorous flax, reseeding itself freely.

L. narbonense is another blue-flowered flax about 1½ to 2 feet high, but with slightly larger, white-eyed blooms. 'Six Hills' bears rich sky blue blossoms. Flowering occurs mainly in summer.

For other colors, try golden *L. flavum* (a perennial) or scarlet *L. grandiflorum* 'Rubrum' (an annual). Both of these plants grow about 1 to 1½ feet high and bloom from spring into summer.

LIRIOPE MUSCARI
Big blue lily turf
Evergreen perennial

Color: Blue, white
Season: Summer
Hardy to: −10°F/−23°C
Exposure: Part shade, shade
Water: Regular to moderate

This largest of the lily turfs produces a clump of narrow, strap-shaped, arching evergreen leaves about 1½ feet high. In summer, it bears 6- to 8-inch, deep violet flower spikes similar to those of grape hyacinth; the spikes rise well above the foliage on young plants, but are partly obscured on older ones.

'Majestic' grows a little taller than the species and bears flattened spikes. For pale purple or white blooms, choose 'Lilac Beauty' or 'Monroe White'. 'Silvery Sunproof' has more upright leaves, striped in gold that ages to white, and showy lavender spikes that jut above the foliage.

Use this heat-resistant plant to edge walks, ring tree trunks, or cover small patches of ground. Clumps thrive for many years undisturbed, though they can be divided for more plants.

LITHODORA DIFFUSA
Lithodora
Small evergreen shrub

Color: Blue
Season: Late spring, early summer
Hardy to: −10°F/−23°C
Exposure: Sun
Water: Moderate

Here's a nice choice for a rock garden or a small-scale ground cover. Sometimes listed as *Lithospermum diffusum*, lithodora is a prostrate, hairy-foliaged subshrub bearing small, tubular blossoms of a particularly brilliant blue. 'Grace Ward' and 'Heavenly Blue' are splendid selections. The plant reaches 6 inches to a foot high and spreads 3 to 4 feet wide.

Lithodora diffusa

Lobelia cardinalis

Lobularia maritima

Lupinus Russell Hybrids

LOBELIA
Lobelia
Annuals and perennials

Color: *Blue, purple, red, orange-red, pink, white*
Season: *Summer, fall*
Hardy to: *Varies; some need winter chill*
Exposure: *Sun, part shade*
Water: *Regular to moderate*

Lobelias range from low spreaders to tall border plants, but all have tubular, lipped blossoms, usually in blue or red shades.

Annual lobelia, *L. erinus,* is a 4- to 8-inch-high edger with flowers in various blues as well as in white, pink, and red. It blooms from summer until frost in cool-summer areas, but tends to die out early in hot climates. For the best blooms, water regularly. Plants take sun or part shade.

Cardinal flower, *L. cardinalis* (−40°F/−40°C), is a summer-blooming perennial. The plant forms a bright green foliage rosette; the leafy 3- to 4-foot flower spikes bear blossoms typically in glowing red, though pink and white forms also exist. Cardinal flower needs regular moisture, part shade, and some winter chill.

Blue cardinal flower, *L. siphilitica* (−30°F/−34°C), is similar to *L. cardinalis,* but it's a little shorter and has vivid blue to purplish flowers in tighter spikes. It too performs best with some chill and in part shade, but it doesn't need as much water.

Various hybrids are derived from these perennial species. 'Bees' Flame' and 'Queen Victoria' have flaming scarlet flowers and reddish purple leaves; others produce purple, violet, pink, salmon, rose, or red spikes and sometimes sport purplish or bronzed foliage. Most of the hybrids are hardy to about −30°F/−34°C.

The sun-tolerant, shrubby, 2-foot Mexican native *L. laxiflora* (10°F/−12°C) is better suited to mild climates than the aforementioned perennials. It bears loose clusters of tubular, orange-red flowers over a long period. A drought-tolerant plant, it becomes invasive if given more than moderate water.

Except for the Mexican species, the perennial lobelias are short-lived when crowded, so divide clumps every year or so after flowering.

LOBULARIA MARITIMA
Sweet alyssum
Perennial grown as annual

Color: *White, pink, purple, lavender*
Season: *Spring, summer, fall*
Exposure: *Sun, part shade*
Water: *Regular*

Clusters of honey-scented, four-petaled blossoms blanket this low, trailing plant throughout the growing season. Various strains and cultivars from 2 inches to a foot high are available in white as well as a range of soft pinks and purples.

Quick-blooming sweet alyssum is wonderful between stepping stones, at the front of borders, and in rock gardens and containers. In mild climates, it's perennial (though it does burn out in hot, dry weather); elsewhere, it may self-sow.

LUPINUS
Lupine
Perennial

Color: *Blue, purple, pink, red, orange, yellow, cream, white, bicolors*
Season: *Spring, early summer*
Hardy to: *−30°F/−34°C; not suited to hot-summer regions*
Exposure: *Sun*
Water: *Regular*

Lupines may evoke images of Victorian cottage gardens, but most types grown today are derived from the Russell Hybrids developed in this century.

A typical plant forms an attractive clump of leaves, each resembling a hand with the fingers spread, and sends up several flower spikes to 4 or 5 feet tall. The spikes are packed with sweet pea–shaped blossoms in a broad range of solid shades and bicolors. Dwarf types grow only about 1½ feet high.

Fairly short-lived, lupines perform best in cool-summer regions.

In warmer climates, set out young plants in fall or early spring so that they'll bloom before hot weather arrives. Plants will self-sow if conditions are favorable, but the offspring usually revert to blue or white.

LYCHNIS CORONARIA
Crown-pink
Perennial

Color: *Magenta, white, gray*
Season: *Late spring, early summer*
Hardy to: *−35°F/−37°C; not suited to Gulf Coast and Florida*
Exposure: *Sun*
Water: *Regular to moderate*

From low rosettes of felted, gray-white leaves, branched flowering stems rise in late spring or early summer, bearing five-petaled, inch-wide, magenta blossoms so vivid they scream for attention. 'Oculata', white with a magenta eye, is a less blatant form. In bloom, crown-pink is about 2 to 3 feet tall.

Plants give out in a few years, but self-sowing maintains the planting.

LYCORIS
Spider lily
Deciduous bulb

Color: *Pink, red*
Season: *Late summer, fall*
Hardy to: *Varies*
Exposure: *Sun, part shade*
Water: *Regular*

Spider lily's narrow, strap-shaped leaves appear well before its blossoms, then die back a couple of months before the leafless flower stalks emerge in late summer or early autumn.

The hardiest species is 2-foot-high *L. squamigera* (−20°F/−29°C), which produces its foliage in spring. The fragrant, bright pink to rosy lilac flowers, borne in clusters, are funnel-shaped and about 3 inches long. Locate this plant in a ground cover such as periwinkle (*Vinca*, page 202), since the dying leaves look messy.

The smaller, more delicate leaves of 1½-foot-high *L. radiata* (10°F/−12°C)

Lychnis coronaria

Lycoris radiata

emerge in fall and live through the winter. Coral red flowers with a golden sheen put on a brief show, their reflex petals and prominent stamens creating a spidery effect.

LYSIMACHIA CLETHROIDES
Gooseneck loosestrife
Perennial

Color: *White*
Season: *Summer*
Hardy to: *−20°F/−29°C; not suited to hot, dry climates*
Exposure: *Sun, part shade*
Water: *Regular*

From a bushy dark green foliage clump up to 3 feet high, gooseneck loosestrife produces white, 6- to 8-

Lysimachia clethroides

inch-long flower spikes arched like a goose's neck. Densely packed with tiny blossoms, the conical spikes provide a long-lasting summer display and can be cut for bouquets.

Because this plant has invasive tendencies, it's unsuitable for small gardens. To help restrain its growth, keep the soil on the dry side and divide clumps frequently.

MAGNOLIA
Magnolia
Deciduous and evergreen trees and shrubs

Color: *White, pink, red, purple, yellow*
Season: *Spring, summer, fall*
Hardy to: *Varies*
Exposure: *Sun, part shade*
Water: *Regular*

Magnolias are prized for their typically big, waxy-petaled, fragrant flowers. Most are deciduous, bloom-

Magnolia × soulangiana

Mahonia aquifolium

ing early in the year; evergreen types bloom from summer into fall.

The following deciduous trees, hardy to about –10°F/–23°C and flowering on bare branches, are among the most striking. The 35-foot yulan magnolia, *M. denudata*, has cup-shaped creamy white blossoms to 7 inches wide. Selections of saucer magnolia, *M. × soulangiana*, bear 6-inch, goblet-shaped blooms in colors from white through pink to purplish red; the plant spends many years as a shrub, gradually reaching 20 to 25 feet. Some newer hybrids boast pale yellow blooms; those of 35-foot *M.* 'Elizabeth' are 6 to 7 inches across.

A couple of deciduous species are shrubby, growing slowly to about 12 feet. Star magnolia, *M. stellata* (–20°F/–29°C), blooms on leafless branches very early in the season, bearing 3-inch, white or pink blossoms with ribbonlike petals. Lily magnolia, *M. liliiflora* (–10°F/–23°C), displays 4-inch, tuliplike, purplish pink or dark purple flowers in mid-spring as leaves emerge. Lily and star magnolia were crossed to produce the Little Girl Hybrids ('Betty', 'Jane', 'Jody'). These are as hardy as star magnolia and, like it, bloom on bare branches—but they evade frost damage by flowering a bit later.

The classic evergreen species is Southern magnolia, *M. grandiflora*

(0°F/–18°C), a leathery-leafed tree to 80 feet tall with many-petaled white flowers up to 14 inches across. Smaller selections are available, as are hardier ones; the most cold-tolerant is 30-foot 'Edith Bogue', surviving to –20°F/–29°C if protected from wind.

Specialty nurseries in the South and West offer many Asian species and hybrids suited to mild-winter climates.

All magnolias have shallow, fleshy roots that are easily damaged by digging and regular foot traffic. For this reason, the best location for these trees is in lawn, with a generous grass-free area around the trunk, or in a border that won't be dug up.

MAHONIA
Mahonia
Evergreen shrubs

Color: *Yellow*
Season: *Winter, spring*
Hardy to: *Varies*
Exposure: *Sun, part shade*
Water: *Moderate*

These prickly-leafed plants, growing from about 2 to 15 feet high, produce clusters of small, slightly cupped, bright yellow blossoms at their branch tips in late winter or early spring. The flowers are followed by

berries (typically blue) covered with a chalky film.

Some mahonias offer a bonus of colorful foliage. Oregon grape, *M. aquifolium* (–10°F/–23°C), a shrub growing to about 6 feet tall, turns bronzy or purplish in winter. The 5-foot 'Orange Flame' has bronzy orange new growth and wine red winter foliage. All types of Oregon grape have showy spring flower clusters.

The 10-foot-tall leatherleaf mahonia, *M. bealei* (0°F/–18°C), remains shiny green in winter, its strong pattern of knobby, vertical stems and horizontal leaflets providing a sculptural element in the garden. Upright, 6-inch flower spikes appear in late winter or early spring. The plant does well in dry shade.

Mahonias are tough, undemanding plants. Locate them where their spines won't wound the unwary.

MALUS
Crabapple
Small deciduous trees

Color: *White, pink, red, orange, yellow*
Season: *Spring, summer, fall*
Hardy to: *Varies; needs some winter chill*
Exposure: *Sun*
Water: *Regular to moderate*

Crabapples are grown for their fleeting but breathtaking springtime display of single to double, white or pink blossoms up to 2 inches across. Those with single blooms usually bear small red, orange, or yellow apples that ripen from midsummer into fall; double-flowered types rarely produce fruit.

The hundreds of cultivars range from about 8 to 30 feet tall and wide. Smaller selections are exquisite in mixed borders, while larger ones work well as specimen trees in lawns or, when closely planted in a row, as blossoming screens. All types are extremely hardy, making them among the most important small flowering trees for northern climates.

Planting crabapples was once a risky venture, since the plants were vulnerable to so many insect pests and diseases—but today, scores of resistant selections are available. Local nurseries can help you choose types that will withstand the troublemakers in your area.

Malus 'Dorothea'

MATTHIOLA
Stock
Biennial grown as annual

Color: *White, cream, pink, red, purple, lavender, bicolors*
Season: *Spring, early summer*
Exposure: *Sun*
Water: *Regular*

This old-fashioned bedding plant forms a clump of narrow gray-green leaves, then puts up sturdy spikes crowded with four-petaled, spicily fragrant single or double blossoms. The most widely sold strains and cultivars are derived from the common species, *M. incana*. Colors include pastels as well as red and purple shades; plant heights range from about 1 to 2½ feet. Most types thrive in cool weather, though some newer varieties are heat-tolerant.

Stock is a lovely choice for cut flower arrangements. The main bloom season runs from spring into early summer, but in mild-winter regions, plants can flower from winter into spring—or even longer if summers are cool.

Matthiola incana 'Column Mix'

MECONOPSIS
Blue poppy, Welsh poppy
Perennial

Color: *Blue, yellow, orange*
Season: *Late spring, summer*
Hardy to: *–20°F/–29°C; best suited to Pacific Northwest*
Exposure: *Part shade, shade*
Water: *Regular*

These plants require just the right conditions to produce their big, gorgeous bowls of color. They flourish in

Meconopsis betonicifolia

climates with mild winters and cool, moist summers—notably, the Pacific Northwest. They also do well on the coast of Maine, where summers are cool and winters very cold. Seaside locations are ideal, as long as the plants are protected from wind.

Given a shady spot in its preferred climate, blue poppy, *M. betonicifolia*, grows as tall as 6 feet and bears 5-inch, sky blue poppies with golden stamens in late spring or early summer. In a less favorable locale, it's a much squatter, shorter-lived plant with smaller flowers verging on mauve.

Welsh poppy, *M. cambrica*, requires the same conditions as blue poppy but is easier to grow. Only 1

to 2 feet tall, it produces 3-inch orange or yellow poppies from early to mid or late summer. The plants self-sow without becoming invasive.

MERTENSIA VIRGINICA
Virginia bluebells
Perennial

Color: *Blue*
Season: *Spring*
Hardy to: *−35°F/−37°C; needs some winter chill; not suited to Gulf Coast and Florida*
Exposure: *Part shade, shade*
Water: *Regular*

Though this woodland shade plant comes and goes quickly, its blossoms are among the much-anticipated joys of spring.

From a clump of oval, pale bluish green leaves, the leafy flowering stems rise 1½ to 2 feet, bearing sprays of nodding, trumpet-shaped flowers that open pink and turn to purplish blue. Plants begin to go dormant soon after blooming and die down completely by midsummer.

There's no need to divide clumps unless you want extra plants—and volunteer seedlings can fill that demand.

Mertensia virginica

MIMULUS × HYBRIDUS
Monkey flower
Perennial grown as annual

Color: *Red, yellow, orange, bicolors*
Season: *Summer*
Exposure: *Part shade, shade*
Water: *Regular*

This classification includes the hybrid strains developed from various *Mimulus* species.

Spreading, low-growing plants 1 to 1½ feet high, monkey flowers are among the few shade-loving summer annuals with big, eye-catching blossoms. Velvety, two-lipped, and measuring up to a couple of inches across, the flowers come in bright, warm colors and are often spotted or mottled with another color; to the fanciful eye, they look like grinning monkey faces.

Mimulus × hybridus

These plants will grow anywhere, but prefer cool, moist regions like the Pacific Northwest.

MOLUCCELLA LAEVIS
Bells-of-Ireland
Annual

Color: *Green*
Season: *Summer*
Exposure: *Sun*
Water: *Regular*

This plant is grown for its unusual flower spikes: upright, 2-foot stems

Moluccella laevis

bearing whorls of bell-shaped, pale green "flowers" delicately veined in white. These are actually enlarged calyxes, the outer leaves at the base of most blossoms; the tiny, purplish or white true flowers are set inside the bells.

Bells-of-Ireland brings subtle beauty rather than a big show to the garden. Its spikes are attractive in both fresh and dried arrangements.

MONARDA DIDYMA
Bee balm
Perennial

Color: Red, pink, violet, lavender, white
Season: Summer
Hardy to: –30°F/–34°C; needs some winter chill; not suited to Gulf Coast and Florida
Exposure: Sun, part shade
Water: Regular

Bee balm's aromatic leaves can be used for herbal tea, but most gardeners grow this member of the mint family for its flamboyant flowers. For several weeks in summer, the spreading clump puts up many leafy, branching stems ending in whorls of tubular blooms. The basic species has scarlet blossoms, but you'll also find selections and hybrids in pink,

Muscari

violet, lavender, and white. When in bloom, the plants range from about 2½ to 4 feet tall.

Though bee balm can stand some dryness, it performs better with regular water. Give it full sun in cool- to mild-summer regions, part shade in hotter areas. Divide the clumps, which spread by running stems, every 2 or 3 years.

MUSCARI
Grape hyacinth
Deciduous bulb

Color: Blue
Season: Spring
Hardy to: –40°F/–40°C
Exposure: Sun, part shade
Water: Moderate

In early to midspring, grape hyacinth produces short spikes covered with urn- or bell-shaped, sometimes fragrant blossoms in blue shades from azure to deep purplish blue. Before the flowers open, the tight buds resemble little bunches of grapes.

The various species range from about 6 inches to a foot tall. In most cases, the grassy leaves appear in fall and live through cold and snow, then die back in summer, well after the flowers have faded. In cold-winter regions, where foliage can look battered by the time spring arrives, provide camouflage by growing grape hyacinth among other plants.

Grape hyacinth naturalizes easily; it's charming in big drifts and in small clusters in rock gardens.

NARCISSUS
Daffodil
Deciduous bulb

Color: Yellow, cream, white, pink, orange, bicolors
Season: Late winter, spring
Hardy to: Varies
Exposure: Sun, part shade
Water: Regular

So many types of these trouble-free bulbs exist that they're grouped in a dozen categories, including trum-

Monarda didyma 'Cambridge Scarlet'

Narcissus 'Scarlet O'Hara'

pets, large cups, small cups, doubles, jonquils, and species. Most types survive to about –30°F/–34°C, though there are a few less hardy exceptions.

The flowers come in assorted sizes and shapes, but all have the same basic structure: six outer petals (the perianth) and a central petal-like structure (the corona), which usually forms an elongated tube or a shallow cup. The perianth may be yellow, cream, or white; the corona may be any of those colors as well as orange or pink. Stem heights range from about 6 inches to 1½ feet.

By planting early, midseason, and late bloomers, you can have daffodils over a fairly long period, starting in winter in mild climates.

Choose a planting spot in full sun or light shade. Clumps will increase over the years, though individual plants may become smaller unless the clump is fertilized or divided. Let the foliage turn yellow before lopping it off.

NEMESIA STRUMOSA
Nemesia
Annual

Color: *White, cream, yellow, orange, red, pink, blue, bicolors*
Season: *Summer*
Exposure: *Sun, part shade*
Water: *Regular*

Nemesia strumosa 'Carnival'

This bedding plant forms 3- to 4-inch clusters of cup-shaped, wide-mouthed flowers in colors including bright jewel tones as well as soft pastels. Plants range from about 8 inches to 1½ feet in height, though modern hybrids tend to fall at the short end of the scale.

Nemesia grows as a summer annual everywhere, performing best where weather is cool. In mild-winter climates, it also flowers from winter to spring. To prolong the bloom period, cut the plants back after the first flush of flowers.

NEMOPHILA MENZIESII
Baby blue eyes
Annual

Color: *Blue*
Season: *Late spring*
Exposure: *Sun, part shade*
Water: *Regular*

This little California wildflower, a trailing plant just 6 to 10 inches high, has inch-wide, cup-shaped sky blue flowers with pale centers.

Suited to the cool coastal and mountain climates of the West, baby blue eyes dies quickly in heat and humidity. It makes a fine bulb cover or rock garden plant, reseeding itself when conditions are favorable.

Nemophila menziesii

NEPETA × FAASSENII
Catmint
Perennial

Color: *Blue*
Season: *Spring, summer*
Hardy to: *–35°F/–37°C; not suited to Gulf Coast and Florida*
Exposure: *Sun*
Water: *Regular to moderate*

Starting in mid to late spring, loose spikes of small, clustered flowers turn this 1- to 2-foot-high, billowy plant into a blue to lavender haze.

A wonderful choice for borders, catmint is a hardier alternative to lavender. Reports vary on feline attraction to the soft, aromatic gray-green foliage—but to be on the safe side, start with larger plants, since cats may wreck smaller specimens.

Cut out the previous year's flowering stems before growth begins in spring, then shear plants after the initial bloom for an encore show. Since this is a sterile hybrid, divide clumps to get more plants.

Nepeta × faassenii

NERIUM OLEANDER
Oleander
Evergreen shrub

Color: *Red, pink, yellow, cream, white*
Season: *Spring, summer, fall*
Hardy to: *15°F/–9°C*
Exposure: *Sun*
Water: *Moderate to little*

A tough, vigorous, coarse-textured shrub with lance-shaped leaves up to a foot long, oleander blooms over a long season, starting in mid to late spring and continuing into fall. The 2- to 3-inch-wide, often fragrant flowers are borne in showy clusters at the branch tips.

The many cultivars, most growing 6 to 12 feet tall, are available in white and shades of yellow, pink, and red. Double-flowered types tend to hold onto faded blossoms, while those with single blooms shed them cleanly.

Oleander succeeds in most conditions, but it won't peform well in shade or in climates with persistent fog. It takes any amount of pruning and can be trained into a small tree. All plant parts are poisonous.

NICOTIANA
Flowering tobacco
Perennial grown as annual

Color: *White, pink, red, purple, green*
Season: *Spring, summer*
Exposure: *Sun, part shade*
Water: *Regular*

Flowering tobacco has traditionally been grown for the powerful fragrance and luminous, almost ghostly appearance it brings to the evening garden.

The classic species is *N. alata*, a sticky-leafed, 3-foot-tall plant with tubular greenish white flowers that open and release a heady perfume at dusk or on overcast days. Modern strains tend to be more compact—usually about a foot high—and bloom during the day. They offer a broader color range than the "unimproved" species, but the flowers aren't nearly as redolent.

Nerium oleander

For intense fragrance day and night, choose 5-foot-tall *N. sylvestris*, with leaves up to a foot long and whorls of very long-tubed white blossoms at its branch ends.

Flowering tobacco is treated as an annual in cold-winter climates, but it's perennial in milder regions. Plant fragrant types under windows, along the border of a patio, or in other locations where the potent scent can be enjoyed.

Nicotiana sylvestris

NIEREMBERGIA HIPPOMANICA
Cup flower
Perennial

Color: *Blue, violet*
Season: *Spring, summer*
Hardy to: *15°F/–9°C*
Exposure: *Sun, part shade*
Water: *Regular*

This spreading, foot-high edging plant blooms from midspring into fall, bearing broadly cup-shaped blue flowers with a yellow throat. The leaves are short and needlelike.

The plant usually offered is the slightly taller wild variant *N. h. vio-*

Nierembergia hippomanica violacea 'Purple Robe'

lacea, which has larger flowers with violet petals. The various selections range from about 6 to 15 inches high.

Give full sun in mild-summer areas, some shade in hotter climates. Cut the plants back after bloom to keep them compact; replace them every few years when performance declines. In cold-winter regions, treat cup flower as an annual.

NIGELLA DAMASCENA
Love-in-a-mist
Annual

Color: *Blue, pink, white*
Season: *Spring, early summer*
Exposure: *Sun, part shade*
Water: *Regular*

Reaching about 2 feet tall, this feathery-leafed annual puts on a misty pastel show in spring in mild-winter gardens, in early summer in colder climates. Each 1- to 2-inch, many-petaled bloom is set in a collar of threadlike foliage. The flowers are followed by puffy pale green seed capsules that are attractive in dried arrangements.

'Miss Jekyll' has clear blue semidouble blossoms. 'Persian Jewels', another semidouble selection, contains a mix of blue, lavender, purple, mauve, rose, and white flowers.

Heat puts a quick end to love-in-a-mist—but the plants reseed themselves easily, making them ideal for wild gardens.

OENOTHERA
Evening primrose, sundrops
Perennial

Color: *Yellow, pink, white*
Season: *Summer*
Hardy to: *Varies*
Exposure: *Sun*
Water: *Moderate*

These carefree plants produce an abundance of silky, four-petaled, bowl-shaped flowers throughout summer. Some types bloom during the day, while others open as the sun wanes in the afternoon, then close the following morning.

The showiest yellow-flowering species is Ozark sundrop, *O. missourensis* (–20°F/–29°C), a sprawling plant about 9 inches high. Its 3- to 5-inch, clear yellow blossoms open in the afternoon. The other commonly available sundrops is a shrubby 2-footer that may be listed as *O. fruticosa* or *O. tetragona*. As hardy as the Ozark species, it has reddish brown buds that open to 1½-inch, shiny yellow flowers during the day.

The 2-inch, rosy pink blooms of *O. berlandieri (O. speciosa childsii)* also open in the daytime, despite the plant's common name of Mexican evening primrose. Hardy to –10°F/ –23°C, this foot-high plant spreads aggressively, so choose a location you won't mind it taking over.

Other *Oenothera* species feature white blossoms. All types do well with little attention, thriving in wild gardens or difficult spots.

ORIGANUM DICTAMNUS
Crete dittany
Perennial

Color: *Silver*
Season: *All year*
Hardy to: *0°F/–18°C*
Exposure: *Sun*
Water: *Moderate*

This foot-high member of the mint family is grown for its aromatic, woolly, silvery white foliage rather than its tiny pinkish blooms. Clothing slender, arching stems, the thick, roundish, somewhat mottled leaves are less than an inch long.

Crete dittany makes a wonderful foliage accent in rock gardens and containers, though some consider it difficult to grow.

Nigella damascena

Oenothera berlandieri

Origanum dictamnus

Osmunda regalis

Pachysandra terminalis

OSMUNDA REGALIS
Royal fern
Deciduous fern

Color: *Green*
Season: *Spring, summer, fall*
Hardy to: *–40°F/–40°C*
Exposure: *Sun, part shade, shade*
Water: *Regular*

A vase-shaped plant to 6 feet tall, royal fern has coarse-textured fronds that emerge pale pink, then turn rich green. Mature plants produce what look like rusty brown flower plumes. 'Purpurascens' has purplish new growth.

This species grows naturally in swampy soils. In cultivation, it requires constant moisture; it can even take sun if given enough water.

PACHYSANDRA TERMINALIS
Japanese spurge
Evergreen ground cover

Color: *Green, white*
Season: *All year*
Hardy to: *–30°F/–34°C*
Exposure: *Part shade, shade*
Water: *Regular*

Widely used as a ground cover and lawn substitute in shady sites, this rugged perennial produces handsome, oval dark green leaves in whorls at the ends of upright stems 6 to 10 inches high. Spikes of tiny, fluffy, fragrant white flowers add sparkle in early summer.

'Green Carpet' is lower growing and more compact than the species.

'Variegata' and 'Silveredge', with creamy white leaf margins, are useful for brightening deep shade.

Japanese spurge isn't weedy, but it spreads rapidly by underground stems to form a dense cover. It thrives under trees and shrubs.

PAEONIA
Peony
Deciduous perennials and shrubs

Color: *Red, pink, white, cream, yellow, orange, lavender, purple*
Season: *Spring*
Hardy to: *Varies; needs some winter chill*
Exposure: *Sun*
Water: *Regular*

These exceptionally long-lived plants flaunt gorgeous, silky, single to double, often fragrant flowers in a tremendous color range each spring. The bloom period typically lasts for a month or more, though it's briefer in mild climates.

Most peonies are the herbaceous type (–50°F/–46°C), 2- to 4-foot plants which sprout from tuberous roots and die to the ground in fall. A shrubby clump of dark green, deeply cut foliage forms early in the season, soon followed by blooms as big as 10 inches across, in colors from white through pale cream and pink to red, and even pure yellow. For a lengthy floral show, choose early, midseason, and late varieties.

Herbaceous peonies need a definite period of winter chill. In borderline areas, early types with single blossoms or Japanese flower forms

Paeonia lactiflora

(one or two rows of petals surrounding a conspicuous, fluffy mass of petal-like stamens) may succeed if given light afternoon shade. Clumps can remain undisturbed indefinitely.

Tree peonies (–30°F/–34°C) are 3- to 6-foot shrubs that bloom in midspring, producing flowers up to a foot across. Types with purple, red, pink, lavender, or white flowers are likely derived from the Chinese *P. suffruticosa*. Those with sunset colors can be traced in part to the Tibetan *P. lutea;* many of these have such heavy blossoms that the stems droop to the ground unless staked. Many double-flowered European hybrids (which come chiefly in pinks and rosy shades) also need staking.

Tree peonies aren't as dependent on winter chill as the herbaceous type and thus can be grown in milder climates. Prune only to remove dead stems in spring.

PAPAVER ORIENTALE
Oriental poppy
Perennial

Color: *Red, pink, orange, white*
Season: *Late spring*
Hardy to: *–40°F/–40°C; needs some winter chill; not suited to Gulf Coast and Florida*
Exposure: *Sun, part shade*
Water: *Regular to moderate*

Papaver orientale

At the end of spring, Oriental poppy's leafy flower stalks rise from a low mound of finely divided, hairy foliage, bearing flamboyant, bowl-shaped blossoms. The blooms, each as big as 8 inches across, typically consist of four to six broad, wavy-edged petals, each with a dark blotch at the base, and a central tuft of stamens.

The original Oriental poppies were bright orange or red with a black center. Modern hybrids include white and pastel colors; some have lighter centers or lack petal blotches. Most cultivars range from 2 to 4 feet tall when in bloom.

Plants die to the ground soon after flowering, but the leaves emerge again in early fall and remain as a small clump over winter. Water regularly while plants are actively growing, less often while they're dormant. Give some shade in hot climates.

PARROTIA PERSICA
Persian parrotia
Deciduous tree or large shrub

Color: *Yellow, orange, red; mottled gray or brown*
Season: *All year*
Hardy to: *–20°F/–29°C*
Exposure: *Sun, part shade*
Water: *Regular to moderate*

Growing 15 to 30 feet tall, often with multiple trunks, this highly pest-resistant plant is a year-round beauty. It looks most dramatic in autumn, when the lustrous dark green foliage turns brilliant yellow, then orange, and finally scarlet. The beautiful mot-

Parrotia persica

tled bark, especially noticeable after leaf drop, has a smooth, dark gray or brown outer layer that flakes off to reveal creamy white patches beneath.

Persian parrotia blooms in late winter or early spring; the small, red-stamened flowers, held in woolly brown bracts, seem to surround the plant with an overall reddish haze. Reddish purple new leaves unfurl following bloom.

PARTHENOCISSUS
Virginia creeper, Boston ivy
Deciduous vine

Color: *Red*
Season: *Fall*
Hardy to: *Varies*
Exposure: *Sun, part shade*
Water: *Regular*

These large-leafed, rambling vines are grown for their brilliant scarlet fall color, most striking in full sun.

The leaves of Virginia creeper, *P. quinquefolia* (–40°F/–40°C), are divided into five leaflets and spaced widely along the stems, making a loose cover. 'Englemannii' has smaller, more closely spaced leaves.

P. tricuspidata (–30°F/–34°C) is the typically three-lobed Boston ivy. 'Green Showers' has burgundy fall color, 'Veitchii' small leaves and new growth that's purplish in color in-

Parthenocissus quinquefolia

stead of the standard reddish. Plants are semievergreen in mild climates.

Whether you grow these plants upward or as ground covers (they root where they touch the soil), provide plenty of room, since they can be invasive. Locate vines carefully—they climb with the help of suction disks that can damage wood and brick surfaces.

PELARGONIUM
Geranium
Perennial grown as annual

Color: Red, pink, orange, purple, white, bicolors
Season: Spring, summer, fall
Exposure: Sun, part shade
Water: Regular

Quite different from true geraniums (see page 151), these popular bedding and container plants generally have big, flashy flower clusters and rounded or heart-shaped leaves with scalloped or fluted edges.

Common geranium, *P. × hortorum*, is sometimes called zonal geranium for the area of contrasting color just inside the leaf margin. It bears rounded or flat-topped clusters of 1-inch-wide, single or double blossoms in white and just about every gradation of pink, red, purple, and orange. The many strains range in height from about 8 inches to 3 feet.

Martha Washington geranium, *P. × domesticum,* is rangier than common geranium and has no zonal markings on its foliage. Reaching about 3 feet tall, it produces loose clusters of 2-inch blooms in white through pink to deep purple, often with contrasting petal blotches. These plants aren't heat-tolerant and usually don't bloom in summer in warm climates.

Ideal for hanging baskets, ivy geranium, *P. peltatum,* has trailing stems to about 3 feet long. Its single or double flowers are similar to those of common geranium; they come in white, lavender, and rosy shades, often with darker markings.

Geraniums can survive light frosts and are often grown as evergreen perennials in mild-winter areas.

Pelargonium × hortorum

PENSTEMON
Penstemon, beard tongue
Perennial

Color: Blue, purple, lavender, red, pink, white
Season: Spring, summer
Hardy to: Varies; most not suited to Gulf Coast and Florida
Exposure: Sun, part shade
Water: Regular

These bushy, narrow-leafed, generally upright plants are fairly short-lived—but to make up for that, they produce lots of color over a long period. The loose spikes of tubular, flaring blossoms come in strong colors and soft pastels, sometimes with a light-colored, decoratively spotted throat.

In humid-summer areas with some winter chill, the late-spring bloomer *P. barbatus* (–30°F/–34°C) is your best bet. Its selections 'Prairie Fire' (scarlet), 'Prairie Dusk' (purple), and 'Rose Elf' (pink) all grow about 2 feet tall.

Two hybrid groups bloom during summer and often into fall. Both are hardy on the West Coast but treated as annuals elsewhere.

The first group, comprising hybrids derived from several Mexican species, thrives where winters are fairly mild (to 15°F/–9°C) and sum-

mers are dry. It includes 2-footers with slender-tubed flowers; good choices are wine red 'Garnet', light pink 'Evelyn', and deep pink 'Alice Hindley'.

More readily available is the category of hybrids known as border penstemon, *P. × gloxinioides,* 2- to 3-footers with wider-tubed blossoms. These include 'Holly's White', red 'Firebird', and purple 'Midnight'.

Another West Coast specialty is *P. heterophyllus purdyi* (0°F/–18°C), commonly sold in nurseries as 'Blue Bedder'. Its stems sprawl, then grow upward to 1 to 1½ feet. Flower color ranges from lavender to sky blue.

Give penstemon some shade in hot-summer regions. Plants usually need to be replaced after 3 or 4 years.

Penstemon × gloxinioides 'Firebird'

Perovskia

Petunia 'Celebrity Orchid Ice'

PEROVSKIA
Russian sage
Small evergreen shrub

Color: Blue
Season: Summer
Hardy to: –40°F/–40°C; needs some
   winter chill
Exposure: Sun
Water: Moderate

Throughout summer, this little shrub's silvery stems and small, grayish leaves are obscured by a haze of blue to purplish blossoms clustered on branched spikes.

P. atriplicifolia is the most commonly listed Russian sage, though the plant sold under this name in the United States is actually a hybrid between this species and *P. abrotanoides* and appears to be identical with the deep violet *P.* 'Blue Spire'. The earliest flowering cultivar is 'Blue Mist', which, along with 'Blue Haze', has lighter blue blossoms than the basic species. Plants grow 3 to 4 feet tall and wide.

Mass Russian sage or use it individually in borders. Extremely resistant to heat and drought, it performs best in warm summers, even where weather is humid. Cut the plants nearly to the ground each spring before new growth begins.

PETUNIA × HYBRIDA
Petunia
Perennial grown as annual

Color: White, cream, yellow, pink,
   red, purple, blue, bicolors
Season: Spring, summer, fall
Exposure: Sun
Water: Regular

These stalwart bedding and container plants bloom lavishly from late spring into fall, especially when faded flowers are removed. Blossoms may be single or double; singles are funnel-shaped, while doubles resemble carnations. Both types are available in Grandifloras, with very large blooms, and Multifloras, with smaller but more numerous flowers.

Colors range from pure white through cream to yellow, from soft pink to deep red, from light blue to dark purple. You'll find blooms with contrasting throats, dark veining, or petals rimmed or striped in another color. Many of the plants available today are organized into series, some containing up to a couple of dozen colors and combinations.

In size, petunias range from about 8 inches to 2½ feet high. Spreading or trailing types are ideal for containers and can even be grown as ground covers.

PHILADELPHUS CORONARIUS
Mock orange
Deciduous shrub

Color: White
Season: Late spring, early summer
Hardy to: –20°F/–29°C
Exposure: Sun, part shade
Water: Regular to moderate

Upright and arching to about 10 feet high and wide, mock orange tends to look straggly and irregular—but all is forgiven in late spring or early summer, when the plant produces its clusters of four-petaled, creamy white, sweet-scented blooms.

For more compact growth without loss of fragrance, choose 3-foot-tall, double-flowered 'Snowflake' or any of these hybrids: single-flowered 'Avalanche', 4 feet tall and wide; double-flowered 'Snowgoose', 4 to 5 feet

Philadelphus coronarius

tall and half that wide; single-flowered 'Belle Etoile', 6 feet tall and somewhat narrower, with extra-large, purple-blotched blooms; and double-flowered 'Minnesota Snowflake', 8 feet tall and wide.

For the best blooms, choose a full-sun location. Blossoms form on old wood, so prune the shrubs after flowering to maintain size and shape. To rejuvenate plants, cut them to the ground periodically.

PHLOX
Phlox
Perennials and annuals

Color: *Blue, purple, red, pink, white*
Season: *Spring, summer, fall*
Hardy to: *Varies; needs some winter chill*
Exposure: *Sun, part shade*
Water: *Regular to moderate*

The many types of phloxes, all showy bloomers, range in height from about 6 inches to 4 feet. Perennial sorts are spring-flowering low spreaders and summer-blooming border plants; an annual species puts on a show throughout the growing season.

Perhaps the best-known spreader is 6-inch-high moss pink, *P. subulata* (–30°F/–34°C); during bloom time, its tiny, needlelike foliage is covered with a blanket of lavender, white, pink, or magenta flowers. The larger-leafed, foot-high sweet William phlox, *P. divaricata* (–35°F/–37°C), bears loose clusters of 1-inch flowers in white or blue shades.

Border phloxes are generally hardy to about –30°F/–34°C. The 3- to 4-foot-tall *P. carolina* and *P. maculata* bloom in early summer, bearing rounded flower clusters in the complete color range. Cultivars and hybrids of *P. paniculata* produce dome-shaped or pyramidal clusters on 2½- to 4-foot stems; some come into bloom before midsummer, while others continue into early fall. All kinds of border phloxes may reward you with a second flowering if you regularly cut off the spent blossom heads. Best suited to areas with cool to mild summers, these plants should be divided every few years.

Phlox drummondii

Annual phlox, *P. drummondii*, is a Texas wildflower that breeders have refined for the garden—though it still reseeds in mild-winter areas. Ranging in size from about 6 inches to a little over 1½ feet, this species offers blooms in the full color palette, often with a contrasting eye.

All phloxes require full sun and regular moisture, with the following exceptions: moss pink does nicely with moderate water, and sweet William phlox prefers light shade.

PHOTINIA × FRASERI
Fraser's photinia
Evergreen shrub

Color: *Red*
Season: *Throughout the growing season*
Hardy to: *0°F/–18°C*
Exposure: *Sun*
Water: *Moderate*

Photinia's new leaves spurt up bright red above the dark green mature foliage, creating a two-toned effect. Growing 10 to 15 feet tall and slightly wider, the plant makes an excellent hedge or screen; compact 'Indian Princess', with new growth that's more orange than red, is about half the size of the common type.

Photinia × fraseri

Fraser's photinia is carefree in dry-summer regions, but it often develops serious leaf spot diseases in moist, humid climates.

PHYSALIS ALKEKENGI
Chinese lantern plant
Perennial

Color: *Orange*
Season: *Fall*
Hardy to: *–40°F/–40°C*
Exposure: *Sun, part shade*
Water: *Regular*

This 2-foot-tall, angularly branched plant is cultivated for its lantern-shaped, bright reddish orange fruit, often used in dried arrangements. The little lanterns, which follow inconspicuous summer flowers, are actually inflated, papery husks surrounding the plant's small berries.

Though it is a perennial, Chinese lantern plant is often grown as an annual, since it spreads by creeping underground stems and can become unmanageable if left to grow undisturbed.

Physalis alkekengi

Physostegia virginiana

Picea pungens

PHYSOSTEGIA VIRGINIANA
Obedient plant, false dragonhead
Perennial

Color: *Pink, red, white*
Season: *Summer, fall*
Hardy to: *–35°F/–37°C*
Exposure: *Sun, part shade*
Water: *Regular*

This exuberant bloomer is a good source of pink for late-summer borders. The usual color is bright bluish pink, but selections in softer rosy pink, rosy red, and white are available.

Plants range from 1½ to 3 feet tall, growing in spreading clumps that send up leafy stems topped by tapering flower spikes from mid to late summer into early fall. The blossoms resemble snapdragons (hence the name false dragonhead) and will remain in place if twisted or pushed out of position—the source of the plant's other common name, obedient plant.

These plants spread rapidly under good growing conditions and should be divided every 2 or 3 years. They tend to flop over unless staked.

PICEA PUNGENS
Blue spruce, Colorado spruce
Evergreen conifer

Color: *Blue*
Season: *All year*
Hardy to: *–40°F/–40°C; needs some winter chill*
Exposure: *Sun*
Water: *Regular to moderate*

Blue spruce is a pyramidal tree that can reach 100 feet tall in the wild but is generally smaller in gardens. The foliage color in seed-grown plants varies, but cultivars offer reliable bluish tones.

'Hoopsii' may be the bluest selection. 'Koster' and the more symmetrical and compact 'Moerheimii' are nearly as blue, as is slow-growing 'Fat Albert', which reaches just 10 feet in about 10 years. 'Thomsen' is an icy blue-white, 'Glauca' a solid blue-gray.

Often grown as a specimen tree in lawns, *P. pungens* is the only spruce species to succeed in the Southwest and lower Midwest. It does not grow well in the humid South.

PIERIS JAPONICA
Lily-of-the-valley shrub
Evergreen shrub

Color: *White, pink, red*
Season: *Winter, spring*
Hardy to: *–10°F/–23°C*
Exposure: *Part shade*
Water: *Regular*

An elegant rhododendron relative, lily-of-the-valley shrub forms tiers of leathery dark green leaves that often emerge pink to red or bronze. In winter or spring, depending on the climate, pinkish flower buds that resemble strings of beads open to drooping clusters of small, urn-shaped white blossoms. The plants grow to about 10 feet tall and not quite that wide.

Named selections offer foliage and flower variations, usually on somewhat shorter plants. Among the many options are 'Variegata', a slow grower with leaves trimmed in ivory (often tinted pink in spring); 'Mountain Fire', noted for bright red new growth; 'Valley Valentine', with maroon buds opening to dark rosy pink blooms; and 'Christmas Cheer', with rosy red and white blossoms.

A tidy, well-behaved plant that rarely needs pruning, lily-of-the-valley shrub is lovely in woodland settings, as a foundation plant, or in borders. The leaves and nectar are poisonous.

Pieris japonica 'Variegata'

Platycodon grandiflorus

Plumbago auriculata

Potentilla fruticosa

PLATYCODON GRANDIFLORUS
Balloon flower
Perennial

Color: *Blue, pink, white*
Season: *Summer*
Hardy to: *–35°F/–37°C; not suited to Gulf Coast and Florida*
Exposure: *Sun, part shade*
Water: *Regular*

Carried at the ends of leafy stems, this plant's balloonlike buds open to star-shaped, dark-veined, deep blue flowers about 2 inches across. Also available are forms with soft blue, pink, or white blossoms, as well as double-flowered types. Selections range from around 1 to 3 feet tall.

Balloon flower is a fine choice for summer borders, since blooming starts early and lasts for a couple of months—or even longer, if spent flowers are removed. Provide some shade in hot-summer regions. Plants die to the ground each fall and regrow quite late the next spring, so be sure to mark their locations.

PLUMBAGO AURICULATA
Cape plumbago
Evergreen to semievergreen shrub

Color: *Blue, white*
Season: *Spring, summer, fall*
Hardy to: *20°F/–7°C*
Exposure: *Sun, part shade*
Water: *Little*

Also sold as *P. capensis*, this mounding, almost vinelike shrub provides easy, carefree color in mild-winter climates. Abundant clusters of inch-wide blue blossoms adorn plants from spring through fall, or even all year long in the mildest areas. Seedlings' flower color varies from light blue to white, but consistently sky blue or white cultivars can also be purchased.

Left to grow naturally, cape plumbago sprawls to about 10 feet across and 6 feet tall; if trained, it will reach about twice that high. It's a good choice for a bank cover or background planting.

Plants are evergreen in frost-free regions, but in colder areas, they'll shed some of their leaves. They regrow quickly if damaged by frost and can be rejuvenated by severe cutting back.

POTENTILLA
Cinquefoil
Evergreen perennials and deciduous shrubs

Color: *Yellow, orange, red, pink, white*
Season: *Spring, summer, fall*
Hardy to: *Varies; not suited to Gulf Coast and Florida*
Exposure: *Sun*
Water: *Regular to moderate*

Cinquefoil's dark green or grayish leaves are often mistaken for strawberry foliage; its small, five-petaled blooms look like wild roses.

The many species vary from about 4 inches to 5 feet tall. Perhaps the most commonly grown is the deciduous shrub *P. fruticosa* (–40°F/–40°C), bush cinquefoil, ranging from 1 to nearly 5 feet high and wide. Its upright to arching stems bear a profusion of single yellow flowers from late spring or early summer until frost. Double-flowered selections and forms in paler and deeper yellow shades, orange, red, and white are also sold. Give bush cinquefoil moderate water.

Among the loveliest herbaceous cinquefoils for summer borders are 1½-foot *P. atrosanguinea* 'Gibson's Scarlet', which has brilliant red single blooms, and 1-foot *P. nepalensis* 'Miss Willmott', which bears pink single flowers with a red center. Plants are hardy to –20°F/–29°C; give them regular water.

The ground cover spring cinquefoil, *P. tabernaemontanii* (–30°F/–34°C), grows to about 6 inches high, forming a glossy green mat dotted with bright yellow blossoms from spring into summer. You can mow the planting occasionally to neaten its appearance. Provide moderate water.

PRIMULA
Primrose
Perennial

Color: *Yellow, cream, white, purple, lavender, pink, red, orange, mahogany, bicolors*
Season: *Winter, spring, early summer*
Hardy to: *–20°F/–29°C; most need some winter chill; not suited to Gulf Coast and Florida*
Exposure: *Part shade*
Water: *Regular*

Primula

Prunus serrulata

Primroses form a rosette of leaves, above which rise circular, five-petaled blossoms; each petal has an indentation at its apex. The flowers may be borne on individual stems, in clusters at stem ends, or in tiered clusters up the stem. Most primroses are spring-blooming, but some start their season in mid to late winter in mild climates, while a few bloom in early summer.

Numerous types of primroses can be cultivated. Some thrive under ordinary garden conditions, while others require plentiful moisture or even boggy soil. Of those in the former group, hybrids of *P. × polyantha* are the easiest to grow, succeeding even in mild-winter regions. Their stocky stems rise to a foot high, ending in clusters of yellow-eyed flowers in a full range of soft and bright colors and bicolors.

English primrose, *P. vulgaris,* is another good performer in average conditions. Its light yellow, scented blossoms are borne individually on stems to 9 inches high. You'll also find double-flowered strains and selections with two or three blossoms per stem, in colors including not only yellow but also red, pink, lavender, cream, white, and mahogany.

Of the primroses requiring damp soil, the Candelabra group is among the most graceful. Foliage clumps reach 2½ feet across, sending up stems as high as 3 feet that bear tiered whorls of flowers. The most widely grown member of this group is *P. japonica,* with purple, red, pink, or white blooms.

The moisture-loving Sikkimensis primroses are valued both for fragrance and for their early summer flowers. Borne in clusters atop thick 1½- to 3-foot stems, the bell-shaped, nodding blooms come in yellow, orange, and red. These plants are suited only to cool-summer regions.

All types of primroses flourish in the Pacific Northwest. In less favorable climates, they are sometimes treated as annuals.

PRUNUS
Flowering cherry, English laurel
Shrubs and trees

Color: *White, pink, red, purple, green; mahogany*
Season: *Varies*
Hardy to: *Varies*
Exposure: *Sun, part shade, shade*
Water: *Regular*

Flowering cherry trees are among the most breathtaking sights of late winter or spring. Clouds of single to double blossoms in white, pink, or rosy red clothe the bare branches—or, in some cases, appear along with the new leaves.

Forms and sizes vary; you can choose from horizontally spreading to narrowly upright canopies and mature heights from 15 to 40 feet. Most types are hardy to –20°F/–29°C; Sargent cherry, *P. sargentii,* survives to –30°F/–34°C. Give all types full sun.

Some species are valued for their striking bark. That of birch bark cherry, *P. serrula* (–20°F/–29°C), is glossy mahogany red with brown stripes. Amur cherry, *P. maackii* (–40°F/–40°C), has shiny golden bark, which often flakes off in thin horizontal strips.

Cherry plum, *P. cerasifera* (–20°F/–29°C), includes several purple-leafed selections, including upright, 18-foot 'Krauter Vesuvius', with black-purple foliage and little or no fruit, and round-headed, 25- to 30-foot 'Atropurpurea', with red-purple leaves and purple plums.

In mild climates, evergreen English laurel, *P. laurocerasus* (5°F/–15°C), makes a handsome, glossy-leafed screen or hedge 4 to 15 feet tall; dwarf forms as well as hardier selections are available. These plants adapt to any light level, though they need some shade in the hottest climates.

Pulmonaria 'Roy Davidson'

PULMONARIA
Lungwort
Perennial

Color: Blue, pink, red, white
Season: Spring
Hardy to: Varies; not suited to Gulf Coast and Florida
Exposure: Part shade, shade
Water: Regular

These quiet charmers are indispensable in moist shade gardens. Just as the broadly oval to lance-shaped leaves (silver-dappled in some selections) emerge in spring, the flower stems appear, topped with nodding clusters of funnel-shaped, typically blue or pink blossoms. After flowering is finished, the plant produces more foliage from the base. If kept well watered, the clump remains ornamental through summer.

Blue lungwort, *P. angustifolia* (–35°F/–37°C), grows 8 inches to a foot high, bearing dark green leaves and blue flowers that open from pink buds. The 1- to 2-foot *P. rubra* (–20°F/–29°C) has coral red blooms and pale green foliage.

Bethlehem sage, *P. saccharata* (–35°F/–37°C), features beautifully spotted leaves. The basic species grows 1 to 1½ feet high, with silver-speckled foliage and blossoms that open pink and mature to blue. Cultivars are more commonly offered; 'Mrs. Moon' and 'Margery Fish' have the same coloring as the species, while 'Sissinghurst White' bears large white blooms for an overall look of silvery white and green.

Divide clumps when they become crowded.

PYRACANTHA
Firethorn
Evergreen shrubs and ground covers

Color: Red, orange, yellow
Season: Late summer, fall, winter
Hardy to: Varies
Exposure: Sun
Water: Moderate

Firethorn's springtime clusters of tiny, fragrant white blossoms are pretty, but its real glory is its brilliant fruit: thick clusters of pea-size orange-red berries that light up the garden beginning as early as late summer. Selections with red, orange, and yellow fruit are also available; in some types, the berries hang on until late winter, when they're finally cleared out by birds, storms, or decay. During the rest of the year, firethorn's tidy, glossy dark green foliage enhances its surroundings.

The following outstanding hybrids are all hardy to –5°F/–21°C. Fireblight-resistant 'Mohave', to 12 feet tall and wide, has orange-red fruit that colors in late summer and lasts into winter. Columnar 'Teton', also resistant to fireblight, reaches 12 feet tall and 4 feet wide and bears yellow-orange berries. 'Watereri', to 8 feet tall and wide, has bright red fruit.

Vivid red berries decorate the arching stems of 'Ruby Mound' (0°F/–18°C), among the most graceful of ground cover firethorns. It grows 2½ feet high and spreads to about 10 feet.

P. coccinea (–10°F/–23°C) is the hardiest firethorn. Selections range

Pyracantha 'Mohave'

Pyrus salicifolia 'Pendula'

from about 3 to 10 feet in height, from pure orange to red and yellow in fruit color.

As shrubs or ground covers, these plants look better and produce more fruit if allowed to follow their natural growth habit. Prune only occasionally to check wayward branches. The plants can also be espaliered.

PYRUS SALICIFOLIA 'PENDULA'
Weeping willowleaf pear
Small deciduous tree

Color: Silvery
Season: Spring, summer, fall
Hardy to: –20°F/–29°C
Exposure: Sun
Water: Regular to moderate

Also sold as 'Silver Frost', this elegant specimen tree is grown for its silvery, willowlike foliage and beautiful weeping habit, showcased in winter when branches are bare. The new leaves are silver, lovely against the tree's white spring flowers; they turn to silvered green in summer and retain their shimmer in autumn, then drop to reveal the pendent branches.

Weeping willowleaf pear reaches 15 to 25 feet high, 10 to 15 feet wide.

Rhododendron

Robinia pseudoacacia 'Frisia'

RHODODENDRON
Rhododendron, azalea
Deciduous and evergreen shrubs

Color: *White, cream, yellow, orange, red, pink, lavender, purple, bicolors*
Season: *Winter, spring*
Hardy to: *Varies*
Exposure: *Sun, part shade*
Water: *Regular*

The countless types of rhododendrons provide spectacular color from midwinter through late spring. In the cool Pacific Northwest, the ideal climate for these plants, blooming can continue through August. All kinds of rhododendrons produce tight clusters ("trusses") of typically funnel-shaped, sometimes fragrant flowers in nearly every color but true blue, often with a contrasting throat.

The plants known as rhododendrons (as opposed to azaleas) are generally large, bold-leafed evergreen species, though some are low growers with tiny blossoms and foliage. Natural rhododendron country includes the Pacific Northwest and down the Northern California coast; the Appalachian highlands from northern Georgia into New York; the Atlantic seaboard from northern Delaware through New England; and highland areas westward through New York, Pennsylvania, and parts of Ohio. For each of these regions, there are suitable rhododendrons.

Azaleas are a class of rhododendron. Generally smaller and finer-textured than the shrubs called rhododendrons, they're adapted to a greater range of climates and come in both evergreen and deciduous types. The most widely sold azaleas are selections from hybrid groups.

Evergreen azaleas are quite heat-resistant, making them landscape staples in the South. Although their flowers come in many colors, they can't match deciduous types in the yellow, orange, and flame red range. Deciduous azaleas offer a bonus of fall color, too—the leaves typically turn bright yellow, orange, bright red, or maroon in autumn.

To find the best rhododendrons or azaleas for your area, visit local nurseries and public gardens. Try to see the plants in bloom, so you'll know just what color you're getting.

Generally, the plants need moist, acidic soil and some shade. The ideal planting site is in the filtered light beneath tall trees; the next best locations are the east and north sides of structures. If grown in too much shade, the plants get leggy and bloom sparsely. Most types can take full sun in cool-summer areas, and some are actually sun-tolerant.

ROBINIA PSEUDOACACIA 'FRISIA'
Golden locust
Deciduous tree

Color: *Chartreuse, yellow*
Season: *Spring, summer, fall*
Hardy to: *–30°F/–34°C*
Exposure: *Sun*
Water: *Moderate*

Robinia pseudoacacia is generally known as black locust, but its cultivar 'Frisia', thanks to its striking foliage, is more commonly called golden locust. The oval leaflets, orange-tinged when they emerge, range from bright chartreuse to butter yellow at maturity—and then turn orange-yellow in autumn. The new wood is orange, the thorns red.

A graceful tree to about 30 feet, 'Frisia' is best suited to mild-summer areas that aren't too arid. Use it as a specimen tree, or position it in the background with tall, deep green or purple-foliaged plants.

ROMNEYA COULTERI
Matilija poppy
Perennial

Color: *White*
Season: *Late spring, summer*
Hardy to: *–10°F/–23°C*
Exposure: *Sun*
Water: *Regular to little*

This large, shrublike California native sends up thick gray-green stems 6 to

Romneya coulteri

Rosa 'The Fairy' *(left and right) and* 'Blaze' *(center)*

8 feet high, clad in irregularly lobed leaves of the same color. From late spring into summer, the upper part of each stem bears enormous, crepe-papery white blossoms centered with a cluster of golden stamens. The flowers have been likened to stunning-looking fried eggs.

Give Matilija poppy plenty of room, since its roots can be invasive. Established plantings can endure extreme drought, but they'll also take regular water. Cut plants down to about 6 inches in late fall or winter.

ROSA
Rose
Deciduous shrubs and vines

Color: *Red, pink, purple, lavender, white, cream, yellow, orange, bicolors*
Season: *Spring, summer, fall*
Hardy to: *Varies*
Exposure: *Sun, part shade*
Water: *Regular*

The "queen of flowers" is grown for the beauty and fragrance of its blooms, available in an astonishing range of sizes, colors, and forms. Some species are evergreen in mild climates.

Species roses. The roses from which all others are descended, these often large plants make good hedges and backdrops. Some flower just once in spring or summer, but others offer a second, less abundant bloom in fall. Species roses usually have five-petaled single blossoms, and many produce especially colorful fruit ("hips") in autumn. Most are hardy in cold climates and are quite care-free compared with modern roses.

Old garden roses. Valued for their strong fragrance and lovely flower forms, the old European roses—gallicas, damasks, albas, and centifolias—generally bloom once in spring or summer. China roses and many of their derivatives, however, are repeat bloomers. Growth habits vary widely; members of the group range from 2-foot bushes to rampant climbers to tall shrubs. Nearly all need winter protection in cold climates.

Modern roses. These prolific bloomers comprise the vast majority of roses sold today. The most popular are hybrid teas, with large flowers on 2- to 6-foot plants; the category includes other bush types (such as miniatures and floribundas) and climbers. Modern roses are so highly bred that, as a group, they aren't as hardy or disease-resistant as most older roses. For best success, seek out cultivars that grow well in your area.

English roses. By crossing old garden roses with modern ones, British nurseryman David Austin produced the flower forms, fragrances, and disease resistance of old roses in repeat bloomers offering the color range of modern hybrids. These roses include 3- to 9-foot shrubs as well as climbers.

All roses need long hours of full sun for best bloom production, but will take some shade for part of the day. In hot-summer areas, blooms last longer with some midday or afternoon shade; in cooler regions, restrict shade to the morning.

ROSMARINUS OFFICINALIS
Rosemary
Evergreen shrubs and ground covers

Color: *Blue*
Season: *Winter, spring*
Hardy to: *0°F/–18°C*
Exposure: *Sun*
Water: *Moderate to little*

Rosemary produces clusters of little blue flowers along stems clothed in aromatic, almost needlelike leaves that are glossy green on top, grayish white beneath. The bloom period usually runs from winter into spring, though it can begin as early as fall.

The basic species is a 3- to 4-foot-high, irregularly shaped shrub with lavender blooms; various selections offer different heights, habits, and shades of blue. Among low spreaders, the best known is 1½- to 2-

Rosmarinus officinalis 'Blue Spire'

Rudbeckia fulgida sullivantii 'Goldsturm'

Salix alba 'Britzensis'

foot 'Prostratus', with light grayish blue blossoms. 'Collingwood Ingram' is slightly taller, with bright blue-violet flowers. Blue-violet 'Tuscan Blue', with candlelabra-like branches, grows upright to 6 feet.

With good drainage, rosemary will tolerate regular watering, but it thrives with occasional or no supplemental water in all but the hottest regions. The leaves of all types can be used for seasoning.

RUDBECKIA
Coneflower
Perennial

Color: *Yellow, gold, mahogany, bicolors*
Season: *Summer, fall*
Hardy to: *–35°F/–37°C*
Exposure: *Sun*
Water: *Regular*

Breeders have tamed *R. hirta*, the wild black-eyed Susan, to produce many superior cultivars for the border, some as low as 8 inches. All selections are short-lived perennials best treated as annuals. One fine choice is the 3-foot-high Gloriosa Daisy strain, featuring dark-centered yellow, gold,

mahogany, or bicolored blooms up to 6 inches across.

For a typical black-eyed Susan–type daisy—golden petals encircling a dark cone—on a reliably perennial plant, choose *R. fulgida sullivantii* 'Goldsturm'. The foliage clump sends up branching, leafy 2- to 2½-foot stems covered with daisies for many weeks. The cultivar is a uniform and predictable performer, but some nurseries offer the taller, more variable seed-grown Goldsturm strain.

A couple of other widely available coneflowers, usually listed as selections of *R. nitida*, have cylindrical green centers. 'Autumn Sun' ('Herbstsonne') bears single yellow daisies on stems to 6 feet; 'Goldquelle' has double yellow blooms on 3-foot stems.

Divide clumps of true perennial coneflowers every 2 to 4 years.

SALIX ALBA 'BRITZENSIS'
Coral embers willow
Deciduous shrub

Color: *Orange-red*
Season: *Winter*
Hardy to: *–40°F/–40°C; needs some winter chill*
Exposure: *Sun*
Water: *Regular*

This willow is prized for its luminous cold-season color: in winter, the bare bark is a radiant orange-red. During the growing season, the clump of upright stems is dressed in bright green leaves with a silvery underside; in many areas, the foliage turns yellow before dropping.

For the best winter display, cut back the clump to about a foot high just before spring growth begins. The stems will grow as much as 8 feet in a single season.

SALVIA
Sage, salvia
Annuals, perennials, and shrubs

Color: *Red, blue, purple, white, silver, green variegation*
Season: *Varies*
Hardy to: *Varies*
Exposure: *Sun*
Water: *Moderate*

Sages are diverse, undemanding plants with whorls of two-lipped, tubular flowers, mainly in blues and reds. The foliage is often coarse and aromatic.

Among the most widely planted hardy perennial sages are summer-blooming, vibrant purple 'East Friesland' and deep indigo 'May Night', both 2½-foot-tall cultivars of *S. × superba* (–20°F/–29°C). To encourage repeat bloom, cut back the spent flower spikes.

Mealy-cup sage, *S. farinacea* (10°F/–12°C), is often grown as an annual in cold climates. The species is a shrubby 3-footer bearing blue spikes in summer. 'Alba' is white; the Victoria series offers 1½-foot-high plants with blue or white blossoms.

Shrubby perennial scarlet sage, *S. splendens,* is a perennial—but even in mild climates, it's usually treated as a summer annual. Besides the original vivid scarlet, you'll find selections in salmon, lilac, purple, and white. Plants range from under a foot to a little over 2 feet tall.

Many free-blooming, drought-tolerant sages are indispensable in

Salvia farinacea

Santolina chamaecyparissus

Sanvitalia procumbens 'Gold Braid'

the arid West. One favorite is 3- to 4-foot-high, shrubby Mexican sage, *S. leucantha* (0°F/–18°C), which also does well in the Southeast. Bearing arching, twisting, velvety purple spikes, the plant puts on a show that starts in late summer and continues until frost kills it to the ground. In frost-free areas, it blooms all year.

Some sages are grown for their leaf color. Silver sage, *S. argentea* (–20°F/–29°C), a short-lived perennial often grown as a biennial, forms a mound of whitish foliage 2 to 3 feet high. Its whitish yellow blooms don't detract from the leaves.

Several selections of culinary sage, *S. officinalis* (–10°F/–23°C), are fancy-leafed. 'Icterina' has gray-green foliage marbled with pale green and yellow; 'Tricolor' is pink, gray-green, and cream; 'Purpurascens' has soft purple leaves; and 'Bergartten' is silvery gray.

SANTOLINA CHAMAECYPARISSUS
Lavender cotton
Small evergreen shrub

Color: Gray, yellow
Season: All year
Hardy to: –10°F/–23°C
Exposure: Sun
Water: Moderate

Too attractive to be restricted to the herb garden, lavender cotton deserves use as a pathway edger or an accent in the front of borders. The plant forms a 2-foot-high, spreading mound of feathery gray foliage; in most areas, it maintains its silvery presence throughout winter. It may die to the ground in the coldest part of its range, but will regrow from the roots.

In late spring to early summer, the foliage clump is studded with small, buttonlike yellow flowers. Trim the plant after flowering to keep it compact; otherwise, it tends to flop outward, leaving a bare patch in the middle. To rejuvenate untidy plants, cut them back in early spring.

SANVITALIA PROCUMBENS
Creeping zinnia
Perennial grown as annual

Color: Yellow, orange
Season: Spring, summer, fall
Exposure: Sun
Water: Moderate

From the onset of warm weather until frost, this small, trailing plant is blanketed with diminutive, dark-eyed, bright yellow single or double daisies. 'Mandarin Orange' is a vivid orange single-flowered form. Plants grow to about 8 inches high and spread about twice that wide.

A delightful choice for edgings, rock gardens, or window boxes, creeping zinnia is a heat-resistant plant that requires only moderate water once established. Don't let it go dry, though; if you do, it will stop blooming.

SARCOCOCCA
Sweet box
Evergreen shrubs

Color: Green
Season: All year
Hardy to: Varies
Exposure: Part shade, shade
Water: Regular

With their dark green, waxy foliage and graceful growth habits, these shade lovers are superior selections for any reduced-light location. The white blossoms that appear in late winter and early spring are very small, but powerfully fragrant. Black or red fruit follows the flowers.

S. confusa and *S. ruscifolia,* both hardy to about 0°F/–18°C, grow about 4 feet tall and a little wider. The former produces black berries, the latter red ones. A hardier species is black-fruited *S. hookerana humilis* (–10°F/–23°C), which reaches about 1½ feet tall and slowly spreads to 6 feet or more.

Sarcococca hookerana humilis

Scabiosa caucasica

SCABIOSA
Pincushion flower
Annuals and perennials

Color: *Blue, lavender, purple, pink, red, white*
Season: *Summer*
Hardy to: *–35°F/–37°C; not suited to Gulf Coast and Florida*
Exposure: *Sun*
Water: *Regular*

Pretty in borders and bouquets, pincushion flower produces unusual blossoms: each has a skirt of shallowly lobed, petal-like bracts surrounding a domed cushion of small flowers. A mass of stamens protrudes from this central disk—hence the plant's common name.

The following two species reach about 2½ feet tall and bloom for several months (or even longer, if spent flowers are removed). Plants perform best in mild-summer climates.

Among the longest-blooming of all perennials, *S. caucasica* bears 3-inch blossoms in sky blue, lavender, or white. The annual *S. atropurpurea* has dusky purple, lilac, red, pink, or white flowers about 2 inches across.

SCAEVOLA
Scaevola
Perennial

Color: *Blue*
Season: *Spring, summer, fall*
Hardy to: *20°F/–7°C*
Exposure: *Sun*
Water: *Moderate*

An Australian plant, scaevola produces a wealth of fan-shaped blossoms in blue shades over a long season.

The hybrid 'Mauve Clusters' resembles a bright green mat about 6 inches high and as much as 5 feet across; it produces clusters of small lilac-mauve flowers nearly year-round in the mildest climates.

Several cultivars of *S. aemula*—'Purple Fanfare', 'Diamond Head', and 'Blue Wonder'—are excellent planted at the tops of walls or in hanging baskets. Fleshy-stemmed, sprawling plants about 1½ feet tall, they bear lavender-blue flowers from spring through fall.

Scaevola can be treated as an annual in cold-winter climates.

Scaevola aemula 'Blue Wonder'

Scilla siberica

SCILLA
Squill
Deciduous bulb

Color: *Blue, pink, white*
Season: *Winter, spring*
Hardy to: *Varies*
Exposure: *Sun, part shade*
Water: *Regular*

These summer-dormant plants all have much the same form—a clump of strap-shaped leaves from which rise leafless stems carrying clusters of star-or bell-shaped flowers.

In areas that receive some winter chill, try the following two very early bloomers (both hardy to –30°F/–34°C). Winter-flowering *S. tubergeniana* has nodding clusters of pale blue, starlike blooms with a stripe down each flower segment. Siberian squill, *S. siberica*, blooms in late winter or early spring, exhibiting loose spikes of flaring bells in bright sky blue; violet-blue, purplish pink, and white forms are also sold. Both species grow about 6 inches high and naturalize well.

A good choice for mild-winter climates is Peruvian scilla, *S. peruviana* (20°F/–7°C). In late spring, the clump of floppy leaves sends up foot-tall stems, each topped by a domed cluster of 50 or more starlike, purplish blue flowers. Use this species as an edger or a pot plant.

Since squills need sun during bloom and part shade at other times, a location beneath deciduous trees is ideal. Water regularly during active growth, then ease off when the foliage yellows.

SEDUM 'AUTUMN JOY'
Stonecrop
Perennial

Color: *Pink, rust*
Season: *Late summer, fall, winter*
Hardy to: *–35°F/–37°C*
Exposure: *Sun*
Water: *Moderate*

Sedum 'Autumn Joy'

This 2-foot-high hybrid really earns its place in a colorful garden. It starts the growing season with fresh green foliage, then puts up broad flower clusters that open pale pink in late summer. In fall, the blossoms turn coppery pink and finally rosy rust, remaining attractive into winter—even if killed by a hard frost. The dried heads can be left in place as winter sculpture, then cut back when new growth emerges in spring.

SENECIO
Dusty miller, cineraria
Perennials and annuals

Color: *Purple, blue, red, pink, yellow, white, bicolors*
Season: *Varies*
Hardy to: *10°F/–12°C*
Exposure: *Varies*
Water: *Regular to moderate*

A sun-loving 2-footer, perennial dusty miller, *S. cineraria*, is grown for its nearly white foliage. Attractive throughout the growing season, the felted, deeply cut leaves may have rounded or blunt-tipped lobes. Remove yellow summertime daisies if they detract from the foliage; shear the plants occasionally to keep them compact. Provide moderate water.

In parts of the country with mild winters and cool summers, cineraria,

Senecio cineraria

S. × *hybridus*, provides brilliant color for shady spots. A perennial usually grown as an annual, this foot-high plant forms domed clusters of velvety blossoms in purple, blue, red, pink, yellow, and white, sometimes with contrasting centers. The bloom season comes in spring and early summer, or, in frost-free areas, in late winter and early spring. Give cineraria regular water.

SKIMMIA JAPONICA
Skimmia
Evergreen shrub

Color: *Red, white*
Season: *Fall, winter*
Hardy to: *0°F/–18°C*
Exposure: *Part shade, shade*
Water: *Regular*

Growing about 3 to 5 feet tall, skimmia has attractive dark green foliage

Skimmia japonica

Solidago sphacelata 'Golden Fleece'

that is aromatic when crushed. Clusters of small, fragrant white flowers appear in early spring, followed by a prominent display of berries that lasts through fall and winter—or even into the following spring.

For fruit production, you'll need both a female plant and a nearby male one to pollinate it. The basic species bears red berries; the more compact 'Fructo-Albo' (to 2½ feet) has white fruit.

SOLIDAGO
Goldenrod
Perennial

Color: Yellow
Season: Summer, fall
Hardy to: −30°F/−34°C
Exposure: Sun, part shade
Water: Moderate

Some very refined relatives of the familiar, cheerful roadside weed make lovely additions to the late-season garden. All such types of goldenrod form clumps of leafy stems topped by arching, feathery plumes made up of tiny daisies.

Various hybrids, ranging in height from about 1 to 3 feet, flower from mid to late summer into fall. Among the most widely available are 3-foot 'Goldenmosa' and 1½-foot 'Cloth of Gold'. The former begins blooming in midsummer, the latter a bit later.

S. sphacelata 'Golden Fleece' flowers in late summer and early fall, standing just 1 to 1½ feet high and wide when in bloom. A low foliage mound makes it a good ground cover.

Goldenrod is equally effective in outlying spots where the soil is poor or close up in borders and beds. Contrary to popular opinion, the plants don't cause hay fever.

SORBUS
Mountain ash
Deciduous trees

Color: White, red, orange, yellow
Season: Spring, fall, winter
Hardy to: Varies; needs some winter chill; not suited to hot-summer areas
Exposure: Sun
Water: Regular to moderate

In cold-winter regions where summers are not too hot, mountain ash puts on a varied color show throughout the year. The display begins with broad, flat white flower clusters scattered over the canopy; these develop into hanging bunches of small, applelike, typically red or orange-red fruits that color up in late summer or early fall—and can last until spring if not eaten by birds. To complete the show, the foliage generally takes on vivid hues before dropping.

The 20- to 40-foot-tall European species *S. aucuparia* (−40°F/−40°C) is

Sorbus aucuparia

the classic mountain ash, with large leaves divided into many leaflets, fall color in shades of yellow, red, and purple, and clusters of orange-red fruit. 'Cardinal Royal' has extra-large, vivid red fruit that colors early. Other cultivars include 'Apricot Queen' and yellow-fruiting 'Xanthocarpa'.

The 35-foot-tall *S. hupehensis* 'Coral Cascade' (−20°F/−29°C) is a red-fruited selection of a normally white-fruited species; its fall leaf color is red as well. This tree is highly resistant to fireblight, a disease afflicting mountain ash and various other rose-family members.

Spiraea japonica 'Little Princess'

Stachys byzantina 'Silver Carpet'

SPIRAEA
Spiraea, bridal wreath
Deciduous shrubs

Color: *White, pink, red*
Season: *Spring, summer*
Hardy to: *Varies*
Exposure: *Sun*
Water: *Regular to moderate*

The bridal wreath type of spiraea blooms in spring or early summer, bearing white flower clusters that cascade down arched branches. *S. × vanhouttei* (–20°F/–29°C) is the typical example; its clusters of single blooms appear on leafy stems that form a fountain 6 feet high by 8 feet wide (or wider). The foliage sometimes turns red in fall.

Another popular bridal wreath, also hardy to –20°F/–29°C, is *S. prunifolia* (often sold as *S. p.* 'Plena'). It's an airy plant with upright but arching stems and double blossoms that appear before the leaves emerge. The foliage turns vivid sunset colors in autumn.

Another spiraea group consists of summer- to fall-flowering, shrubby plants with pink or red blossoms clustered at the ends of upright branches. One member of this category is *S. japonica* (–10°F/–23°C); selections are usually sold rather than the basic species. Choices include 'Little Princess', a 1½-footer with pinkish red flowers, and the 3-foot 'Shirobana' ('Shibori'), which bears white, pink,

and rosy red blooms all on the same plant.

S. × bumalda (–20°F/–29°C) is a group of hybrids derived in part from *S. japonica*. 'Anthony Waterer', 2 to 3 feet high and 4 feet wide, has clusters of carmine red flowers and pinkish new growth. 'Limemound' is a 2-footer with pink blooms carried above lime green foliage that turns orange-red in fall.

Prune bridal wreath types of spiraea when they finish blooming; prune shrubby types in late winter or earliest spring.

STACHYS BYZANTINA 'SILVER CARPET'
Lamb's ears
Perennial

Color: *Gray*
Season: *All year*
Hardy to: *–30°F/–34°C; not suited to Gulf Coast and Florida*
Exposure: *Sun, part shade*
Water: *Moderate*

This nonflowering form of lamb's ears is grown strictly for its thick, velvety, tongue-shaped, whitish gray leaves. Use it as an accent, edging plant, or small-scale ground cover. Each plant forms an 8-inch-high clump that expands by underground stems; if bare spots develop, simply divide the clump and replant the pieces.

Stewartia monadelpha

STEWARTIA
Stewartia
Deciduous trees

Color: *White, red, orange, yellow; mottled browns and creams*
Season: *All year*
Hardy to: *–10°F/–23°C*
Exposure: *Part shade*
Water: *Regular*

Unbeatable for year-round color, stewartias feature camellialike white blossoms in summer, bright fall foliage, and smooth bark that flakes off to reveal a patchwork of green, gray, brown, rust, terra-cotta, and cream. For the most colorful bark, choose pyramidal Japanese stewartia, *S. pseudocamellia,* which may reach 30 to 40 feet after many years. Its leaves turn purplish in fall. *S. koreana* (sometimes considered a form of Japanese stewartia instead of a separate species) is more open in structure, with bright yellow to orange-red fall color.

Despite its name, tall stewartia, *S. monadelpha,* reaches only about 25 feet. Its branches angle upward; foliage turns bright red in fall.

Stewartias are lovely in woodland gardens and as foreground trees against a darker background. Success is limited to the West Coast, Southeast, and Mid-Atlantic states.

STOKESIA LAEVIS
Stokes' aster
Perennial

Color: *Blue, white*
Season: *Summer, fall*
Hardy to: *–20°F/–29°C*
Exposure: *Sun*
Water: *Regular to moderate*

Stokes' aster is a vigorous bloomer: loose clusters of 3- to 4-inch blossoms that resemble cornflowers or true asters keep coming all summer long. In seed-grown plants, flower color ranges from pale to fairly deep

blue, shading to cream in the middle, but cultivars in specific blue shades and white are available. In established clumps, the flowering stems grow 1½ to 2 feet high.

Plants bloom well into fall in mild climates; in frost-free areas, they'll flower intermittently all year if spent blossoms are removed. The foliage is evergreen in mild regions, only partly so in colder areas. Divide and replant crowded clumps.

STYRAX JAPONICUS
Japanese snowbell
Small deciduous tree

Color: *White*
Season: *Spring*
Hardy to: *–10°F/–23°C; not suited to hot, dry regions*
Exposure: *Sun, part shade*
Water: *Regular*

In spring, this tree's canopy is decorated with rich green, oval leaves and pendent clusters of lightly fragrant, bell-shaped white flowers. The foliage angles up from the branches, while the blossoms hang below; because of the tree's horizontal branching habit, the effect is one of parallel tiers of green and white. A lesser show comes in fall, when the leaves turn yellow or rusty red.

Small size (20 to 30 feet tall) and graceful appearance make Japanese snowbell an ideal choice for a patio, foundation, or understory tree. Deep, noncompetitive roots make it easy to garden under.

SYRINGA
Lilac
Deciduous shrubs

Color: *Blue, purple, magenta, pink, white, yellow, bicolors*
Season: *Spring*
Hardy to: *Varies; needs some winter chill*
Exposure: *Sun*
Water: *Regular*

A garden staple in cold-winter regions, lilacs are cherished for their big, flamboyant, fragrant flower clusters; once out of bloom, they're just plain bushes with no particular appeal. The blossoms appear at branch tips in early spring to early summer, depending on the climate.

Common lilac, *S. vulgaris* (–40°F/–40°C), is the classic species. Growing 8 to 15 feet tall and nearly as wide, it produces single or double flowers in clusters up to 10 inches long. The hundreds of cultivars come in white, pale yellow, and many gradations of blue and purple, including

Stokesia laevis

Styrax japonicus

Syringa vulgaris

Tagetes tenuifolia 'Lemon Gem'

Teucrium fruticans 'Azureum'

rosy shades. Those with dark buds opening to lighter blossoms give a bicolor effect, and true bicolors are available as well. Some types are more intensely fragrant or disease-resistant than others. The Descanso Hybrids, including the popular 'Lavender Lady', were developed for areas with little winter chill.

Other lilac species and hybrids vary in size and hardiness. Two compact types for borders are *S. patula* 'Miss Kim', 6 to 8 feet high and wide, with clusters of purple buds that open dark and fade to palest blue; and *S. meyeri* 'Palibin', 4 to 5 feet tall and a little wider, with reddish purple buds that open to light bluish pink. Both survive to –30°F/–34°C.

Since lilacs bloom on wood formed the previous year, prune them just after flowering ends. Remove spent blossom clusters and thin out stems at the base, leaving only the most vigorous ones.

TAGETES
Marigold
Annual

Color: *Orange, yellow, cream, bronze, red, bicolors*
Season: *Summer, fall*
Exposure: *Sun*
Water: *Regular*

These popular bedding and edging plants bloom quickly from seed, producing a bounty of color throughout summer—and even until frost, if you keep faded flowers snipped off.

Though associated with intense, hot shades of orange and yellow, marigolds also come in softer versions of those hues as well as in cream, various reds, and bicolors. Rising well above the dark green, finely cut leaves, the blossoms range from daisylike single blooms to double flowers resembling pompoms or carnations.

The myriad selections, most of them with strongly scented foliage, range from 6 inches to 4 feet in height. The various categories include generally tall, large-flowered African types; low-growing French marigolds; dwarf, small-blossomed signets; and sterile triploid hybrids, which bloom especially prolifically because they don't set seed.

Marigolds flourish in full sun, though those with creamy white blossoms need some afternoon shade in hot-summer climates.

TEUCRIUM FRUTICANS
Bush germander
Evergreen shrub

Color: *Gray, blue*
Season: *All year*
Hardy to: *0°F/–18°C*
Exposure: *Sun*
Water: *Moderate to little*

Bush germander forms a loose, airy jumble of silvery stems bearing little

leaves that are gray-green on top, silvery white beneath. Spiky new growth juts out here and there. The plant grows 4 to 8 feet tall and equally wide (or wider); 'Compactum' is a 3-footer.

Small lavender-blue flower clusters appear at branch tips sporadically throughout the year. 'Azureum' has deeper blue blossoms.

THALICTRUM
Meadow rue
Perennial

Color: *Purple, rosy lilac, yellow, white*
Season: *Late spring, summer*
Hardy to: *–20°F/–29°C; most need some winter chill; not suited to Gulf Coast and Florida*
Exposure: *Sun, part shade*
Water: *Regular*

Meadow rue's clump of ferny foliage produces leafy 2- to 6-foot stems topped by airy, many-branched flower clusters. The 2- to 3-foot *T. aquilegifolium* is the first species to bloom, showing off clouds of fluffy stamens (the light-colored sepals drop off) for a couple of weeks in late spring. Rosy lilac is the usual color, though white and purple selections are also available. If you leave the spent flowers in place, they'll be followed by attractive seed heads.

The 5-foot *T. speciosissimum* flowers in summer, bearing clouds that are lemon yellow in color but otherwise similar to those of *T. aquilegifolium*. Other summer-blooming species have petal-like sepals surrounding a cen-

Thalictrum

tral tuft of stamens; one such choice is 5-foot *T. rochebrunianum* 'Lavender Mist', with lavender sepals and yellow stamens. The 4- to 5-foot plants sold as *T. dipterocarpum* and *T. delavayi*, with sepals that may be dark lilac to violet, are the only meadow rues that really succeed in mild-winter regions. Double lilac 'Hewitt's Double' has a bloom period lasting for 2 months or more.

All the meadow rues thrive in the dappled sunlight at woodland edges. They can take full sun in cool-summer regions. Divide clumps every 4 or 5 years.

THUNBERGIA ALATA
Black-eyed Susan vine
Perennial vine grown as annual

Color: *Orange, yellow, white*
Season: *Summer*
Exposure: *Sun*
Water: *Regular*

This rapidly growing tropical vine blooms the first year after planting, making it useful as a colorful annual in all regions. Its flaring inch-wide trumpets are typically orange with a black eye, though yellow and white selections as well as sorts without the dark center are sold.

Covered with triangular, furry, bright green leaves, the plant twines rapidly to about 10 feet up any available support—even the stem of an open-structured shrub. It lives over in the warmest climates, where it's sometimes used as a ground cover.

THYMUS PSEUDOLANUGINOSUS
Woolly thyme
Evergreen ground cover

Color: *Gray*
Season: *All year*
Hardy to: *–30°F/–34°C*
Exposure: *Sun*
Water: *Moderate*

A pleasing choice for rock gardens, the edges of raised beds, or the spaces between stepping stones, woolly thyme covers a small area with an undulating, aromatic gray mat 2 to 3 inches high. The tiny, fuzzy leaves are closely spaced, creating a dense covering. The plant only occasionally produces small pink flowers.

Provide some shade where summers are hot.

TITHONIA ROTUNDIFOLIA
Mexican sunflower
Perennial grown as annual

Color: *Orange*
Season: *Summer, fall*
Exposure: *Sun*
Water: *Regular*

Glowing orange, 3- to 4-inch daisies with yellowish orange centers decorate this profusely blooming, coarse-leafed species from summer until frost. The plant is a robust 6-footer, though some lower-growing selections are available.

Mexican sunflower is extremely heat-resistant, growing well even in desert gardens. Stake it to maintain upright growth.

Tithonia rotundifolia

Thunbergia alata

Thymus pseudolanuginosus

Trachelospermum jasminoides

Trollius ledebourii 'Golden Queen'

TRACHELOSPERMUM JASMINOIDES
Star jasmine
Evergreen vine or ground cover

Color: *White*
Season: *Late spring, early summer*
Hardy to: *15°F/–9°C*
Exposure: *Sun, part shade*
Water: *Regular*

Though not a true jasmine, this plant has the intensely sweet fragrance associated with jasmines. Plentiful clusters of small, pinwheel-shaped white blossoms appear for a couple of months starting in late spring; the shiny, oval dark green leaves are handsome all year.

Given support, star jasmine twines to about 20 feet high, but it's more often used as a ground cover. Each plant spreads 4 to 5 feet and mounds to about 2 feet high; pinch back upright shoots to maintain a neat, horizontal appearance. Star jasmine is especially attractive under trees or spilling over walls.

TROLLIUS
Globeflower
Perennial

Color: *Yellow, orange*
Season: *Late spring, summer*
Hardy to: *–30°F/–34°C*
Exposure: *Sun, part shade*
Water: *Regular*

Given ample moisture, this buttercup relative forms a robust clump of fine-ly cut leaves, then sends up tall stems topped by roundly cupped to globular blooms in rich yellow and orange shades.

The classic globeflower is *T. europaeus* 'Superbus', a 2-foot-tall midspring bloomer with 2-inch, butter yellow blossoms. Various hybrids listed as *T. × cultorum* bloom from late spring into summer; these include 2-foot 'Lemon Queen' (soft yellow), 2½-foot 'Golden Monarch' (canary yellow), and 3-foot 'Etna' (orange). Blooming in summer is *T. ledebourii* 'Golden Queen', with 4-inch yellow-orange flowers on 3-foot stems. Removing spent blooms from all types prolongs the flowering period.

Plants don't tolerate heat or drought, and they accept full sun only in cool-summer climates. Divide clumps when they thin out in the middle.

TROPAEOLUM MAJUS
Nasturtium
Annual

Color: *Orange, yellow, cream, red, pink, bicolors*
Season: *Summer*
Exposure: *Sun*
Water: *Regular*

These familiar favorites are known for their round, bright green leaves and bountiful long-spurred, single or double blooms in orange, yellow, creamy white, and various red shades.

Climbing types trail over the ground or climb to 6 feet by coiling their leafstalks around supports. The more widely sold dwarf forms, which grow from under a foot to about 15 inches high, make good edgers. The young foliage and flowers of both types have a peppery flavor and can be used in salads.

In cold-winter regions, nasturtiums bloom primarily in summer, though they don't thrive in extreme heat and humidity. The best show comes from winter into spring in milder climates, where the plants live over and often self-sow.

Tropaeolum majus

Tulipa 'Blue Heron'

TULIPA
Tulip
Deciduous bulb

Color: Purple, red, pink, lavender, yellow, orange, cream, white, green, bicolors
Season: Late winter, spring
Hardy to: –40°F/–40°C; most need some winter chill
Exposure: Sun, part shade
Water: Regular

The thousands of different tulips are grouped into more than a dozen hybrid categories and upwards of a hundred species. The flowers come in all colors except true blue; plant height ranges from 6 inches to 3 feet. Bloom time varies, too—so by planting a selection of early, midseason, and late types, you can enjoy tulips from late winter through spring.

All tulip hybrids and most species do well the first year if they receive sufficient cold (refrigerate them first in mild climates), but they peter out in subsequent years and should be replaced. Some of the smaller species tulips, however, are truly perennial and return year after year.

The hybrid groupings include tulips with the traditional egg-shaped blooms as well as those with more unusual forms, such as lily-flowered (with pointed petal tips), parrot (with feathery petals), and double late (with peonylike blossoms).

Among the most widely available species (along with their varieties and hybrids) are *T. fosterana*, bearing huge blooms up to 8 inches across on stems to 20 inches high; *T. greigii*, with large flowers and beautifully mottled leaves on plants 10 to 14 inches tall; and *T. kaufmanniana*, producing pointy-tipped, wide-open blossoms on 4- to 8-inch stems.

One of the best perennial types for climates with little winter chill is the lady tulip, *T. clusiana*. Its 9-inch stems are topped with two-tone blooms that are creamy white inside, striped rosy red outside; *T. c. chrysantha* substitutes yellow for white. These bulbs don't require refrigeration.

Tulips need regular water while actively growing and blooming, but little moisture while dormant. The ideal planting site is beneath deciduous trees that leaf out after the tulips have finished flowering. Light shade will help prolong the bloom of late-flowering types.

VERBASCUM
Mullein
Perennial

Color: Yellow, white, purple, pink, gray
Season: Spring, summer
Hardy to: –20°F/–29°C
Exposure: Sun
Water: Moderate

For striking vertical accents, look to these undemanding plants. From rosettes of broad, grayish leaves rise upright, 1- to 6-foot spires closely set with nearly circular blossoms about an inch across. Depending on the species, the flower spikes may be single or branched.

V. chaixii has woolly gray-green foliage and 3-foot-high, unbranched stems that bear red-eyed, light yellow flowers in late spring or early summer. 'Album' is a white-petaled form.

Verbascum chaixii (center) and V. c. 'Album'

Hybrids of purple mullein, *V. phoeniceum*, grow 3 to 5 feet tall and produce blooms in white, yellow, and warm pink as well as purple.

The fuzzy gray-white leaves of *V. olympicum* are attractive throughout the growing season. Branched spikes to 6 feet high bear yellow flowers for up to a couple of months in summer.

Cut off spent spikes of perennial mulleins to encourage a second round of blooming. When growing biennial species, though, leave the spikes in place for reseeding. Keep all types on the dry side.

VERBENA
Verbena
Perennials, some grown as annuals

Color: Purple, blue, pink, red, orange, yellow, white, bicolors
Season: Spring, summer, fall
Hardy to: 10°F/–12°C
Exposure: Sun
Water: Moderate

The low, spreading plants grouped as *V.* × *hybrida* are treated as annual

Verbena × *hybrida*

Veronica 'Blue Charm'

bedding plants everywhere—even in mild climates, where they can live over for a few years. From summer into fall, the plants are blanketed with flat clusters of fragrant flowers in nearly every color of the rainbow, as well as bicolors. Among the most subtle is 9-inch 'Peaches & Cream', with blooms in a blend of apricot, cream, orange, and yellow.

Fast-spreading, 1½- to 2-foot *V. rigida* produces tight clusters of little purple blossoms in branching sprays at the ends of stiff, upright stems. Pale lilac and white selections also exist. The plants can be treated as annuals or perennials; they bloom from mid or late spring until frost.

V. bonariensis resembles a taller, airier version of *V. rigida*. Its clusters of purple blooms are carried on stiffly branching sprays at the ends of 4- to 6-foot, nearly leafless stems. A short-lived perennial that reseeds itself in mild climates, this plant is grown as a summer annual in colder regions.

VERONICA
Speedwell
Perennial

Color: *Purple, blue, pink, white*
Season: *Late spring, summer, fall*
Hardy to: *–30°F/–34°C*
Exposure: *Sun, part shade*
Water: *Regular*

There are some 250 speedwell species, ranging from 4 inches to 4 feet high and bearing flowers mainly in blue shades. They can be divided into upright and sprawling types; the former are lovely in borders, while the latter are suitable for rock gardens and edgings.

Upright speedwells form foliage clumps, which send up tall, candle-like spikes made up of tiny star-shaped flowers. Midsummer is the prime bloom time, though some types begin flowering in late spring, especially in mild climates. A notable hybrid is foot-high *V.* 'Goodness Grows', which produces long dark blue spikes from spring until the first hard frost in fall.

Since there's confusion about names, it's easiest to choose speedwells based on the stated plant height, flower color, and foliage color. Most upright kinds are in the 1½- to 2½-foot range; flowers typically come in purple and blue shades, though some selections are white or pink. Leaf colors include green and gray-white.

The more sprawling speedwells, which grow from about 6 inches to 1½ feet high and feature shorter flower spikes, are associated with *V. latifolia*. Perhaps the best-known selection is foot-high 'Crater Lake Blue', which produces its vivid true-blue blossoms earlier than most speedwells.

Remove faded spikes from any speedwell to encourage additional flowering on secondary spikes. Divide clumps when their vigor declines. Provide light shade in the hottest regions.

VIBURNUM
Viburnum
Deciduous and evergreen shrubs

Color: *White, red, pink*
Season: *All year*
Hardy to: *Varies*
Exposure: *Sun, part shade*
Water: *Regular*

Attractive as both specimen and background plantings, these handsome shrubs range in height from about 2 to 20 feet.

Deciduous species are grown for their showy white or pink flower clusters, bright berries, and vivid fall foliage. The following three are among the most dramatic.

Korean spice viburnum, *V. carlesii* (–20°F/–29°C), blooms in early and midspring, bearing 3-inch, rounded clusters of fragrant white blossoms that open from pink buds. Blue-black berries ripen in summer; in fall, the

Viburnum plicatum tomentosum 'Mariesii'

Vinca minor

oval dark green leaves turn bright red. The basic species is 8 feet high, while 'Compactum' is about half that size.

Cranberry bush viburnum, *V. opulus* (–40°F/–40°C), is an upright, arching plant reaching 10 to 20 feet high. A midspring bloomer, it shows off 4-inch white "lace caps" (larger sterile flowers encircling tiny fertile blossoms) against maplelike foliage. Showy red berries decorate the branches in fall and winter; the leaves also redden in fall. The fruitless form 'Roseum' bears 3-inch snowballs composed of sterile flowers only.

Horizontal branching gives 15-foot doublefile viburnum, *V. plicatum tomentosum* (–20°F/–29°C), a graceful, layered look during midspring bloom. Its oval dark green leaves point down, while the 4- to 6-inch, white lace cap clusters are held above the branches. The berries that develop are red, aging to black. 'Mariesii' has larger flower clusters, and 'Pink Beauty' has pale pink blooms fading to white. White-blossomed, 6-foot 'Summer Snowflake' flowers from midspring through summer.

Evergreen viburnums are valued mainly for their outstanding foliage; flowers and fruit are a bonus. One of the finest species for unclipped hedges and screens is laurustinus, *V.*

tinus (0°F/–18°C), an upright grower to 12 feet tall and half that wide. Dressing up the oval, leathery dark green leaves from midfall into spring are 3- to 4-inch, lightly fragrant clusters of white flowers that open from pink buds; blue berries follow the blossoms and last through summer. More compact cultivars and those with variegated foliage also exist.

VINCA
Periwinkle
Evergreen ground cover

Color: *Blue, white*
Season: *Spring*
Hardy to: *Varies*
Exposure: *Part shade, shade*
Water: *Moderate*

This evergreen perennial's trailing, arching stems root where they touch the soil. The shiny dark green leaves are oval to oblong; lavender-blue, five-petaled, pinwheel-shaped blooms appear in the leaf joints in spring.

V. major (10°F/–12°C) is the larger species, with leaves up to 3 inches long and flowers as big as 2 inches across. It's an aggressive plant, spreading rapidly and mounding 1 to 2 feet high—and should be sheared close to the ground occasionally. A form with creamy leaf variegation exists.

Dwarf periwinkle, *V. minor* (–30°F/–34°C), is a miniature version with smaller leaves and flowers and a height of just 6 inches. Because its growth is much more restrained than that of *V. major*, it's less likely to invade adjacent plantings. Forms with variegated leaves and selections with white, deeper blue, and double flowers are available.

Both species tolerate sun if given ample water.

VIOLA
Violet, pansy
Annuals and perennials

Color: *Violet, purple, blue, pink, red, orange, yellow, white, bicolors*
Season: *Spring, summer*
Hardy to: *–10°F/–23°C*
Exposure: *Sun, part shade, shade*
Water: *Regular*

These low-growing plants, all of which produce five-petaled blooms during cool weather, can be divided into two major groups: violets and pansies.

True violets are perennial. All bear a spur on the lower flower petal, though it may be fairly short in some modern selections. Prolific self-seeding makes them ideal for woodland gardens: let them meander through plantings or colonize the ground beneath deciduous trees and shrubs.

Sweet violet, *V. odorata,* is typical of the category. Sweet-scented, spurred blossoms rise above long-stalked, nearly round leaves in early spring. Violet is the standard flower color, but dark blue, rosy pink, and white forms also exist. Selections range from about 2 to 10 inches high. Provide some shade.

True species pansies aren't grown as often as the modern hybrids known as *V.* × *wittrockiana.* Above heart-shaped or oval leaves, the flowering stems rise about 8 inches high, bearing big, velvety blooms with overlapping petals. Up to 3 inches across, the flowers come in a wide variety of colors—sometimes solid-colored, sometimes with contrasting blotches or centers. Lovely in beds and borders, these short-lived perennials are treated as annuals. Give sun or part shade.

The main bloom time for pansies traditionally comes in early spring to early summer. However, they grow well in late winter and spring on the West Coast as well as in the Southeast and mild parts of the Mid-Atlantic.

WEIGELA FLORIDA
Weigela
Deciduous shrub

Color: *Pink, red, white*
Season: *Spring*
Hardy to: *–20°F/–29°C*
Exposure: *Sun*
Water: *Regular*

An unassuming plant most of the year, weigela erupts into spectacular bloom in spring. The cascading branches are cloaked in clusters of funnel-shaped, pink to rosy red blossoms. Two noteworthy hybrids are 'Bristol Ruby', with red flowers, and 'Mont Blanc', bearing fragrant white blooms. The selection 'Variegata' has white-edged leaves and deep rose blossoms.

Plants grow to about 10 feet high and as wide or a little wider. More compact forms are also commonly available.

Use weigela singly in a mixed border or mass it for a background planting. Since the plant blooms on wood formed during the previous year, prune it right after flowering is finished.

WISTERIA
Wisteria
Deciduous vine

Color: *Blue, white, pink*
Season: *Spring, summer*
Hardy to: *–20°F/–29°C*
Exposure: *Sun, part shade*
Water: *Regular to moderate*

A big, woody vine that ascends by twining, wisteria can also be trained as a sprawling shrub or a tree. It produces huge, drooping clusters of sweet-scented, sweet pea–shaped flowers, either before or as the foliage emerges. The large leaves are divided into many leaflets.

Japanese wisteria, *W. floribunda,* flowers in early to midspring during leaf-out, producing violet or blue-violet, quite fragrant blossoms in 1½-foot clusters. Forms in various other blue shades, white, and pink are also available. In all types, the clusters open gradually, starting from the base. These plants grow best in sun.

Chinese wisteria, *W. sinensis,* blooms before its leaves emerge, producing slightly fragrant, violet-blue

Viola × *wittrockiana*

Weigela florida

Wisteria sinensis

Zantedeschia aethiopica

Zephyranthes candida

Zinnia elegans

clusters up to a foot long. Though smaller than those of the Japanese species, they open all at once and so provide a more dramatic display. White forms also exist. This species blooms in sun or part shade.

Wisteria is so vigorous that it should be pruned twice yearly—once after flowering and again in mid to late winter. In cold-winter climates, the plants can take many years to bloom.

ZANTEDESCHIA AETHIOPICA
Calla lily
Rhizomatous perennial

Color: White, cream
Season: Spring, summer
Hardy to: 10°F/–12°C
Exposure: Sun, part shade
Water: Regular

A bold accent plant, calla lily forms a handsome clump of huge, arrow-shaped leaves to 1½ feet long and 10 inches wide. The flower stems appear in early spring to early summer, extending slightly above the 3-foot foliage mass and each bearing an 8-inch-long, pure white or creamy bract resembling an upturned bell. 'Green Goddess' is white toward the base of the bract, green toward the tip. You'll also find smaller varieties, some as low as a foot.

Calla lilies are sold as dormant rhizomes or nursery plants. Evergreen in mild-winter climates, the clumps should be divided every few years.

ZEPHYRANTHES CANDIDA
Fairy lily
Deciduous or evergreen bulb

Color: White
Season: Late summer, early fall
Hardy to: 0°F/–18°C
Exposure: Sun, part shade
Water: Regular

Fairy lily makes a delicate show in rock gardens or at the front of borders. In late summer and early fall,

flowering stems rise about level with the foot-high clump of stiff, rushlike leaves, each holding a solitary, 2- to 3-inch white bloom with orange stamens. The exterior of the petals is sometimes brushed with pink.

In frost-free regions, encourage additional bloom cycles by letting the plants dry out briefly after flowering.

ZINNIA ELEGANS
Zinnia
Annual

Color: White, yellow, orange, red, pink, lavender, purple, bicolors
Season: Summer, fall
Exposure: Sun
Water: Moderate

This elegant border plant blooms profusely through the heat of summer, providing splendid color until the first frost. Choose from hundreds of cultivars with single or double blossoms, colors in every shade but true blue, flower shapes ranging from flat-petaled to dahlialike, and heights varying from 6 inches to 3 feet.

The rough-textured, light green leaves are handsome—except when afflicted with mildew. Be sure to buy resistant strains in areas where this disease typically ravages zinnias.

These plants are heat-tolerant, though they decline quickly in very hot, humid climates. They require less water than many other flowering annuals.

Index

All photographs except those in the encyclopedia, pages 113–205, are indicated by *italicized* page numbers.

Acacia baileyana, 71, 114
Acer, 10, 14, 15, 63, 90, 91, 96, 107, 114
Achillea, 39, 46, 47, 61, 70, 83, 84, 97, 101, 102, 103, 111, 115
Aconitum, 34, 55, 115
Agapanthus, 47, 53, 55, 115–116
Ageratum houstonianum, 55, 116
Ajuga reptans, 55, 96, 97, 116
Alcea rosea, 60, 63, 65, 116
Alchemilla mollis, 76, 76–77, 78, 99, 117
All-America Selections, 109
Allium, 53, 54, 55, 71, 117
Alstroemeria, 34, 71, 117
Alyssum. See Lobularia maritima.
Amaranthus, 61, 63, 78, 118
Amelanchier, 47, 118
Amethyst flower. See Browallia speciosa.
Amsonia tabernaemontana, 55, 118
Anaphalis, 46, 47, 84, 118
Anchusa azurea, 36, 55, 119
Anemone × hybrida, 47, 98, 99, 119
Angelica archangelica, 76, 78, 119
Annuals, explained, 106
Anthemis tinctoria, 71, 119–120
Antirrhinum majus, 36, 47, 63, 71, 120
Aquilegia, 9, 54, 55, 71, 101, 120–121
Arabis caucasica, 47, 102, 121
Arbutus, 12, 14, 63, 121
Arrhenatherum elatius 'Variegatum', 47, 99, 121
Artemisia, 44, 82, 83, 83, 84, 98, 121–122
Arum italicum 'Pictum', 76, 78, 122
Aruncus dioicus, 46, 46, 47, 122
Asclepias tuberosa, 71, 103, 123
Aster, 55, 63, 97, 123
Astilbe, 47, 63, 98, 108, 123
Aurinia saxatilis, 71, 124
Autumn crocus. See Colchicum autumnale.
Autumn fern. See Dryopteris.
Avens. See Geum.
Azalea. See Rhododendron.

Baby blue eyes. See Nemophila menziesii.
Baby's breath. See Gypsophila paniculata.
Bachelor's button. See Centaurea.
Balloon flower. See Platycodon grandiflorus.
Ballota pseudodictamnus, 84, 124
Baptisia australis, 53, 55, 124
Barberry. See Berberis.
Basket-of-gold. See Aurinia saxatilis.
Beach wormwood. See Artemisia.
Beard tongue. See Penstemon.
Beauty bush. See Kolkwitzia amabilis.
Beds and borders, 26, 92–94, 102
Bee balm. See Monarda didyma.
Belamcanda chinensis, 125
Bellflower. See Campanula.
Bells-of-Ireland. See Moluccella laevis.
Berberis, 4, 25, 63, 65, 71, 72, 96, 99, 102, 125
Bergenia, 63, 99, 125

Bethlehem sage. See Pulmonaria.
Betula, 14, 15, 89, 126
Biennials, explained, 106
Big blue lily turf. See Liriope muscari.
Birch. See Betula.
Birch bark cherry. See Prunus.
Blackberry lily. See Belamcanda chinensis.
Black-eyed Susan. See Rudbeckia.
Black-eyed Susan vine. See Thunbergia alata.
Blanket flower. See Gaillardia.
Bleeding heart. See Dicentra spectabilis.
Bluebell. See Endymion.
Blue color category, 50–57
Blue fescue. See Festuca ovina glauca.
Blue marguerite. See Felicia amelloides.
Blue poppy. See Meconopsis.
Blue spruce. See Picea pungens.
Blue star. See Amsonia tabernaemontana.
Boston ivy. See Parthenocissus tricuspidata.
Botanical name, explained, 108
Botanical wonder. See × Fatshedera lizei.
Bougainvillea, 37, 47, 107, 126
Boxwood. See Buxus.
Brachycome, 55, 126
Brassica oleracea, 10, 38, 63, 127
Bridal wreath. See Spiraea.
Browallia speciosa, 55, 127
Brunnera macrophylla, 53, 55, 127
Buddleia, 55, 101, 128
Bugbane. See Cimicifuga racemosa.
Bulbs, explained, 106–107
Burning bush. See Euonymus.
Bush germander. See Teucrium fruticans.
Bush morning glory. See Convolvulus cneorum.
Busy Lizzie. See Impatiens wallerana.
Butterfly bush. See Buddleia.
Butterfly weed. See Asclepias tuberosa.
Buxus, 50, 76, 78, 102, 128

Cabbage, flowering. See Brassica oleracea.
Caladium bicolor, 10, 128
Calceolaria crenatiflora, 8, 71, 129
Calendula officinalis, 71, 100, 103, 129
California poppy. See Eschscholzia californica.
Calla lily. See Zantedeschia aethiopica.
Calluna vulgaris, 63, 96, 129
Camellia, 47, 61, 63, 76, 78, 107, 129–130
Campanula, 53, 54–55, 101, 130
Campsis, 63, 71, 130
Candytuft. See Iberis.
Canna, 71, 131
Cardinal flower. See Lobelia.
Cardoon. See Cynara cardunculus.
Carnation. See Dianthus.
Carpet bugle. See Ajuga reptans.
Catalogs, ordering from, 108–109
Catananche caerulea, 55, 101, 131
Catharanthus roseus, 46, 47, 131
Catmint. See Nepeta × faassenii.
Ceanothus, 53, 131–132
Celosia, 60, 63, 71, 103, 132
Centaurea, 44, 55, 82, 83, 83, 84, 132
Cerastium tomentosum, 44, 46, 47, 80, 83, 84, 97, 132–133

Ceratostigma plumbaginoides, 54, 55, 133
Cercis, 63, 133
Chaenomeles, 63, 133
Cherry plum. See Prunus.
Chinese forget-me-not. See Cynoglossum amabile.
Chinese lantern plant. See Physalis alkekengi.
Christmas rose. See Helleborus.
Chrysanthemum, 44, 45, 46–47, 47, 71, 83, 84, 98, 134
Cimicifuga racemosa, 47, 134
Cineraria. See Senecio.
Cinquefoil. See Potentilla.
Cistus, 44, 47, 134–135
Clematis, 16, 43, 47, 54, 55, 58, 61, 63, 102, 109, 135
Cleome hasslerana, 47, 60, 135
Clethra alnifolia, 47, 91, 135–136
Climate zones, 108
Cobaea scandens, 55, 136
Cockscomb. See Celosia.
Colchicum autumnale, 63, 136
Colorado spruce. See Picea pungens.
Color, locations for displaying, 19–27
Color schemes, 33–39, 88–89
Color, sources of, 105–111
   bark and stems, 14–15, 87
   flowers, 8–9, 87
   foliage, 10–11, 87,89, 90, 91, 96
   fruit, 12–13, 87, 89
   landscaping materials, 16–17, 90
Color, special uses of, 37
Color spectrum, 32–33
Color terms, explained, 31–32, 42
Color theory, 30–36, 91
   pigments and, 31, 91
Color, timing of, 88–90
Color wheel, 32
Columbine. See Aquilegia.
Common name, explained, 108
Coneflower. See Rudbeckia.
Convallaria majalis, 47, 101, 136–137
Convolvulus cneorum, 47, 84, 137
Cool colors, 33, 97
Coral bells. See Heuchera.
Coral embers willow. See Salix alba 'Britzensis'.
Coreopsis, 54, 67, 71, 103, 111, 137
Cornelian cherry. See Cornus.
Cornflower. See Centaurea.
Cornus, 8, 14, 47, 48, 63, 64, 70, 70, 71, 89, 99, 137–138
Cosmos, 9, 47, 63, 71, 90, 98, 138
Cotinus coggygria, 10, 50, 55, 56, 138
Cotoneaster, 12, 13, 63, 64, 78, 89, 138–139
Cottage gardens, 36, 36, 90, 101
Crabapple. See Malus.
Cranesbill. See Geranium.
Crape myrtle. See Lagerstroemia.
Crataegus, 12, 47, 59, 63, 64, 139
Cream color category, 42–49
Creeping zinnia. See Sanvitalia procumbens.
Crete dittany. See Origanum dictamnus.
Crocosmia × crocosmiiflora, 68, 71, 139
Crocus, 55, 93, 139–140
Crown imperial. See Fritillaria imperialis.
Crown-pink. See Lychnis coronaria.
Cultivar, explained, 109
Cup-and-saucer vine. See Cobaea scandens.
Cup flower. See Nierembergia hippomanica.
Cupid's dart. See Catananche caerulea.

Cynara cardunculus, 84, 140
Cynoglossum amabile, 55, 140

Daffodil. See Narcissus.
Dahlia, 18, 23, 44–45, 48, 63, 71, 140
Daphne, 63, 141
Daylily. See Hemerocallis.
Dead nettle. See Lamium maculatum.
Delphinium, 18, 22, 23, 28, 34, 39, 50, 53, 54, 55, 101, 141
Design
   examples, 96–103
   formal, 92, 94
   informal, 92, 93, 94
   planning and, 88, 94–95
Dianthus, 48, 62, 63, 98, 102, 103, 106, 141–142
Dicentra spectabilis, 42, 48, 63, 142
Dictamnus albus, 48, 63, 97, 102, 142
Digitalis, 36, 48, 57, 58, 61, 63, 71, 99, 101, 106, 142–143
Diospyros kaki, 13, 71, 72, 143
Dogwood. See Cornus.
Doronicum, 71, 143
Drifts, 93, 111
Dryopteris, 78, 143–144
Dusty miller. See Artemisia, Centaurea, Chrysanthemum, Senecio.
Dutch hyacinth. See Hyacinthus.
Dwarf plumbago. See Ceratostigma plumbaginoides.
Dwarf witch alder. See Fothergilla gardenii.

Echinacea purpurea, 61, 64, 102, 144
Echinops, 8, 54, 56, 144
Edible garden, 100
Elaeagnus, 11, 84, 96, 144–145
Endymion, 53, 54, 56, 145
English ivy. See Hedera helix.
English laurel. See Prunus.
Eranthis hyemalis, 71, 72, 145
Erica, 64, 145–146
Erigeron, 28, 31, 37, 56, 146
Eryngium, 56, 146
Erysimum, 72, 146–147
Eschscholzia californica, 36, 46–47, 68, 72, 77, 101, 147
Euonymus, 48, 62–63, 64, 72, 89, 91, 96, 147
Euphorbia, 72, 73, 78, 79, 147–148
Evening primrose. See Oenothera.
Everlasting, pearly. See Anaphalis.

Fairy lily. See Zephyranthes candida.
Fall color, 10, 91, 107.
False dragonhead. See Physostegia virginiana.
False indigo. See Baptisia australis.
False oatgrass. See Arrhenatherum elatius 'Variegatum'.
False spiraea. See Astilbe.
False sunflower. See Heliopsis helianthoides.
× Fatshedera lizei, 76, 78, 148
Felicia amelloides, 56, 148
Festuca ovina glauca, 56, 148–149
Filipendula rubra, 61, 64, 101, 149
Firethorn. See Pyracantha.
Flax. See Linum.
Fleabane. See Erigeron.
Floss flower. See Ageratum houstonianum.
Flowering cabbage. See Brassica oleracea.
Flowering cherry. See Prunus.
Flowering kale. See Brassica oleracea.
Flowering quince. See Chaenomeles.

Flowering tobacco. See Nicotiana.
Forsythia, 72, 149
Fothergilla gardenii, 48, 149
Foxglove. See Digitalis.
Fritillaria imperialis, 72, 150

Gaillardia, 67, 70, 72, 150
Galanthus, 46, 48, 150
Gas plant. See Dictamnus albus.
Gaura lindheimeri, 31, 44, 48, 97, 150–151
Gayfeather. See Liatris spicata.
Gazania, 8, 72, 151
Gentiana asclepiadea, 56, 151
Genus, explained, 108
Geranium, 39, 55, 58, 62, 63, 64, 151–152. See also Pelargonium.
Geum, 68, 72, 103, 152
Ginkgo biloba, 11, 72, 91, 152
Gladiolus, 72, 103, 152
Globe amaranth. See Gomphrena globosa.
Globeflower. See Trollius.
Globe thistle. See Echinops.
Goatsbeard. See Aruncus dioicus.
Goldenchain tree. See Laburnum × watereri.
Golden locust. See Robinia pseudoacacia 'Frisia'.
Golden marguerite. See Anthemis tinctoria.
Golden mimosa. See Acacia baileyana.
Goldenrod. See Solidago.
Gomphrena globosa, 64, 153
Gooseneck loosestrife. See Lysimachia clethroides.
Grape hyacinth. See Muscari.
Gray color category, 80–85
Green color category, 74–79
Ground covers, explained, 107
Gypsophila paniculata, 44–45, 46, 48, 98, 101, 115, 153

Hamamelis, 5, 9, 10, 70, 72, 153–154
Hawthorn. See Crataegus.
Heath. See Erica.
Heather. See Calluna vulgaris.
Hedera helix, 78, 107, 148, 154
Helenium, 72, 154
Helianthemum nummularium, 64, 154
Helianthus, 70, 72, 154–155
Helichrysum bracteatum, 72, 155
Heliopsis helianthoides, 72, 155
Heliotrope. See Heliotropium arborescens.
Heliotropium arborescens, 56, 155–156
Helleborus, 44, 48, 64, 76, 78, 99, 156
Hemerocallis, 20, 38, 62, 66, 70, 72, 97, 102, 109, 156
Heuchera, 64, 97, 156–157
Hibiscus, 48, 56, 97, 111, 157
Holly. See Ilex.
Hollyhock. See Alcea rosea.
Hosta, 11, 42, 48, 56, 65, 77, 78, 96, 99, 157–158
Houttuynia cordata 'Variegata', 158
Hyacinthus, 54, 56, 68, 72, 158
Hybrid, explained, 109
Hydrangea, 9, 48, 56, 57, 76, 78, 91, 108, 158–159
Hypericum, 72, 159

Iberis, 48, 97, 159–160
Ilex, 12, 64, 76, 78, 160
Impatiens wallerana, 35, 48, 60, 64, 72, 95, 106, 160

Imperata cylindrica 'Rubra', 64, 96, 160–161
Ipomoea tricolor, 56, 161
Iris, 48, 56, 69, 72, 97, 98, 99, 102, 161–162
Italian bugloss. See Anchusa azurea.
Ivy, English. See Hedera helix.

Jacaranda mimosifolia, 56, 162
Japanese anemone. See Anemone × hybrida.
Japanese blood grass. See Imperata cylindrica 'Rubra'.
Japanese persimmon. See Diospyros kaki.
Japanese snowbell. See Styrax japonicus.
Japanese spurge. See Pachysandra terminalis.
Jasminum, 72, 162
Jekyll, Gertrude, 50, 92, 93
Judas tree. See Cercis.
Juniperus, 52, 56, 78, 162–163

Kale, flowering. See Brassica oleracea.
Kalmia latifolia, 64, 163
Kerria japonica, 72, 163
Kniphofia uvaria, 38, 66, 68, 72, 163–164
Kochia scoparia, 78, 164
Kolkwitzia amabilis, 64, 164

Laburnum × watereri, 70, 72, 164–165
Lady's mantle. See Alchemilla mollis.
Lagerstroemia, 56, 102, 165
Lamb's ears. See Stachys byzantina 'Silver Carpet'.
Lamium maculatum, 44, 48, 83, 84, 98, 99, 165
Lantana, 56, 72, 165–166
Lathyrus odoratus, 22, 64, 166
Lavandula, 34, 51, 54, 56, 85, 100, 101, 102, 166–167
Lavatera trimestris, 44, 46, 48, 64, 103, 167
Lavender. See Lavandula.
Lavender cotton. See Santolina chamaecyparissus.
Lawn, 25, 76–77, 78, 86, 107
Lenten rose. See Helleborus.
Leopard's bane. See Doronicum.
Liatris spicata, 64, 68–69, 102, 167
Ligularia, 66, 72, 167
Lilac. See Syringa.
Lilium, 9, 44, 46, 48, 69, 72, 101, 168
Lily. See Lilium.
Lily-of-the-Nile. See Agapanthus.
Lily-of-the-valley. See Convallaria majalis.
Lily-of-the-valley shrub. See Pieris japonica.
Lily turf, big blue. See Liriope muscari.
Limonium latifolium, 56, 97, 168
Linum, 56, 101, 169
Liriope muscari, 56, 97, 99, 169
Lithodora diffusa, 53, 56, 169
Lobelia, 31, 54, 56, 64, 82, 95, 103, 170
Lobularia maritima, 46, 48, 170
Love-in-a-mist. See Nigella damascena.
Love-lies-bleeding. See Amaranthus.
Lungwort. See Pulmonaria.
Lupine. See Lupinus.
Lupinus, 8, 56, 64, 170–171
Lychnis coronaria, 58, 60, 64, 83, 85, 108, 171
Lycoris, 64, 171
Lysimachia clethroides, 9, 48, 171

Madagascar periwinkle. See Catharanthus roseus.
Madrone. See Arbutus.
Magnolia, 48, 64, 171–172
Mahonia, 12, 56, 72, 172
Maidenhair tree. See Gingko biloba.
Mail order, 107–109
Male fern. See Dryopteris.
Mallow, annual. See Lavatera trimestris.
Malus, 13, 44, 48, 64, 172–173
Maple. See Acer.
Marguerite. See Chrysanthemum.
Marigold. See Calendula officinalis, Tagetes.
Matilija poppy. See Romneya coulteri.
Matthiola, 39, 48, 60, 64, 173
Meadow rue. See Thalictrum.
Meadow saffron. See Colchicum autumnale.
Meconopsis, 52, 53, 56, 173–174
Mertensia virginica, 33, 52, 56, 174
Mexican sunflower. See Tithonia rotundifolia.
Michaelmas daisy. See Aster.
Mimulus × hybridus, 72, 174
Mock orange. See Philadelphus coronarius.
Moluccella laevis, 76, 79, 174–175
Monarda didyma, 64, 100, 101, 175
Monkey flower. See Mimulus × hybridus.
Monkshood. See Aconitum.
Montbretia. See Crocosmia × crocosmiiflora.
Morning glory. See Ipomoea tricolor.
Moss pink. See Phlox.
Mountain ash. See Sorbus.
Mountain laurel. See Kalmia latifolia.
Mullein. See Verbascum.
Muscari, 52, 54, 56, 68, 93, 175

Narcissus, 20, 45, 46, 48, 69, 72, 93, 175–176
Nasturtium. See Tropaeolum majus.
Nemesia strumosa, 72, 176
Nemophila menziesii, 56, 176
Nepeta × faassenii, 51, 54, 56, 97, 102, 176
Nerium oleander, 48, 64, 177
Nicotiana, 42, 44–45, 48, 74, 79, 177
Nierembergia hippomanica, 56, 177–178
Nigella damascena, 34, 56, 101, 178

Obedient plant. See Physostegia virginiana.
Oenothera, 64, 72, 178
Oleander. See Nerium oleander.
Orange color category, 66–73
Oregon grape. See Mahonia.
Oriental poppy. See Papaver orientale.
Origanum dictamnus, 85, 178
Osmunda regalis, 79, 179
Oxeye. See Heliopsis helianthoides.

Pachysandra terminalis, 79, 179
Paeonia, 48, 58, 62, 64, 72, 179–180
Painted daisy. See Chrysanthemum.
Pansy. See Viola.
Papaver orientale, 9, 44, 46, 46–47, 48, 64, 72, 98, 180
Parrotia persica, 15, 180
Parthenocissus, 11, 22, 64, 91, 180–181
Pearly everlasting. See Anaphalis.
Pelargonium, 33, 62, 64, 95, 181
Penstemon, 36, 39, 56, 58, 64, 103, 181

Peony. See Paeonia.
Perennials, explained, 106
Periwinkle. See Catharanthus roseus, Vinca.
Perovskia, 54, 56, 182
Persimmon, Japanese. See Diospyros kaki.
Peruvian lily. See Alstroemeria.
Petunia × hybrida, 18, 44–45, 48, 61, 64, 98, 103, 106, 109, 182
Philadelphus coronarius, 48, 98, 182–183
Phlox, 44, 49, 56, 65, 183
Photinia × fraseri, 64, 65, 96, 183
Physalis alkekengi, 12, 72, 73, 183
Physostegia virginiana, 65, 184
Picea pungens, 30, 56, 184
Pieris japonica, 49, 79, 184
Pincushion flower. See Scabiosa.
Pink. See Dianthus.
Pink color category, 58–65
Plantain lily. See Hosta.
Plant lists, compiling, 94 examples, 96–103
Plants, types of, 106–107
Platycodon grandiflorus, 56, 185
Plumbago auriculata, 56, 185
Pocketbook plant. See Calceolaria crenatiflora.
Poppy. See Eschscholzia californica, Meconopsis, Papaver orientale, Romneya coulteri.
Potentilla, 73, 185
Pot marigold. See Calendula officinalis.
Primrose. See Primula.
Primula, 38, 39, 49, 52, 65, 73, 86, 98, 185–186
Prunus, 15, 49, 64, 65, 96, 186
Pulmonaria, 10, 48, 49, 56, 99, 187
Purple coneflower. See Echinacea purpurea.
Purple color category, 50–57
Pyracantha, 12, 13, 64, 65, 72, 73, 89, 187
Pyrus salicifolia 'Pendula', 81, 83, 85, 187

Queen-of-the-prairie. See Filipendula rubra.
Quince, flowering. See Chaenomeles.

Redbud. See Cercis.
Red color category, 58–65
Red-hot poker. See Kniphofia uvaria.
Rhododendron, 26, 46, 49, 54, 56, 62, 65, 73, 107, 110, 188
River birch. See Betula nigra.
Robinia pseudoacacia 'Frisia', 75, 76, 79, 99, 188
Rockcress. See Arabis caucasica.
Rock gardens, 21, 27
Rockrose. See Cistus.
Romneya coulteri, 44, 46, 49, 188–189
Rosa, 18, 23, 34, 36, 38, 48, 49, 54, 56, 62, 65, 69, 70, 73, 98, 101, 102, 109, 189
Rose. See Rosa.
Rose-mallow. See Hibiscus.
Rosemary. See Rosmarinus officinalis.
Rose of Sharon. See Hibiscus.
Rosmarinus officinalis, 54, 57, 100, 189–190
Royal fern. See Osmunda regalis.
Rudbeckia, 71, 73, 73, 107, 190
Russian olive. See Elaeagnus.
Russian sage. See Perovskia.

Sage. See Salvia, Perovskia.
St. Johnswort. See Hypericum.
Salix alba 'Britzensis', 190

Salvia, *11, 31, 40,* 49, 54, 57, 60, 65, *74, 76,* 79, *80,* 85, *95,* 97, 100, 102, 109, 190–191
Santa Barbara daisy. *See Erigeron.*
Santolina chamaecyparissus, 85, 96, 191
Sanvitalia procumbens, 71, 73, 191
Sarcococca, 79, 191
Scabiosa, 39, 57, 65, 97, 192
Scaevola, 57, 192
Scilla, 54, 57, 93, 192–193
Sea holly. *See Eryngium.*
Sea lavender. *See Limonium latifolium.*
Sedum 'Autumn Joy', 61, 65, 102, 193
Seed, growing from, 110–111
Senecio, 44, 65, 82, 85, 193
Series, explained, 109
Serviceberry. *See Amelanchier.*
Shasta daisy. *See Chrysanthemum.*
Shrubs, explained, 107
Siberian bugloss. *See Brunnera macrophylla.*
Silverberry. *See Elaeagnus.*
Silver color category, 80–85
Silver lace. *See Chrysanthemum.*
Sissinghurst, 44, *47,* 49
Skimmia japonica, 13, 49, 193–194
Smoke tree. *See Cotinus coggygria.*
Snapdragon. *See Antirrhinum majus.*
Sneezeweed. *See Helenium.*
Snowdrop. *See Galanthus.*
Snow-in-summer. *See Cerastium tomentosum.*
Solidago, 73, 194
Sorbus, 13, 64, 65, 194

Speedwell. *See Veronica.*
Species, explained, 108
Spider flower. *See Cleome hasslerana.*
Spider lily. *See Lycoris.*
Spindle tree. *See Euonymus.*
Spiraea, 45, 49, 65, *73,* 98, 102, 195
Spruce, blue or Colorado. *See Picea pungens.*
Spurge. *See Euphorbia, Pachysandra terminalis.*
Squill. *See Scilla.*
Stachys byzantina 'Silver Carpet', *80,* 83, 85, 89, 97, 102
Star jasmine. *See Trachelospermum jasminoides.*
Statice. *See Limonium latifolium.*
Stewartia, 11, 15, 195–196
Stock. *See Matthiola.*
Stokes' aster. *See Stokesia laevis.*
Stokesia laevis, 57, 196
Stonecrop. *See Sedum* 'Autumn Joy'.
Strawberry tree. *See Arbutus unedo.*
Strawflower. *See Helichrysum bracteatum.*
Styrax japonicus, 49, 196
Summer cypress. *See Kochia scoparia.*
Summersweet. *See Clethra alnifolia.*
Sundrops. *See Oenothera.*
Sunflower. *See Helianthus.*
Sunrose. *See Helianthemum nummularium.*
Swan River daisy. *See Brachycome.*
Sweet alyssum. *See Lobularia maritima.*

Sweet box. *See Sarcococca.*
Sweet pea. *See Lathyrus odoratus.*
Sweet William. *See Dianthus.*
Syringa, 49, 57, 65, 98, 196–197

Tagetes, 60, 68, *71,* 73, 90, 103, 109, 197
Tetraploid, explained, 109
Teucrium fruticans, 85, 96, 197
Thalictrum, 57, 99, 197–198
Thunbergia alata, 68, 73, 198
Thyme. *See Thymus pseudolanuginosus.*
Thymus pseudolanuginosus, 83, 85, 198
Tithonia rotundifolia, 73, 198
Tobacco, flowering. *See Nicotiana.*
Trachelospermum jasminoides, 49, 199
Trees, explained, 107
Triploid, explained, 109
Trollius, 73, 199
Tropaeolum majus, 22, 73, 100, 199
Trumpet vine. *See Campsis.*
Tulipa, 33, 49, 54, 57, 62, 65, 73, 76, 79, 98, 107, 200

Variety, explained, 108
Verbascum, 49, 73, 85, 200
Verbena, 57, *61,* 65, 103, 200–201
Veronica, 50, 52, 54, *57,* 57, 201
Viburnum, 12, 49, 65, 201–202
Vinca, 53, 57, 79, 202
Vines, explained, 107
Viola, 33, *36,* 38, 39, 49, 54, 57, *57,* 65, 73, 98, 101, 106, 202–203
Violet. *See Viola.*

Virginia bluebells. *See Mertensia virginica.*
Virginia creeper. *See Parthenocissus.*
Virgin's bower. *See Clematis.*

Wallflower. *See Erysimum.*
Wall rockcress. *See Arabis caucasica.*
Warm colors, 33, 103
Washington thorn. *See Crataegus.*
Weeping willowleaf pear. *See Pyrus salicifolia* 'Pendula'.
Weigela florida, 65, 203
Welsh poppy. *See Meconopsis.*
White color category, 42–49, 98
Wild lilac. *See Ceanothus.*
Willow gentian. *See Gentiana asclepiadea.*
Winter aconite. *See Eranthis hyemalis.*
Wisteria, 49, 54, 57, *112,* 203–205
Witch hazel. *See Hamamelis.*
Wood fern. *See Dryopteris.*
Wood hyacinth. *See Endymion.*
Woolly thyme. *See Thymus pseudolanuginosus.*

Yarrow. *See Achillea.*
Yellow color category, 66–73

Zantedeschia aethiopica, 49, 205
Zephyranthes candida, 49, 205
Zinnia, creeping. *See Sanvitalia procumbens.*
Zinnia elegans, 40, 60, *65,* 65, 73, *74,* 76, 79, 82, *95,* 103, 106, 109, 205

Photographers

Scott Atkinson: 86, 104, 110; **Marion Brenner:** 122 top left, 130 bottom center, 133 bottom left, 146 bottom right, 151 top center, 178 bottom center, 191 top center, 198 top left; **Lisa Butler:** 184 top right; **Charles Cresson:** 204 bottom left; **Claire Curran:** 155 bottom left, 167 top right; **Alan Detrick:** 187 top left; **William Dewey:** 126 bottom center; **Goldsmith Seeds:** 109; **Saxon Holt:** 11 middle right, 12 top right and bottom right, 13 middle center and bottom, 24 top, 26 bottom, 40, 43, 45 bottom, 50 bottom, 65 left, 73 right, 107, 114 top, 117 top right and bottom, 118 top right, 119 top right, 120 top left, 122 top right, 124 top left and top right,125 middle right, 126 bottom right, 130 top left and bottom right, 131 top left, 132 top left, 136 top right, 139 bottom left, 140 center, 141 top and bottom right, 143 left, 145 left, 149 top and bottom right, 151 top left, 152 bottom right, 153 top left, 154 top right, 155 top center, 162 right, 163 bottom left and top right, 164 bottom left and top, 165 bottom left and bottom right, 174 top, 177 top, 178 right, 179 top and bottom right, 186, 188 left, 189 right, 191 top left, 193 top right, 197 left; **Charles Mann:** 8 middle right, 10 bottom left and bottom right, 11 top left and middle left, 15 middle right, 16 top and middle left and bottom, 17 top, 20 top center and top right and bottom, 22 left, 23 top, 24 bottom, 25 top left, 26 top right, 28, 35 left, 36 top right, 37, 49 left, 53 right, 57 bottom, 65 right, 66 top, 68 right, 70 bottom, 76 top, 79, 92, 94 top, 112, 115 bottom center, 116 right, 119 left, 120 top, 133 top left and top right, 135 top left and top center, 137 bottom left, 138, 142 center and right, 144 top right and bottom, 145 right, 146 top left, 150 center, 151 bottom, 157 bottom left and bottom right, 159 bottom right, 162 left, 166 bottom, 172 right, 176 bottom right, 178 left, 180 right, 182 top left, 184 top left, 189 left, 190 center, 194 bottom, 195 top left, 199 top left, 202 right, 203 left and right; **Ells Marugg:** 159 bottom left; **David McDonald:** 154 bottom, 169 bottom, 197 center; **Park Seed Co.:** 171 bottom left; **Jerry Pavia:** 1, 9 middle left and bottom left, 10 middle left, 13 top left and middle left, 16 bottom right, 17 middle left and right, 25 bottom and top right, 27, 49 right, 54 bottom, 62 top, 76 bottom, 77 right, 80 top, 88, 94 bottom, 120 top right, 127 top and bottom left, 128 bottom, 129 top, 134 left, 136 bottom right, 137 top, 139 top left and bottom right, 140 right, 141 bottom left, 147 center, 148 bottom right, 150 left, 156 top, 158 top, 160 bottom right, 161 right, 164 middle, 169 top right, 171 bottom right, 175 bottom right, 177 bottom left, 180 center, 183 top left, 185 right, 188 right, 190 left, 191 top right and bottom, 194 top right, 196 left, 197 right, 198 bottom right, 201

right; **Joanne Pavia:** 20 top left, 22 top right and bottom right, 35 right, 36 bottom, 53 left, 116 left, 132 right, 156 bottom, 167 left, 170 bottom, 179 bottom left; **Norman A. Plate:** 51, 136 bottom left, 158 bottom; **Susan Roth:** 8 bottom left and top right, 9 top left and top right and middle right, 10 top, 11 top right and bottom, 12 bottom left, 13 top right, 14 bottom left, 15 bottom left, 33, 34 left, 42 bottom, 44 bottom, 45 top, 47 top, 50 top, 52 right, 54 top, 55 top, 57 top right, 59, 60, 61 top left and bottom, 62 bottom, 66 bottom, 68 left, 70 top, 71 top, 74 bottom, 80 bottom, 81, 82 left, 83 top and bottom, 89, 90, 114 bottom, 117 top left, 118 left and top center and bottom, 122 bottom, 123 bottom, 124 bottom, 125 top, 128 top left, 129 middle, 132 center, 134 top, 135 bottom, 137 bottom right, 139 top right, 140 left, 144 middle right, 148 top, 149 bottom left, 150 right, 153 top right, 155 bottom right, 159 top, 160 top, 161 left, 165 top, 166 top, 167 bottom right, 168 top, 170 middle, 171 top, 172 left, 173 top and bottom left, 175 top, 177 bottom right, 181 top, 182 bottom, 185 left, 187 bottom, 192 top right, 198 middle left and bottom left, 200 left; **Strybing Arboretum:** 185 middle; **Michael S. Thompson:** 2, 4, 5, 8 middle left and bottom right, 9 middle center, 10 middle right, 11 middle center, 12 middle left and middle right, 13 middle right, 14 top and middle and bottom right, 15 center and bottom right, 16 middle right, 17 bottom left, 18, 21, 30, 31, 36 top left, 42 top, 44 top, 46 top, 52 left, 57 top left, 58 top, 61 top right, 63 bottom, 67, 69 right, 73 left, 74 top, 95, 106, 108, 116 center, 121, 123 top, 125 bottom, 126 top left, 127 bottom right, 128 top right, 129 bottom, 131 bottom right, 133 bottom right, 142 bottom left, 144 top left, 145 center, 148 bottom left, 151 top right, 152 top, 153 bottom right, 157 top, 160 bottom left, 162 center, 163 bottom right, 169 top left, 173 bottom right, 174 bottom, 175 bottom left, 176 bottom left and top right, 182 top right, 183 top right and bottom, 184 bottom, 192 bottom, 193 bottom, 195 top right, 196 right, 199 bottom, 200 right, 204 top right and bottom right; **Wayside Gardens:** 168 bottom, 190 right; **Peter O. Whiteley:** 17 bottom right; **Doug Wilson:** 147 left, 180 left, 194 top left; **Cynthia Woodyard:** 6, 9 bottom right, 15 top, 23 bottom, 26 top left, 34 right, 46 bottom, 58 bottom, 75, 78, 80 bottom, 82 right, 83 bottom, 84, 85, 91, 115 top left and bottom right, 119 bottom right, 123 middle, 131 top right, 135 top right, 143 right, 146 top right, 147 right, 152 bottom left, 154 top left, 155 top right, 170 top, 174 middle, 181 bottom, 187 top right, 192 top left, 195 bottom, 199 top right, 201 left, 202 left; **Josephine Zeitlin:** 204 top left.